S0-AOW-373

DESIGNING GUI APPLICATIONS FOR WINDOWS

BY ALEX LEAVENS

M&T BOOKS

M&T Books
A Division of MIS:Press, Inc.
A Subsidiary of Henry Holt and Company, Inc.
115 West 18th Street
New York, New York 10011

© 1994 by M&T Books

Printed in the United States of America

All rights reserved. No part of this book may be reproduced or transmitted in any form
or by any means, electronic or mechanical, including photocopying, recording, or by
any information storage and retrieval system, without prior written permission from
the Publisher. Contact the Publisher for information on foreign rights.

Limits of Liability and Disclaimer of Warranty
The Author and Publisher of this book have used their best efforts in preparing the
book and the programs contained in it. These efforts include the development, research,
and testing of the theories and programs to determine their effectiveness.

The Author and Publisher make no warranty of any kind, expressed or implied, with
regard to these programs or the documentation contained in this book. The Author and
Publisher shall not be liable in any event for incidental or consequential damages in connection with, or arising out of, the furnishing, performance, or use of these programs.

Trademarks
All products, names and services are trademarks or registered trademarks of their
respective companies.

Library of Congress Cataloging-in-Publication Data

```
Leavens, Alex.
    Designing GUI applications for Windows / Alex Leavens.
      p.  cm.
    Includes index.
    ISBN 1-55851-328-0 : $39.95
    1. General user interfaces (Computer systems)  2. Windows
  (Computer programs)  3. Microsoft Windows (Computer file)
  1. Title.
  QA76.9.U83L43  1994
  005.2-dc20                                      94-30874
                                                     CIP
```

Publisher: Brenda McLaughlin   **Project Editor:** Michael Sprague
Development Editor: Margot Pagan   **Technical Editor:** Kevin Goodman
Production Editor: Anthony Washington **Associate Production Editor:** Maya Riddick

97   96   95   94   4   3   2   1

TABLE OF CONTENTS

WHY THIS BOOK IS FOR YOU 1

INTRODUCTION 3

CHAPTER 1: Understanding the User Interface 7

CHAPTER 2: Interface Design Philosophy..11

    Make it Consistent: Don't confuse the user 11

    Make it make sense: Guiding the user along the right path 15

    Make it robust: Don't let the user get lost or surprised 19

    Make it friendly: Give good feedback 21

    What the user has done 22

    How has the user done it..23

    What happened...24

    Make it powerful: Give the user the strength of 10 29

CHAPTER 3: What, Why and How: Three Questions You Have to Be
ble to Answer..35

    What task will users be performing? 36

    How will they accomplish the iasks 36

Why will they be performing those tasks 37

Summary 39

CHAPTER 4: Events and Event-Driven Programming **41**

What is event-driven programming? 41

Linear programming 42

Event-driven programming 43

Why are event-driven interfaces better? 47

Types of events in windows 48

    System Events 48

    Control Events 49

    User Events 49

    Other Events 50

Summary 50

CHAPTER 5: Menus, and Their Uses..**51**

Step 1: Standard entries 52

    The File menu 53

    The Edit menu 57

Drag-rights and other things 59

Menu structures 60

Examples 60

    The menu DIL example 61

Putting it together: The DIL in action 101

Other things to do with menus 103

Undo and Redo, how do you do? 104

Graying a menu entry 105

Summary 106

CHAPTER 6: Buttons **199**

Text buttons, graphic buttons 110

The three kinds of graphic buttons 112

Using buttons 117

Text button examples 117

Graphic buttons: An example 123

Looking at the graphic example 143

Creating the buttons 144

Handling the buttons 145

How the button class works internally 146

Summary 181

CHAPTER 7: Dialog Boxes **183**

Introduction 183

The Good, the Bad, and the Ugly 186

Now what? 191

Rules of thumb: Things to do, things not to do 191

Dialog boxes—from simple to complex 193

The message Box: Care and feeding thereof 194

More complex dialog boxes 201

Dealing with Dialogs (and their controls) 202

Handling the controls 221

Handling the radio buttons 223

Handling the Czech boxes 233

Keeping the user around 234

Summary 322

CHAPTER 8: Radio Buttons and Check Boxes **237**

Buttons and boxes: An introduction 237

Using radio buttons in your program 243

Shooting the Moon: Our application in action 246

Checking out the Moon: Our application with check boxes 274

Summary 294

CHAPTER 9: List Boxes and Combo Boxes **285**

Listbox and combobox do's and don'ts 285

Flavors of List boxes and Combo boxes 288

Using a listbox 293

The listbox application in action 321

Using Listbox Item data elements 328

DlgDirList: A warning 332

Listboxes and third party controls 335

Combo boxes 336

Dealing with combo boxes: Some examples 348

Combo boxes and Item data 358

Summary 359

Index 361

WHY THIS BOOK IS FOR YOU

Are you trying to design a good user interface for your Windows product? Then you need this book. If you're looking to understand both the theoretical and practical aspects of user interface design (especially in Windows) then you need this book. You'll find lots of the "Why should I do this this way?" questions answered for you, as well as lots of the "How do I do this?" questions answered. In other words, I'll be explaining not only how you accomplish certain user interface behaviors (such as programming a list box), but why you should use particular user interface pieces (as well as some places that you shouldn't be using them). While I can't pretend to cover every single user interface question in detail, I will try to instill in you the ability to discern between good user interface design and bad, and, more importantly, how to communicate that to others.

Finally, if you're looking for a good primer on the basics of user interface design and development, then this book is for you. Enjoy!

INTRODUCTION

This, if you haven't already guessed from the title, is a book about user interfaces. It came into being mainly because of what I consider the really poor state of user interface design today. That may seem like an odd statement, given the current nature of the Windows marketplace. However, I've been programming for close to 14 years, and there are more programs today that look like they've been designed in a Blend-O-Matic than I care to think about. It's not that there weren't bad user interfaces years ago—there were. It's just that today a bad user interface gets much greater exposure (because of greater market awareness, and because of a greater understanding of the importance of the interface). This being the case, it behooves all of us as programmers to do a better job. This book will show you how.

There are really two sides to the user interface problem—understanding what one is, and understanding how to build one. This book addresses both concerns. If you've never considered the philosophical implications of designing software, then don't worry—I've got lots of handy crates of user interface design philosophy sitting here in the corner, and you're welcome to take home as many of them as you like. And don't worry about getting bogged down—I'll keep it light, I promise.

This book, being primarily about Windows, will also show you how to build really great user interfaces in Windows—not just the theoretical aspects, but the real nitty-gritty, nuts and bolts details. How do you handle a listbox within the context of a dialog? What do you do when the user double-clicks on a tool button? We'll explore answers to all these things. All of this will be illustrated with lots of code fragments— and in some cases, full program examples.

I really want you to get a good feel for what it takes to design great user interfaces. To do this, I'll be discussing all sorts of things that may seem totally unconnected to user interface design, but which really are. There'll be lots of examples, a few bad puns, some Zen riddles and other assorted things. All of this is purposeful—I want to loosen up your thinking and get you thinking in different ways about your problem. Some of the best solutions to user interface design come from lateral thinking— thinking about the problem in totally new ways, in ways that you hadn't thought of before. I'm really trying to induce the "A-ha!" experience to you—the point at which the light bulb goes off in your head.

At this point you may be thinking to yourself, just who *is* this guy? Sure, what he's saying sounds great, but what are his qualifications? In short, why should I listen to what he has to say?

In my own defense, all I can say is that I've been designing user interfaces for software for more than 14 years. Some of the products that I've designed and built have sold more than 100,000 copies each (one sold more than a million units), and one product that I and my partner Shirley A. Russell designed and wrote ended up in the Smithsonian Institution (National Museum of American History) as part of a permanent collection of software—almost solely because of the user interface that we built. I've designed and programmed a pair of moderately successful commercial Windows applications, and I've consulted with companies on half a dozen more Windows products.

This doesn't mean I'm infallible, of course. I've made lots of mistakes in the course of designing software—software that I thought was just great other people treated like road-kill. (I'll talk about a few of them as we go.) The best designs I've done were the ones where I was able to let go of my very proprietary feelings about the software ("It's mine, mine, all mine!"), and really listen to what other people had to say about the way the product should work.

But I'm getting ahead of myself here. Before we delve into how to best design a user interface, we need to truly understand what one is. So loosen your tie, get comfortable, and be prepared to get your feet wet. The user interface swamp lies just ahead.

CHAPTER 1

UNDERSTANDING THE USER INTERFACE

Welcome to the user interface swamp. I call it that for a couple of reasons. One is that I've seen the design of user interfaces drain so much time and energy away from what were otherwise productive people and companies, it seemed like they were drowning in mud. The other is that I've seen too many interfaces (and I'm sure you have, too) that looked like they were designed in a swamp, without much consideration for what the product was going to do, who was going to do it, or how.

This is Not Good.

Fortunately, it doesn't have to be this way. User interface design is not black magic nor alchemy, although I admit that it can sometime seem that way. Fundamentally, user interface design is about building an interface the user can use.

On the face of it, that's such an obvious statement it's almost dismissable. But it's really the truth—it doesn't matter how pretty the interface is, or how well-drawn the icons are. If the product isn't *useable* by the person who's using it, then the user interface is pointless—it's just that simple.

A good exercise to learn about the nature of user interface design is to think about the user interfaces for various common products (not software products).

For example, what's the user interface for a door?

This usually generates lots of puzzled looks. What on earth do I mean, what's the user interface for a door? You put your hand on the handle, turn or push, and the door opens. Nothing to it.

But there is, actually. Both the placement of the door handle and it's shape give the user of the door clues about the workings of the door—which way the door swings and what you have to do to open it. Don Norman, in his excellent book, *The Design of Everyday Things*, talks about a set of doors that were completely missing these cues. As a result, they were almost impossible to open. Not that they wouldn't work perfectly well once you figured out which way they went, but there was absolutely no information that would have helped you determine which way that was.

The door handles were long flat metal rods placed directly in the center of the door, which was glass. There were no visible hinges. There was no clue as to:

✦ the side of the door you had to apply pressure (left or right), or

✦ the way the door swung (in or out).

People couldn't use the door. This is an extreme example, but there's an even better one—Candid Camera once did a stunt where they put the doorknob on the side of the door where the hinges were. The door itself would swing open easily if you pushed on the *other side* of the door—the one where the doorknob wasn't. People couldn't open that door either. They would stand there, struggling with the doorknob, pushing and pulling, but to no avail.

The reason this stunt worked, of course, is because the door deliberately violated people's model of how a door should work. This brings us to the first important point about user interfaces:

✦ The people who use your interface are going to make assunmptions about the way it works.

This is common to people everywhere, and it doesn't just apply to software. We all carry inside our heads models about how the world works. If we didn't, life would become pretty chaotic, that's for sure. We have models about how we use an elevator, about how we dial a phone, about how we use a door. We have models for almost everything we do. And if our model doesn't agree with the way the world actually works, then we can be in trouble.

For example, we all have a model of how we drive a car. But what if everyone else's model is different than ours? Don't laugh—this can happen. What if you learned to drive in the United States, but you've just moved to Great Britain? They all drive on the *wrong side of the road*! Or at least that's how it looks to you—to them, they're driving on the *right* side of the road, and you're the bloomin' idiot who can't quite figure it out.

Of course, the whole point is that neither way is the "right" way to drive—both are just socially accepted models that prevail in the society that's created them. That's the important thing about models—they give us a way to work with something that may be slightly unfamiliar. They give us a framework that allows us to understand an object and how it behaves.

What's this got to do with software? Very simply, people will make assumptions about how your software works. They may or may not be *accurate* assumptions, but regardless of how accurate they are, people will still make them. It's your job as an interface designer to make sure the assumptions your users make accurately reflect what the software's going to do.

There are several things that do this:

✦ Make your software consistent.

✦ Give guidelines about how to use the software.

✦ Don't let the user get lost or confused.

✦ Give good feedback.

✦ Empower the user to get things done.

Each of these topics requires a little more explanation, and each one is the subject of its own section in Chapter 2—call them the "five user interface dwarves," if you want (I do). None of these topics is massively heavy; pretty much everything I have to say about them can fit into two or three pages. But they are very important points, because without them, you won't be able to design software that really works.

The first dwarf is the one named Consistency.

CHAPTER 2

INTERFACE DESIGN PHILOSOPHY

MAKE IT CONSISTENT: DON'T CONFUSE THE USER

Consistency is one of the cornerstones of good user interface design. Consistency is the ability of the user to predict what the software is going to do in a given situation, based on past experience with the product.

Consistency in an interface is something we take for granted in other products, yet rarely give enough thought to when we're developing our software. Think about how bad it would be, for example, if every time you got in your car you had to guess which way to turn the steering wheel. Sometimes you might have to turn the wheel left to move the car left, and sometimes you might have to turn it right. If I really had a car like this, I'd get it fixed in a hurry.

Such an interface on a car is obviously terribly wrong, but there are software equivalents of this car that don't raise much fuss. Some software packages use the function keys on the keyboard extensively, and yet don't provide any consistent mappings. Sometimes F9 means yes, and sometimes it means delete (I really saw this on one software package). Apparently it never occurred to the programmer that having the same key mean both yes and delete would prove terribly confusing, not to mention dangerous.

One of the biggest items that Microsoft addressed when creating version 3.1 of Windows was the lack of consistent interfaces for such things as opening and saving files, choosing colors, and other common operations. Prior to this time, there hadn't been a consistent method of opening and saving files.

If you wanted a File Open dialog box in your program (and most everybody does), you had to write your own. Since everybody was writing their own File Open (and Save) dialog boxes, you had a bunch of different ways you could open and save files.

In Windows 3.1, Microsoft made available what are known as the *common dialog boxes*. As a programmer, you now had a way of presenting the same File Open dialog box other applications were presenting to the user. This created an interface for opening or saving a file that is consistent across applications.

I can already hear a couple of people out there griping, "Yeah, but I can write a better file open dialog box than that!" That may be true, but from the user's perspective, it's irrelevant. Users don't want a *better* way to open files only in your program, they want a *consistent* way to open files in all programs. Once users have learned one model of how a file open dialog box works, they don't want to learn a different one.

This consistency between applications is very important. Studies have shown that users tend to use more applications in a graphical environment such as Windows than they do in a command-line environment such as DOS. The more applications they use, the more they tend to expect them to behave the same—and woe to the application that doesn't. Users won't use it, even if it accomplishes very powerful things. Why not? It's not consistent with the way they've become accustomed to doing things.

If there's a mechanism that already exists for accomplishing a task, such as the common file open dialog box, then by all means use that mechanism. If the standard mechanism doesn't do quite what you want it to do, think very carefully about trying to replace it.

Consistency is also very important when designing the tools the user is going work with. Many applications today have toolbars that give users a selection of tools. Yet sometimes the way these tools work isn't consistent. If the tool performs one function at one time, and a different function at another time, the user is going to find it difficult to use the tool.

This has a flip side, too. If similar tools work in similar ways, make sure that the user can see that consistency. Slight variations in the way a tool works is not a reason to have two tools—have one tool that can work both ways.

For example, in a paint program I wrote, I built a Pencil tool. This tool allows you to draw single-pixel lines in the currently selected color. One of the people who used this tool suggested that it would also be nice to have the Pencil have a built in eraser. This user wanted it so when the user starts drawing, if the color the tool currently on is

+ not the currently selected drawing color, then draw the currently selected drawing color.
+ is the currently selected drawing color, then erase (draw white).

This was very simple behavior to build, and it also followed a consistent and simple model. The user understood right away how it worked.

However, some users didn't like it. They understood it all right, they just didn't want it to work that way. So I added an option to the Pencil tool that allowed them to turn it off—now the Pencil tool would always draw the selected color, no matter what color the drawing started on. See Figure 2-1.

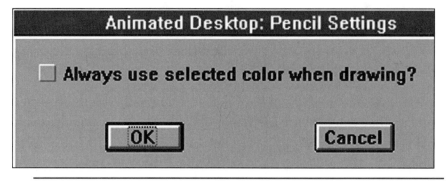

FIGURE 2-1   A SCREEN SHOT OF THE DIALOG THAT LETS YOU SET THE OPTIONS FOR THE PENCIL TOOL. THIS ALLOWS THE USER TO DEFINE THE BEHAVIOR.

This ability to choose the behavior of the Pencil allowed users to build models of how the tools worked that was most consistent with how they wanted the tool to work. It was a flexible consistency.

**Make it consistent,
or your users will curse you.**

CONSISTENCY

Of course, sometimes this isn't going to be possible. In cases where you can't let the user tailor the product to meet their needs (and this is possible more often than you might think), it's still very important to keep the way your product works consistent. Remember, if you don't, they won't use it.

MAKE IT MAKE SENSE: GUIDING THE USER ALONG THE RIGHT PATH

The second user interface dwarf, Helpful, is an obvious cousin of the first once, Consistency (I tell you, it's going to become increasingly difficult to think up cute names for these little buggers!). Where Consistency demands that you provide the same sets of behavior in response to user actions, Helpful demands that you provide clear and obvious paths for the user to get something done.

What do I mean by this? Very simply, a good user interface gives the user clues about what to do next in a given situation. Why do this? So the user won't get lost, or confused while attempting to do whatever it is they're trying to do (which the user *will* do, anyway, despite your best efforts to prevent it. I know. I'm that user).

In everyday life, of course, there are lots of clues (also known as *cues*) about what to do next. For example, if I'm driving along a road, I have clues about where the road goes next by the shape of the road, the road signs along the road, the stripes on the road, the little knobbly things on the road that make your tires go bump-a-bump-a-bump every time you run over them, and so on.

By contrast, if you take your car out into the middle of a salt flat and start driving, it's an eerie experience. There are no roads, no road signs, no lines, *nothing* to tell you where to go. In fact, you can go anywhere—which can be more than a little overwhelming (I did this once and it made the hairs on the back of my neck stand up) because it's hard to know where to go. Since you can go anywhere with equal freedom, there isn't any way to tell which way would be best to go—or even if there *is* a best way.

Without any sort of guidelines for driving, it's possible to become completely lost and disoriented. True story: During the African campaign in World War II, people would become lost in the desert and die, while only being hundreds of yards from a city or a tent. The desert was so featureless and so uniform in appearance that people had no way of figuring out their direction.

This can happen to your users, too. Well, they won't die—but they will get lost—sometimes badly lost. Think about the C:> prompt, for example. Not very helpful, is it? Doesn't give any sort of clue as to what you're supposed to do, does it? It was this lack of any sort of guidelines that eventually led designers in search of a more "intuitive" interface, such as the Macintosh or Windows.

By allowing people to see their environment in a visual way, windowed interfaces provide more feedback about what the user can (and cannot) do. It's still not intuitive, of course, it has to be learned. But it does provide guidelines for the user—ways of organizing and displaying information so that they can be logically navigated.

List boxes will always provide a set of choices for the user—that's consistency. But a list box also provides a set of choices about things that are *related*—file names, for example. That's being helpful—guiding the users towards the right path. If you have users select wildly different items from the same list box at different times, then you haven't violated the principal of consistency—after all, you're always using a list-box—but you've certainly violated the principal of helpfulness, because you haven't given the user any way of distinguishing which items are currently important, and which are not.

Guidelines, then, can be seen as a way of *narrowing* the available range of choices for a user. This gives the user the necessary information about what is possible at the current point, and what isn't, about what makes sense (and what doesn't), about what is logical to do right now (and what isn't).

This is more important than you might think, because, as the designer of the product, you *already know how it works.* You already know which actions are mutually incompatible with other actions, which things make sense in which context. The user, on the other hand, does not. Therefore, it's your responsibility to make sure the internal dependencies of the program of importance to the user are exposed to the user. This does *not* mean that every internal dependency be exposed, only those that are important for the user to know about.

For example, take a look at Figure 2-2, which shows a paint program I wrote. It's got a set of drawing tools, such as a Pencil, a Paint Bucket, a Spray Can, a Paint Brush, and so on. These tools are grouped together, because logically, they perform similar functions. When the user selects one method of drawing, they are also not selecting the other methods of drawing. The grouping of the tools makes this clear.

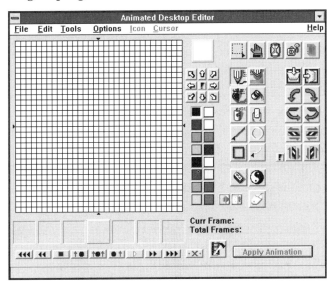

FIGURE 2-2   THE ICON/BITMAP EDITOR I'VE WRITTEN. NOTICE THAT GROUPS OF TOOLS THAT PERFORM LOGICALLY RELATED FUNCTIONS (SUCH AS DRAWING) ARE GROUPED TOGETHER. THIS ALLOWS THE USER TO DETERMINE BY VISUAL INSPECTION WHICH TOOLS ARE LOGICALLY RELATED, AND WHICH ARE SEPARATE AREAS OF FUNCTIONALITY.

If they are using the Pencil tool, they cannot be using the Paint Brush tool. If they are using the Paint Brush tool, they cannot be using the Paint Bucket (fill) tool. If they are using the Paint Bucket tool, they cannot be using the Spray Can tool, and so on. The tools themselves are built so the user can only select one at a time. When they select a new tool, the old tool deselects itself.

This is important because it provides the user with clear guidelines about how the product works. When you are using one drawing tool, the user will discover, you cannot be using another one. Thus, when presenting users with a set of functions mutually exclusive in use, *make sure they can detect that fact.* The fact that a group of tools works mutually exclusively is a very important point—don't forget to inform the user about it!

A second set of tools (the Arrow keys above the drawing tools) is separate, because they perform a different set of functions (they allow the user to move the image around). Note, however, that moving the image around is a separate, unrelated function to the drawing tools. In other words, you can move the image around at any time, regardless of which drawing tool you happen to be currently using.

From the user's standpoint, this makes obvious sense, and is easily learned. "I can move the image around at any time," they will think, and indeed come to expect this behavior. Suppose, however, that I had grouped the Arrow keys *with* the drawing tools. I would have created a dependency in the user's mind where none actually existed. "These are part of the drawing tools," the user would think, since that's what my visual cues would indicate.

The user could probably learn over time that the Arrow keys really weren't part of the drawing tools, which would make the interface poorly designed, but not unusable. However, suppose I actually did make the Arrow keys dependent upon the drawing tools, say by preventing the user from shifting the image unless they had first selected the Pencil tool. This would make the interface really appalling, since:

+ There is no visual clue to the fact that you have to select the Pencil tool to use the Arrow keys.
+ There is no apparent reason for doing so, either. What does the Pencil tool have to do with shifting the image?

As you can see, if I really built my interface this way, it would be terribly confusing and frustrating to the user. Sure, users would probably learn to use it, but it certainly wouldn't win much praise. Yet the functionality of the program would not have changed at all! It would still perform the same functions of painting and shifting.

HELPFUL

Design your software so that it guides the users to the proper use of the product.

The fact that nothing except the interface has changed in this example points out that the interface, and nothing else, can make the difference between a product that is helpful and guides the user, and one that is virtually unusable.

MAKE IT ROBUST: DON'T LET THE USER GET LOST OR SURPRISED

The third user interface dwarf is Confused, so named because he's always saying things like "Uh, now how did I get here again? Where's that menu option? Which button do I have to push?" and other, similar things. Confused is the user interface dwarf that you see in lots of naive users—as well as some not-so-naive users!

Confused is really the anti-dwarf of Helpful; Helpful guides users along the right path, but Confused is the one who shows up when users get lost in the interface. I've just talked about how important it is for your product to guide your users along the correct path for doing a particular task; however, it's also important to make sure that you don't artificially limit what users can do in an attempt to be helpful. This is where Confused comes in—your interface should be directed enough that naive users (I don't mean that in a pejorative sense—merely that they are users who are new to your product) can accomplish meaningful tasks in the interface with a minimum of fuss. However it should be loose enough for power users to accomplish more complex tasks without the interface getting in the way.

I have an anecdote that I relate to people when I'm discussing user interface issues with them. Simply put, I ask them, "do you want the helpful poodle interface or the Porsche Turbo interface?" The helpful poodle is the one that is constantly dashing between your legs, jumping up in your lap, licking your face, yipping at the slightest noise, and in general making you completely and totally aware of his presence every instant of the day. I'm sure you've seen interfaces like this, too: "Do you want to continue? Are you sure you want to reformat your hard drive? Is you hair wet?" etc. They demand a response to everything—from the trivial to the dangerous—and they are constantly pushing, prodding, and poking you about your work.

Well, this can be fine for a very naive user, but a little bit of this goes a long way. After a short exposure to the product, people start filtering these messages out, ignoring the trivial and the important alike.

The Porsche Turbo interface, on the other hand, is named after the famous sports car, which is very powerful, but also very difficult to drive well (almost anyone can drive it badly, but that's beside the point). This is akin to the interface that will let you do almost anything, but which will give you no feedback about whether what you are doing is good, bad, or innocuous. Where the helpful poodle interface asked you about *every-thing*, the Porsche Turbo interface asks you about *nothing*, assuming that you know what you are doing in all cases. Drive 130 miles an hour? Fine. Put the car tail end first into the weeds? Also fine.

These are the two extremes of user interface design; hopefully, your product's interface will lie somewhere in the middle. This is the real trick—making your interface powerful enough to get the job done, without making it so powerful that the user is overwhelmed and confused about everyday tasks. Confused is the dwarf that shows up when you've erred on the side of too much power and not enough guidelines. (His brother, Rigid, is the dwarf who shows up when you've got too many guidelines and not enough power.)

Confused is also the user interface dwarf who rules over things like menus and dialog boxes. Although you may think you've done a good job laying things out, Confused is off there in the wings, just waiting to sneak in. Do you have things like a "View" entry under the "Edit" menu? Unless you can make a darn good case that that's the right place for it, Confused has just reared his head.

> **Make your interface powerful, so that people can get their work done, but not so powerful that they can get easily lost.**

CONFUSED

As I've already mentioned, it's very important for you to group things in your product logically; people are very willing to explore a product to find out how it works, but you must provide them a way of doing that which makes sense. If you have related functionality scattered hither and yon throughout your interface, people will come to hate your product.

MAKE IT FRIENDLY: GIVE GOOD FEEDBACK

A very important part in designing a good user interface is providing the right level and right kinds of feedback to the user. This leads us to the next user interface dwarf, Hungry, who is starving for good information about the user interface.

If you've designed your interface well, then feedback is a highly visible component of it. Feedback, quite simply, is the information that the user receives back from the product which tells them what they've done, how they've done it, and what the results were. Without these three components, the feedback is deficient. Let's look at each of these pieces in detail.

What the user has done

When the user performs an action they need to know what it is they've done. Have they selected an object? Sent a file to the printer? Picked up the paint bucket tool? The user needs to know.

Much of this information comes about in a passive fashion—that is, the user is not informed directly of their actions, but as a by-product. For example, when the user selects "Print" from the "File" menu, a printing dialog comes up to gather more information from the user. At this point, the user has been informed by the appearance of the printing dialog that they selected the "Print" entry. They probably will notice this only in passing, because they've already received feedback that they did something by the appearance of the dialog itself.

Suppose, however, that when they selected the "Print" menu entry that no dialog came up—the file was sent directly to the printer with no further interaction. The user might be very confused—nothing appears to have happened. Of course, when a piece of paper appeared out of the printer, the user might realize that the document had, in fact, been printed. But suppose the printer were down the hall in another room (as is common in many offices)? Then the user might repeatedly select "Print," in the mistaken notion that nothing was happening, with the result that many copies of the document would end up in the paper tray!

This lack of feedback can be a big problem—when nothing appears to have happened, users are likely to repeat the same sequence of steps several times, in a vain attempt to "get something to happen." Of course, something *is* happening, it's just not visible to the user.

This is also why the images on toolbar buttons appear to "depress" when the user clicks on them with the mouse—it's visual feedback, showing the user that, yes, you have pressed this button. Without that feedback, a user could sit there pressing the button with no visible evidence of success. All of the code which is responsible for the drawing of the button image in the proper state (up or down) does nothing *except* provide feedback to the user—we could very easily write a program in which toolbar buttons didn't depress but where actions were carried out anyway. Don't kid yourself—even though the code does nothing except provide visual feedback, it's a very important part of your interface. Why? Because it works at an almost unconscious level. The user doesn't notice the interface itself, they just notice that it works the way they think it should.

The user very quickly becomes accustomed to this "secondary" feedback layer—that is, when you click on something, it appears to "click," when you select a menu entry (such as "Print"), you get a dialog box querying you for more information. This secondary layer is important because, as I've just mentioned, it works in accordance with the user's expectations. That is, when the user does something on the screen, they expect that something will happen—the changing appearance of your controls indicates to the user that an action has indeed occurred.

How has the user done it?

The second piece of information important to the user is how they've done something. In our example of printing above, they selected the "Print" menu entry. But suppose someone in the user interface design group had decided the word "Print" wasn't quite accurate, and had substituted the word "Output" instead?

Don't laugh—I worked at one company where this happened. This user interface developer had to be gently persuaded that "Output" would seriously hamper the users. Although they might stumble on getting something printed, they certainly wouldn't be able to really repeat that set of actions for quite a while.

Why is that? Because almost every *other* program running under Windows uses "Print." Maybe it isn't the best word, but it's the one users have learned (remember the first interface dwarf, Consistency?) and the one that they'll expect. By putting a different path in place, this person made the product that much harder to learn. (We eventually got it changed back—but not before conducting user trials in which users could be seen vainly trying to find the "Print" entry.)

The moral here is simple—make it learnable by your users. In other words, a set of consistent actions will always generate the same results, with the same feedback each time. Do they click on the printer icon? Do the select the "Print" menu entry? However they do it, make sure that their path to that task is clear.

What Happened

The third part of the equation is what the results of the user's action were. In something like printing, the results are fairly obvious—the user selects "Print," fills out the dialog box (even if it's just clicking on OK), and eventually their document is printed. However, for tasks which are more ephemeral (i.e., they don't end up with paper in their hands), it's appropriate to provide on-screen feedback about the results of an action.

In my paint program ICE/Works, I indicated the fact that the user had selected a new drawing tool by changing the shape of the cursor to that tool—for the pencil tool, the cursor became a pencil. For the paint bucket tool, the cursor became a paint bucket, pouring paint. For the spray paint tool, the cursor became a spray paint can, complete with paint coming out of the nozzle. As soon as the user had selected the tool, the cursor would change shape.

In order to get a clearer idea of how this can work, let's summarize the three user interface pieces, and see how they relate to changing tools in ICE/Works. For this example, we'll use the case of the user switching from the paint bucket tool to the pencil tool. (See figures 2-3 through 2-5)

FIGURE 2-3   THE USER SWITCHES FROM THE PAINT BUCKET TOOL TO THE PENCIL TOOL. THE PAINT BUCKET TOOLS STARTS OUT DEPRESSED (INDICATING THAT IT IS CURRENTLY SELECTED). THE CURSOR IS IN THE SHAPE OF THE PAINT BUCKET.

FIGURE 2-4   AS THE USER SELECTS THE PENCIL TOOL, IT ALSO DEPRESSES—HOWEVER, UNTIL THE USER RELEASES THE BUTTON, NO SELECTION HAS TAKEN PLACE. AT THIS POINT, BOTH BUTTONS ARE DEPRESSED, BUT THE PAINT BUCKET TOOL IS STILL THE "ACTIVE" TOOL.

FIGURE 2-5   THE USER RELEASES THE MOUSE BUTTON OVER THE PENCIL TOOL—THE PENCIL TOOL
STAYS DOWN, INDICATING THAT IT IS SELECTED, AND THE PAINT BUCKET TOOL RAISES ITSELF, INDICATING
THAT IT HAS BEEN TURNED OFF. AT THE SAME TIME, THE CURSOR IS CHANGED TO THE SHAPE OF A PENCIL,
FURTHER INDICATING TO THE USER WHAT DRAWING MODE THEY ARE IN.

1). What has the user done? (User performs an action). The user
"mouses down" (presses the left mouse button down while the
cursor is on the button) on the pencil tool button, and the pencil
tool button appears to become depressed. Note that until the
user releases the mouse button ("mouses up") on the pencil tool,
no selection has taken place.

2. How has the user done it? (What step(s) did the user take to perform the action?) The user had to click down and then release the
mouse button on the pencil tool in order to change to it. If the user
only "moused down" on the pencil tool, and then moved the
mouse off of the button without releasing the button, the pencil
tool would not become selected (this is a important feature which
is sometimes overlooked in designing buttons like this). The user
can quickly learn the necessary steps to activate a tool—mouse

down on the tool, then mouse up. The user can also abort a selection by mousing down, and then moving off of the tool.

3. What were the results of the user's action? (What happened?) When the user has successfully moused down and moused up on the pencil tool, it becomes depressed to indicate that it has been selected; the paint bucket tool button raises itself to indicate that it has become de-selected, and the cursor changes to a pencil shape.

All of this feedback is very important in giving your product a "responsive" feel. However, it is only one kind of feedback. Another kind of feedback lies in providing visual clues to the user about where they are in the program right now. This kind of feedback is related to the second user interface dwarf, Helpful, who guides the user along the right path.

This kind of feedback is less temporal and more structural in nature. What I mean by that is that whereas the first kind of feedback we've discussed occurs at a given point in time to a specific action on the part of the user, this second kind of feedback provides ongoing information about what the user is doing.

For example, in ICE/Works, each drawing tool has its own cursor which indicates what mode the user is currently in. As I've already mentioned, the pencil tool has its own cursor—a pencil shaped cursor which serves to indicate that the user is in "pencil mode." As long as the user doesn't change the tool, the cursor will remain in the shape of the pencil. What's important about this visual feedback mechanism is that it exists right at the point of focus for the user—since the user is constantly focusing on the cursor (because that's where the drawing is occurring), the user is constantly getting subtle feedback about which tool they are using.

Another example of visual feedback is what I do in response to turning on "mirroring mode." Mirroring is a drawing tool that allows the user to reflect the currently drawn image about an axis as they draw. Because mirroring applies to all drawing operations, it's important to be able to distinguish between drawing in mirrored mode and non-mirrored (normal) mode. I do this by placing a small mirror in the cursor of the current drawing operation. Thus, if the user is in pencil mode and mirroring is turned on, a little mirror will appear next to the pencil in the cursor. If mirroring is off, then no mirror appears in the cursor. This behavior is reflected in all the drawing tools. (See figure 2-6).

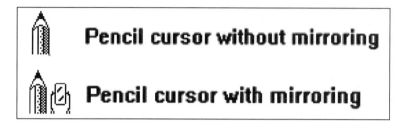

FIGURE 2-6   THE PENCIL TOOL CURSOR WHEN MIRRORING IS OFF, AND WHEN IT IS ON. NOTICE THAT ALTHOUGH THERE IS ONLY A SMALL DIFFERENCE BETWEEN THEM, THE VISUAL CUE TO THE USER IS VERY OBVIOUS ABOUT WHAT MODE THEY ARE CURRENTLY IN.

This visual cue lets the user know at a glance if the next thing they are going to draw is going to be mirrored or not. They don't need to move their eyes anywhere else on the screen (thereby breaking their concentration), they know right away what's going to happen.

HUNGRY

Your users are hungry for good feedback about what your program is doing. Don't be shy about giving it to them!

You'd obviously use this second kind of feedback in a different fashion than the first kind of feedback—they are for different things. However, both kinds of feedback are very important in providing the user clear information about what's going on, and how the program is responding to their inputs.

MAKE IT POWERFUL: GIVE THE USER THE STRENGTH OF 10

This section talks about the last user interface dwarf, Powerful. Powerful's role in life is to ensure that the user is getting his/her work done quickly and easily. Put another way, this means that the user should be able to concentrate on getting the task at hand done with a minimum of interruption and distraction.

In order to help determine what this should be, I like to use what I refer to as the "80% rule." The 80% rule states that any task which the user spends 80% of his or her time doing should be as easy and transparent to do as possible. This means that if a task is one that is often performed by your users in the product, make it simple to do!

One company I consulted with had to wrestle with this issue. They are a company which makes software to analyze seismic data (typically used for oil drilling operations). A major portion of their product allows users to make what are known as "synthetic seismograms." Under the DOS version, this process was incredibly complex—ranges of values had to be chosen, seismic traces picked, starting and stopping points entered. In all, more than 5 screens worth of data had to be input before the user could see the end result.

"This is way too complex," I told them. "You're driving the users out of their minds."

They insisted that the user had to do this each time. "Come on." I said, "are you telling me that there aren't any reasonable default values for any of this?" To make a long story short, they finally were able to come up with good default values for most of the inputs. This meant that users now only had to enter a couple of pieces of information before they saw the end result. This made the task much simpler.

This is one of the best actions that you can do to make your product simple for the user to use—provide sensible defaults. Imagine, if you will, what would happen if a word processor (like Word for Windows, for example) forced you to input every piece of information every time you wanted to create a document. You'd have to input the margins. The headers. The footers. The number of columns. The tab stops. The vertical spacing. The font. The pitch. The point size. The—AAAAAARGH!!! Can you imagine having to input all this stuff every time you wanted to write something??

If it really worked this way, users would be dropping like flies. Fortunately, Word for Windows doesn't do this—it has sensible defaults for all of these things, so that if you need to write something, you can just fire it up and type away.

Of course, the second piece of having sensible defaults is the ability to easily change them. In a word processor, all of the pieces that I've just mentioned (font, and so on) have defaults, but are easy enough to change. This means that if you like the defaults, great—just get to work. If you don't, then change them; and *then* get to work. By giving a user sensible defaults, but also allowing him/her to change them, you've provided the user the flexibility to get the job done without being intrusive.

The third part of having sensible defaults is making them "sticky." What do I mean by this? Simple—when the user changes a default setting, that setting should become the new default, until changed again. If the program is shut down and restarted, the new default value should be saved and reloaded. In other words, the new default value behaves just as the old one did.

The reason for this is simple. If the user doesn't like the defaults that you've provided, then it's easy enough to change them, and have those changes become the new defaults. If, however, the changes to the defaults that the user makes are not sticky, then each time the user starts the program, s/he'll have to change the default values all over again. Believe me, this is not something that most users will want to do!

To give you an example, in ICE/Works (my much-discussed paint program), the user has the ability to shift the bitmap image around. By default, this shift process is a single pixel shift; however, by bringing up a dialog box, the user can change this value to be any value up to 32 pixels. The user also has the option of saving this shift value as the new default value—in other words, the next time the user runs the program, the new shift value will be the default.

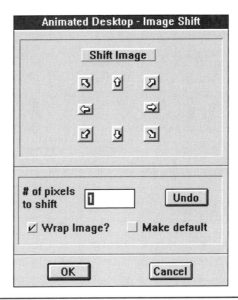

FIGURE 2-7   AN EXAMPLE OF A SENSIBLE DEFAULT VALUE COMBINED WITH THE OPTION OF CHANGING IT. THE USER WILL AUTOMATICALLY GET A SINGLE PIXEL SHIFT UNLESS HE/SHE SPECIFIES OTHERWISE. THE "MAKE DEFAULT" SETTING ALLOWS THE USER TO SAVE THIS VALUE AS THE DEFAULT.

This kind of flexibility conforms very well to the 80% rule. Let's take a look at why:

1. 80% of the time, the user is only going to want to shift the image by a single pixel. The default value for the shift operation is 1. The user can simply shift the image, and get the expected results.

2. Some small percentage of the time, the user is going to want to routinely be able to shift the image more than 1 pixel at a time; in this case, the user can bring up a dialog box and change the shift value. Unless the user selects the "Make Default" checkbox, this new value will only be in effect for as long as the user is running the program. Next time the user starts the program, the default will again be 1 pixel.

3. In an even smaller percentage of the time, the user will want the new value to be the default for all future editing sessions. In this case, the user can select the "Make Default" check box. At this point, the shift value has been changed, and will stay in effect for this session (and all future sessions of the program) until the user changes it again.

As you can see, the difficulty of the action increases as the frequency of the action decreases. For the action that's going to be used a majority of the time, the action is very simple—just shift the image. Next in difficulty is the case where the user needs to change the default value; however, this case is used far less frequently. Finally, the most difficult case (requiring three user actions: setting the shift value, checking the check box and shifting the image) is the least used action. Ramping the difficulty level versus the frequency of the action is a way of providing a great deal of flexibility without impeding the user's progress.

An alternative method of providing defaults to your users is something known as a "style sheet." This is the technique that many word processing programs use. Instead of having one set of defaults, you can have several sets, each with its own identifier. This way, the user can set up defaults for radically different tasks, and switch between them easily.

For example, most word processors use style sheets. Each style sheet has a full set of word processing attributes—font, pitch, margins, layout, etc. This means that you can have one style sheet for a business letter (with formal font and no indention on the paragraph heads) and another one for personal correspondence, and yet another for envelopes, and so on. The word processor makes it easy for you to define a new style, or to inherit from an old one.

POWERFUL

Make sure that your users can get the job done without a lot of interference from your product.

The whole point of defaults is to empower the user, and remove the burden of drudgery. Computers, after all, are very good at mindless, repetitive tasks, and people are not. By eliminating the repetitive tasks, you free the user to concentrate on the essence of the task, not the details of the implementation.

Chapter 3

What, Why and How: Three Questions You Have to Be Able to Answer

Now that you have taken a look at the five user-interface dwarves, it's time to look at the three questions you have to be able to answer when building a user interface:

- ✦ What task(s) will users be performing?
- ✦ How will they accomplish the tasks?
- ✦ Why will they be performing those tasks?

Each of these questions is fairly straightforward, but it's important to be able to answer all of them. If you can't answer one (or more) of these questions, you're going to have problems in designing the interface for your product. To understand why, let's look at each of these questions in a little more detail.

WHAT TASK WILL USERS BE PERFORMING?

This question is really at the heart of what your application is and does. It's a question that has layers, much like an onion. The outer layer is the broad overview—what kind of an application is this? If you want users to be able to push words, then this is a word processing application. If you want users to be able to create images, then this is a painting or drawing application.

Really, that's the easy part. The harder part is nailing down specifics. If users are going to paint things, for example, how do they accomplish this? What tools should be made available? Where should they be located? On the left, or on the right? Top or bottom? Should the tools be available all the time, or only in response to an action?

HOW WILL THEY ACCOMPLISH THE TASKS

This is where you're going to have to start prototyping the application, to get a feel for what task(s) users are going to be doing. There are a number of prototyping tools on the market, and several of the major compilers can also be used to do the job. Visual Basic is also a tool that can be used for rapid prototyping. Whatever tool you use, however, you're going to have to spend a bit of time hooking it up and making it work pretty close to the way you think the final application will work.

The reason for this, of course, is that you want to start getting a feel for the application. And please get it out of your head that you're going to be reusing this code—you're not. Right now, all you're doing (and it's a lot) is figuring out how the interface is probably going to work. Notice that I said *probably*—once you start actually building the application with real code (as opposed to the throw-away prototype), you're going to find that it needs to be changed again. And again. Many times.

So why build a prototype in the first place? Why not do it the old-fashioned way, and write it out (in excruciating detail) on paper?

Well, for starters, it won't work. I have yet to see a product that was spec'd out on paper in great detail that ever turned out to be worth a darn as a product, and I've been in this business a long time. Half of the products that have been set up this way have never even made it off the launching platform. Of those that do, most of them are so cumbersome, unwieldy, and excessive they fit the description of a mouse designed by committee—an elephant.

This is not to say that doing a software product this way can't be done—it's just that I've never seen it happen yet. If the project in question is one at a large company where the greatest hazard to your well-being is rigor mortis of the brain, then go ahead. Paper specifications of a product can be dragged out almost endlessly. If, on the other hand, the biggest task ahead of you is to get a product out the door, and you need to do it within (say) six months, then forget paper. You need to see how this thing is going to live and breathe on the screen.

Once you've got a shell or prototype up on the screen—I don't much care what you call the thing, just so long as you understand that it's something that you can actually interact with—you can begin to start answering your second question, which is how is the user going to go about accomplishing a task?

By this, I mean the actual mechanics of the task at hand. Since I have no idea of what the task is, I'm not going to be able to tell you how to solve it. I can give you some guidelines, however, and probably most important, I can tell you how *not* to do it.

How do you go about designing the mechanics of the interface (how it's going to work)? First, sit down and figure out *what* your users are trying to do. Hopefully, you've just done this by building a rapid prototype of your application. If not, go back and do it right now. I'm not kidding, either—without having anything to look at on the screen, all you've really got are nebulous ideas and plans. For this to work right, you've got to have something concrete to go on. (If you're lucky enough to have a user-interface expert available, consult him or her a lot. I don't mean a self-styled expert, either, I mean someone who's had real experience designing and shipping successful commercial software.)

Okay, you've got your prototype up and running. First thing to do is analyze the problem you're trying to solve. Are you trying to let users print a file? Copy entries from one place to another? Cut and paste? In other words, broadly (and I mean broadly) describe the problem space you're trying to cover. Do *not* use specifics. Do not say something like "We want to use OLE to let users copy files from one place to another." (For OLE, simply insert the hot buzzword of the month). This is gobbly-degook. Do not say "We'll just use drag-and-drop." (I once saw a desktop shell that used nothing *but* drag-and-drop to accomplish tasks, and it was horrendously unuseable.) Resist the temptation to resort to smoke and mirrors or large amounts of handwaving.

You may buffalo your way out of a meeting using one of these stratagems, but you will not be able to buffalo your customers. The interface does not lie. If it is horribly clunky, it will show that fact in its use. It may look pretty—almost anything improves with the application of cosmetics—but there will be no hiding its underlying inadequacy.

How do you avoid this horrible fate? By focusing on the general tasks that need doing, and then, and only then, coming up with appropriate metaphors that let users accomplish that task. The tasks should be easy to perform, with a minimum of fuss, and they should be natural. (One of the big problems with the shell that used drag-and-drop for everything was its insistence on treating *everything* as an object. If I wanted to open a file, I had to drag the file object on the opener object and then try to find the file I wanted. I couldn't use the file-viewer—oh, no. That wouldn't have been object-oriented.)

As a practical matter, this means providing multiple ways of doing things. Many people who use Windows products hate the mouse. Strange, I know, but it's true. They want a keyboard method of doing things, most often because they don't want to lift their hands off the keys. Others prefer to do almost everything via the mouse, and not the keyboard. They don't mind moving their hands back and forth. This means you should provide both mouse and keyboard methods of getting your tasks done. And do not think for a minute that just because you are biased either for or against the mouse that all your customers will be biased the same way. They won't.

WHY WILL THEY BE PERFORMING THOSE TASKS

Once you start having a clearer idea of what and how users are going to perform a task, it's time to ask the third question, why are they going to perform this task? In even simpler words, you're asking "do users need to do this task at all, never mind the how of it?" This is the question that lets you really get to the heart of what you're doing. By answering it, you are defining for yourself whether:

1. This is a task that really needs doing, and users have to be able to do it, so a mechanism needs to be created to let them do it.

2. This is a task that really needs doing, but most of the time the computer has all of the information available about what needs doing, so the mechanics of the task can be hidden from the user.

3. This is a task that doesn't really need doing.

You'll notice only in the first case does a method of doing the task need to be created and made visible to the users. The other two cases are ones where users should never be burdened with excess or irrelevant information. Many tasks are handed over to users that should not be handed over—dull, boring, or repetitive tasks that people are ill-suited for, but which computers are tremendously well-suited for. Sure, it's easier to think up a clunky interface to an irrelevant task than it is to figure out that the task itself is pointless, and then programmatically eliminate that task, but being easier doesn't mean it's better. In short, never build anything in the interface without a good reason.

Summary

To recap this section, remember you need to be able to answer three questions about each interface part that you build—what the interface piece is there for, how it will be used, and why (or if) it is even necessary at all.

You need to be able to answer these questions in addition to being able to deal with the five user-interface dwarves: Consistency, Helpy, Confused, Hungry, and Powerful. If you skipped over those sections, go back and read them now—trust me, it won't take much time, and without a good grounding in each of them, your interface will suffer.

The next chapter of this book deals with some of the fundamental concepts of Windows programming, which is to say event-driven programming. Event-driven programming is very different from traditional, DOS-style programming, and even some people who have been writing Windows code for a while don't get it. Events are the cornerstone of Windows, and it's crucial to understand them, and how they work, in order to design good Windows applications.

CHAPTER 4

EVENTS AND EVENT-DRIVEN PROGRAMMING

Before I get into the nature of user-interface design in Windows, you need to have a better understanding of the event-driven nature of Windows programming. Why? Quite simply, because it's impossible to develop good user interfaces in Windows if you don't know how Windows itself handles things. Developing an interface for an event-driven environment is rather different than developing one for a more traditional environment, such as DOS. To understand the differences, and what is required for them, let's take a look at what event-driven programming is, and how it's different from an environment like DOS.

WHAT IS EVENT-DRIVEN PROGRAMMING?

To understand what event-driven programming is, let's first take a look at the way it used to work, in a traditional, linear program.

Linear programming

Traditional programming, or, as I like to refer to it, linear programming, worked something like this:

1. Start the program, and set up the initial variables.

2. Read some data from a user or from a file

3. Process the data

4. Display the results

5. Exit the program or loop to Step 2.

This is enormously oversimplified, of course, but it represents the heart of linear programming, which is this: A linear program has a direct linear flow of control through the program, and only certain things may be accomplished at certain times. Operations not allowed are ignored (in the best case) or cause the program to crash or exhibit other strange behavior (in the worst case). Figure 4-1 shows a simple flow chart of how a linear program operates.

The biggest problem with linear programs is as they grow linearly in complexity, they grow exponentially in size: The more complex they are, the bigger they are. This also tends to exacerbate the problem of bugs and maintenance. The single biggest reason for all of this is that a linear program must not only manage the task it was designed for (such as solve a mathematical equation), but it must also manage the task of interacting with users in all forms. The program must deal with keystrokes, mouse movements (if the program supports the mouse), output to the screen, file operations, and so on. If the program supports a windowed environment, it must manage the windows, perform all of the calculations needed for the window placement and drawing, and a host of other chores.

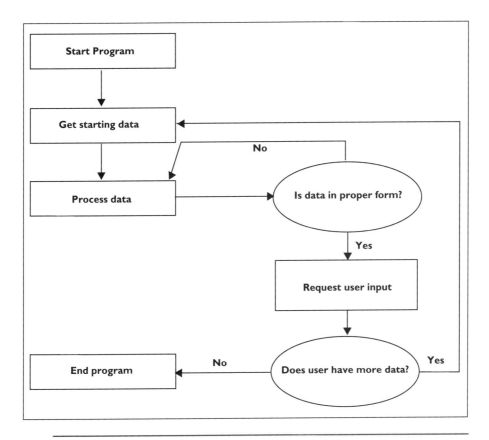

Figure 4-1   A LINEAR PROGRAM TENDS TO BE QUITE SIMPLE: THERE IS SOME INPUT, SOME PROCESSING AND SOME OUTPUT. EVEN THE MOST COMPLEX LINEAR PROGRAMS, SUCH AS STATE MACHINES, STILL TEND TO BE FAIRLY STRAIGHTFORWARD. THERE ARE A CERTAIN NUMBER OF STATES ONE CAN ENTER, AND A LIMITED NUMBER OF OPERATIONS ONE CAN PERFORM IN EACH STATE.

Event-driven programming

An event-driven program has to do this too, of course. It's just the way an event-driven program does this makes it much easier to maintain and develop.

While a linear program is, by nature, an *active* program—querying the user, processing data—an event-driven program is *passive*. Nothing happens in an event-driven program until an event is received that causes something to happen. This implies an important point: For an event-driven program to work, there must be something that provides events.

In Windows, this something is Windows itself, in this case, the Event Manager. The Event Manager is the piece responsible for seeing that events are created and dispatched to the proper places (such as programs that need to receive those events). The Event Manager is responsible for things such as key clicks and mouse movements—it then generates events for these things, and dispatches them to the proper place. In this case, the proper place is an event-driven program waiting to receive such an event.

Let's take a look at how an event-driven program would be described. Using the same idea as a linear program, here's the breakdown of an event-driven program:

1. Start the program, and set up the initial values.
2. Start the event loop,
3. Wait for an event.
4. Process the event.
5. Go to Step 3.

Unlike a linear program, most of an event-driven program's life is spent in Step 3, waiting for an event. This is because as soon as an event is received, an event-driven program processes it, and then returns and waits for more events. Step 4, is where the real work of handling the event is done.

An event-driven program has what are known as *event handlers*, which are simply routines that handle specific events. For example, if you wanted an event-driven program to handle mouse movements, you would create a mouse movement event handler. This is the piece of code that would actually respond to a mouse movement—this code is responsible for handling the way in which a mouse movement is significant to us. In a spreadsheet program, a mouse movement might indicate a user is highlighting some cells. In a paint program, a mouse movement might indicate a user is painting some lines on the screen. Regardless of the significance of the action, our program will be able to respond at any time to a mouse movement event.

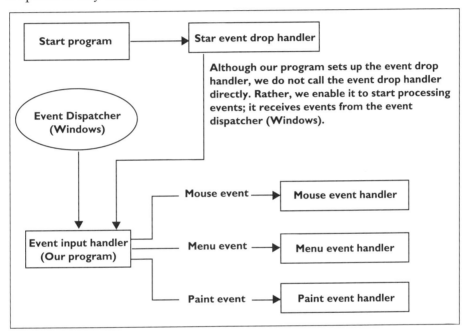

FIGURE 4-2. AN EVENT-DRIVEN USER INTERFACE CAN PROCESS A VARIETY OF EVENTS AT ANY TIME. WHAT EVEN GETS PROCESSED DEPENDS UPON WHAT EVENT IS DELIVERED TO THE PROGRAM BY THE EVENT MANAGER. THIS, IN TURN, IS DEPENDENT UPON WHAT ACTIONS HAVE OCCURRED IN THE SYSTEM (USER GENERATED AND SYSTEM GENERATED).

This leads to another big difference between event-driven programs and linear programs, which is this: an event-driven program is ready at any time to process any sort of event, whereas a linear program is not. You may be scratching your heads at this, so I'll explain in a little more detail.

Let's use the example I just talked about—wanting to know if the mouse has moved. In an event-driven world, we do it this way:

1. Create a mouse movement event handler (some code that handles what happens when users move the mouse).
2. Run the program.

You don't have to do anything else, because you've already got an event-driven program—you've simply added the ability to handle one more type of event, that of responding to a mouse movement. Now, whenever the user moves the mouse, a mouse-movement event is sent to our program (by the system's Event Manager), and our mouse-movement handler processes it, and does whatever is appropriate for our program at that time.

By contrast, in order for a linear program to handle mouse movements, you would have to do something like this:

1. Create some code that handles what happens when the mouse moves
2. Create some code that *"polls"* the mouse to find out what its state is.
3. If the mouse state has changed, call the code written for Step 1.
4. Every place we want to check the mouse, make a call to the code written in Step 2.
5. Run the program.

This is quite a bit more complex. Not only do you have to write the code that responds when the mouse has moved, but you also have to write code to actively go out and interrogate what the current state of the mouse is. On top of that, you have to make sure you call the code that checks the mouse every place you want to do so. And even this doesn't catch everything you might be interested in; after all, you only know what the mouse is doing at the times you check it. In between those times, you will have no idea whether the user has moved the mouse or not.

Of course, there are ways around some of these technical difficulties. You could write a mouse-interrupt routine, for example, to make sure you polled the mouse often enough so as not to miss any important user movements. But this merely adds to the complexity of the task that you are trying to accomplish.

WHY ARE EVENT-DRIVEN INTERFACES BETTER?

In this case, it's clear an event-driven environment makes it easier to build a program that can respond to discontiguous events at all times. For user interfaces, this is clearly an important consideration. Graphic user interfaces are, after all, very much at the whim of users—many different things can be done at any time. In a painting program, for example, users could open a file, save a file, undo the previous operation (if there was one), move the mouse, select a painting tool, begin painting and more.

Because the event-driven interface can respond to any of these events at any given time, it makes developing a program with this interface much simpler. Put another way, a program with a comparable level of interface complexity is much more difficult to write in a linear programming fashion than in an event-driven fashion.

This is because an operating system like Windows provides much of the basic functionality of creating menus, moving windows, generating mouse movements, and so on. All of these things are built into the Windows system, so you, as a programmer, don't have to build them yourself. This, in turn, means you can focus on the task of creating a product that solves a problem or task you (or your users) have, rather than focusing on the mechanics of building an interface. Really, it's a very liberating thing to have an operating system like Windows available.

Types of Events in Windows

Now that you have a better idea of the basic nature of the event-driven nature of Windows programming, let's take a closer look at the kinds of messages Windows provides programmers. These are the kinds of messages you'll need to respond to in your program; I'll talk about these messages in greater detail later in the book when we get to the examples. In the meantime, however, I'll begin with a discussion of the general types of events Windows provides, and some examples of what those messages are.

Broadly speaking, events can be classified into one of four different groups:

1. System events
2. Control events
3. User events
4. Other events.

Let's take a look at system events first.

System events

System events are primarily classified events generated by the system to provide your program with information about something that needs doing. For example, one of the messages Windows provides to you is called WM_PAINT. It specifies that all or part of the display area of your program needs to be repainted. Another message generated by the system is WM_INITMENU, which is sent to your program when a menu is about to become active.

These messages are sent to your program by the system when something has occurred, or is about to occur, to which your program might need to respond. In the first example, the WM_PAINT message lets your program know some or all of the screen needs to be repainted. These events are called *system events*, and are generated by the system itself in response to internal decisions, such as another window was moved and uncovered part of your window, which must now be repainted.

Control events

You may have gotten the impression that only the Windows Event Manager can dispatch messages. This is not the case. Any program can dispatch messages (including your own). Controls, such as buttons, list boxes, and menus (all of which I'll talk about in more detail) are particularly copious generators of messages.

These messages are particular to the given control: Each control has its own set of messages that indicate current state, transition to a new state, or are messages sent to the control to get it to perform a task.

Sending control events and responding to other control events can often make up the bulk of your user-interface code. This is because controls often make up a large portion of the interface. For example, most of the objects inside a dialog box are controls, and most of the code that handles that dialog box is going to deal with the individual controls in the dialog box.

User events

The third type of event your program will get is one generated by users. These events typically have to do with something users have done to the program, such as move the mouse, or move a window. In these cases, your program gets a message such as WM_MOUSEMOVE or WM_MOVE. These messages contain information about the new state of the mouse or window, which your program can then use to determine what to do.

User events, obviously, are generated by users, and as such, occur only when users do something to generate an event. This means that if the machine is sitting idle, there won't be any user-generated events coming in.

Other events

The final type of event your program can receive is what are loosely termed *other* events. These include things such as a WM_TIMER event, which occurs in response to a timer your program has set up. Another kind of event that fits into this category are events defined specifically for your program (these are known as *user-defined events*, although properly speaking they should be called *programmer-defined events*).

Other events is really a catch-all area, including any event that doesn't fall into the other three categories. If an event doesn't seem to fit into any of the other three categories, then it probably belongs here.

SUMMARY

An event-driven program is one in which the key components of the interaction with users (and with the system) are driven by a messaging system that provides messages, known as *events*, to your program. These events are pieces of information to let your program know something specific has happened and your program might need to perform some other action in response to the message.

Different events are triggered by different things—some are generated by the system to let you know that something important has occurred (or will occur), some are generated by other programs or controls, and some are generated by users. These events are what trigger your program to perform various actions.

Probably the most important pieces from a user-interface standpoint are the various controls Windows provides for you—menus, listboxes, and so on. Let's take a look at these in more detail, starting with menus, which are the subject of the next chapter.

CHAPTER 5

MENUS, AND THEIR USES

Menus are one of the most important components in any user interface. Menus provide—or at least they *should* provide—a way for users to navigate among the structures of your program. Menus can provide coherence to a user interface, by shaping the outlines of your program in a way that makes sense to users. Alternatively, menus can make a perfectly logical and understandable structure utterly incoherent to everyone, including the designer of the program. Careless layout of the menu structures can hide the significance of some items, while emphasizing other, less important ones. In short, menus can be either a boon or a boondoggle for your users.

Knowing this, why do some developers put so little thought into their menu structures? Some of the most common reasoning I hear is that menus aren't really all that important, that the important pieces of the user interface lie elsewhere. Speaking from experience, all I can say is that this attitude is misguided. Perhaps because it's so easy to get a basic menu up (as compared with some other, more esoteric user-interface pieces that are much harder to build) programmers tend to dismiss the importance of menus.

So what can we do to help alleviate this sad state of affairs? Quite simply, give menus the attention they deserve. There are a couple of fairly simple steps that, if followed, may not give you the absolute best menu structure (that'll probably take a lot of tweaking close to when your product is done), but will certainly give you a good workable base to go from.

STEP 1: STANDARD ENTRIES

Make sure any of your basic menus in your program (such as File or Edit) have the standard entries. Just what are these standard entries? Take a look at figures 5-1 and 5-2, which show the minimal standard entries for File and Edit menus, respectively.

FIGURE 5-1   THE BASIC FILE MENU. THERE ARE FIVE ENTRIES, BROKEN INTO THREE GROUPS.

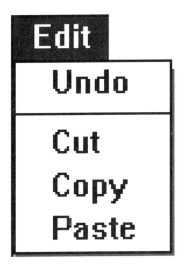

FIGURE 5-2   THE BASIC EDIT MENU. THERE ARE FOUR BASIC ENTRIES, BROKEN INTO TWO GROUPS.

The File menu

The entries for the basic File menu are these: New, Open, Save, Save As..., and Exit. Assuming your program works in some way with files, you'll want at a very minimum these five entries. If you have these five entries, here's what they should do:

1. *New.* Creates a new <whatever it is> in your program. For example, if your program edits graphic images, this menu entry would create a new graphic image in your program's workspace. If there is a current image that has not been saved, you should probably query users to see if they want to save it.

53

HELPFUL

Helpful. A very important point in many products is they sometimes won't get out of the way when users want them to. For example, in the New menu above, I suggest that if an unsaved image is in the buffer, you should query users before creating a new image. I have to tell you, though, that I absolutely hate that behavior. It just drives me nuts. Remember what I said about the puppy-dog interface behavior? I consider this a prime example of it. I already know that I have an unsaved image in the buffer, and if I wanted it saved, I would have saved it. In my product ICE/Works, I have a toggle that turns this sort of querying off (see figure 5-3). If the mode is set for novice, then my product queries users before loading a new image—if the mode is set for expert, it won't. Guess what mode I run it in? Right. So if you build in this interface to your product for New (and really, it's a good idea for new users), please let your expert users have a way of turning it off.

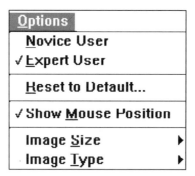

FIGURE 5-3   THIS MENU SHOWS TWO ENTRIES—NOVICE USER AND EXPERT USER—AND ALLOWS THE USER TO SELECT BETWEEN THEM. WHEN THE USER SELECTS ONE MENU ENTRY, THE OTHER ENTRY IS DESELECTED. THIS WAY, NOVICE USERS CAN BE PROMPTED FOR POTENTIALLY DANGEROUS OPERATIONS, WHILE POWER USERS CAN TURN OFF THIS FEATURE.

2. *Open.* Opens an already existing file of whatever type is appropriate for your program. This menu entry typically pops up a File Open dialog box so users can select the file and path they want. Again, you'll probably want to query users if the current <whatever it is> will be erased and it hasn't been saved.

3. *Save.* Saves the current <whatever it is> into the file it lives in. If the <whatever it is> doesn't already have an existing file, this menu option behaves exactly like the Save As... option following. Otherwise, it just saves the file. (An alternative behavior is to have the Save entry grayed out until the <whatever it is> has a filename.) The Save menu entry should be grayed out for files that have been loaded, but not altered. This saves users the dilemma of wondering if they have made any changes that need to be saved. If the entry is gray, they'll know that they haven't.

POWERFUL

Powerful. Some programs query you each time you save a file, with something like *File already exists. Overwrite it?* This is another example of the friendly puppy-dog interface at work, only this one I'll have no truck with whatsoever. Don't put this query into your program—of course users want to overwrite the file; otherwise they wouldn't have used Save, they would have used Save As...

4. *Save As....* Similar to Save, this version first queries users for a filename to save the <whatever it is> to. Typically, this means displaying a File Save dialog box, which lets users select a file name and path. One important note—the File Save dialog box not only lets users create a new file name, it also lets them select an already existing file name. In this case, it's an extremely *good* idea to query them about whether they really meant to overwrite the current file, as opposed to the Save command, where it's a really *bad* idea. The reason it's a good idea here is because the Save As... command is really used only when the user is cre-

ating a new file for the <whatever it is>. If they pick an already existing file, it either means:

- they made a mistake or
- they meant to do it.

In this case, since they're creating a new file, it's a lot more likely they made a mistake. (This follows the 80 percent rule I've developed—respond to what the user is likely doing 80 percent of the time. In this case, most of the time they've made a mistake. It's best to check it out.)

5. *Exit.* Exits the program. Depending upon how you do it, exiting the program can either be *right now*, without saving work, or the program can query the user ("Document <foo> has not been saved. Do you wish to save it? [Yes][No]") about whether to save any unsaved work or not. Again, there are two schools of thought on this; me, I want out right now. Other people are less sure, and some want to be prompted. The best solution: Prompt the user, but give them a way to turn it off. (See figure 5-3 and my comments, above). This entry is also sometimes labeled Quit, which is acceptable, but why not stick with the default standard?

Now that I've talked about each entry, let's also take a quick look at why menu entries are separated the way they are. First, New is separate because it's doing something special—creating a completely new instance of a document. It isn't doing any of the things associated with the next three menu entries (Open, Save, and Save As...), so it doesn't belong with them. Hence the separator.

The next three entries, (as I just said, Open, Save, and Save As...) *do* belong together, because they are all performing similar, related functions—opening and saving currently existing files. Save As... belongs here because it's also file related. The last entry, Exit, (or Quit) is again a different kind of item, so it gets its own little space.

So that, in a nutshell (assuming rather large shells), is the basic layout of the basic File menu, and the few standard entries that it should have. What should you do if these entries aren't appropriate for your program (that is, you won't be opening and closing files)? Simple. Don't put a File menu in your program. This is one of those hard and fast rules that I try to insist on—if it doesn't let you open and save files, then it shouldn't be labeled File. I know some designers who are adamant that File should come first, even if there aren't any file saving capabilities in it, simply because "users are expecting it." I can pretty much guarantee you users are *not* expecting to have a File entry with no file capabilities in it. All you end up doing is confusing them. This sort of "consistency" is one that's lacking in common sense—just because File is the first menu entry on most programs doesn't mean it has to be first on yours—unless you have file capabilities, in which case it *must* be first. Don't put it second or third. In short, don't label the menu File if it doesn't have file related capabilities in it.

The Edit menu

Now that I've thoroughly dealt with the File menu, let's take a look at the basic Edit menu entries. I'm going through both of these in some detail, because I want you to understand and begin to use the sort of thinking processes that go into making these sorts of decisions. What entry goes where, and why, that sort of thing. After going through these two sets of entries in detail, you'll hopefully have a much better grasp of how to go about this process for your other menus and menu entries.

Now, the Edit menu. First, let's understand what the Edit menu is for. It's for basic editing functions of your program. Let's say you're building a graphics editing program—you wouldn't put all your graphics editing tools here. Why not? Because many of them (quite properly) belong under something like a Tools menu. They are tools, not the actual act of editing itself. That's what should go here. Let's take a look at the basic menu entries for Edit, and you'll see what I mean.

1. *Undo.* If your program supports an Undo capability, then this is the first menu entry you should have. Of course, if your program *doesn't* support undo, then you won't have this menu entry. Some programs support and Undo/Redo capability. That is, if users Undo an action, they have the option of undoing the Undo—thus redoing whatever action was performed. (See the code on p. xx.) See also Figure 5-4, which shows the Undo and Redo menu entries. You'll want to be able to gray out the Undo menu entry if nothing's been done.

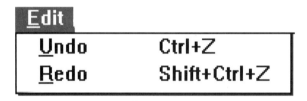

FIGURE 5-4   A MENU ENTRY SHOWING UNDO AND REDO. THIS CAPABILITY ALLOWS
THE USER TO 'UNDO' THE UNDO.

2. *Cut.* This menu entry allows users to cut something from your program to the Windows clipboard. If there's nothing to cut, or users first have to select something to cut, then you'll want to gray out this entry. Some programs gray out this entry if you've already cut something to the clipboard—that is, each cut (or copy) operation must be followed by a paste operation. I tend to dislike this paradigm. What if I cut the wrong thing? I don't want to have to paste something I don't want just to be able to cut the thing I do want.

3. *Copy.* This menu entry is like Cut, only instead of a cut operation, it copies the selected material to the Windows clipboard. In other respects, it behaves just the same as Copy—it should be grayed if there's nothing to copy (either there's nothing there, or the user

has not made a selection). Like Cut, Copy is grayed out by some programs when you've just performed a copy operation—once you copy something, you can't copy something else until you paste the first thing that you copied. Again, I don't much like this feature, and I don't recommend you do it this way.

4. *Paste*. The last of the four standard Edit menu entries, this option lets users paste a previously cut or copied object from the Windows clipboard into the program. If nothing is currently in the clipboard, this menu entry should be grayed out.

Remember that I told you there were a couple of basic steps you could take to ensure your menus came out okay? (I bet you thought I forgot, didn't you?) We've covered Step 1, which was to standardize your basic menus. There are two more steps that follow.

DRAG-RIGHTS AND OTHER THINGS

If there's a way to manipulate something on screen, make sure there's a way to do it from the menu also. What do I mean by this? Let me give you an example—in my icon editor ICE/Works, there are a series of tools you can adjust the settings of, such as the Pencil tool. You do this by double-clicking on the tool, which brings up a dialog box where you adjust the tool's features. However, if you never double-click on a tool, you probably don't know this feature is available. In earlier versions of the program, I didn't have a menu method of accessing these tool setting features. As a result, people kept asking me to put in features that already existed. Finally, I got wise, and put in menu entries for these features, too, so people just browsing the menu structures could find them (see Figure 5-5). This brings us to the next important step:

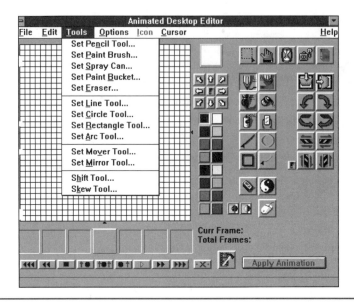

FIGURE 5-5   A SCREEN SHOT OF ICE/WORKS. NOTE THE PULL-DOWN MENU FOR TOOLS, WHICH LETS YOU SET THE PROPERTIES OF THE VARIOUS TOOLS IN THE PROGRAM. YOU CAN ALSO SET THESE FEATURES BY DOUBLE-CLICKING ON EACH TOOL—BUT UNLESS YOU KNOW THIS, YOU WON'T DISCOVER IT.

MENU STRUCTURES

Many people are going to try and figure out how your product works by browsing the menu structures. (I know, because I do it all the time. So do many of the people I've seen in focus groups.) Since people are going to be browsing the menus, it's a good idea to make as much of the functionality of the product *visible* in the menus.

EXAMPLES

Now that you have explored some of the things you can do to make your menus work more effectively in your product, let's take a look at some examples. These examples are working code and code fragments you can use to make your life easier and more productive. Again, I want to concentrate on specific user-interface design issues and how those issues relate to code—you don't want just theory, after all—you want some practical hands-on as well. Here it is.

The menu DIL example

The first example is what's known as a *display information line*, or DIL. A DIL provides you with a method of giving users feedback about actions in a small status line at the bottom of the screen. Many commercial applications use these to very good effect—I'm going to show you how you can build your own DIL, and I'm going to give you a stand-alone C++ class that does all of the hard work for you. All you need to do is provide a couple of pieces of information in your program, and the DIL automatically works. (Pretty cool, eh?) I'm also going to give you a sample program that shows the DIL in action, so you'll know what you need to do.

First, let's take a look at the listings for the DIL example, and then we can check it out in action and touch on the interesting bits. Listings 5-1 through 5-11 are the code for the DIL (skeleton) application.

Since the most interesting piece in all of this is the object class that handles most of the real work in our application, I've listed that first, followed by the other files.

The DIL class itself provides a convenient method of encapsulating DIL behavior; you give it the window handle of your main window, and some string tables and ID tables, and it handles the busy work of figuring out what item to display for a given menu entry, as well as determining if the DIL window has been moved.

Listing 5-1   Dil.hpp

```
//
//  Dil.hpp
//
```

Listing 5-1 *continued*

```
//    This object class provides basic support
// for the creation of a DIL (Display
// Information Line).
//
// Written by Alex Leavens, for ShadowCat Technologies
//
//


//
//
//————————————————————-
//
//
// History: $Log: $
//
//
//
//
//—————————————————————————
//


#ifndef __DIL_HPP

#define __DIL_HPP

#ifdef __cplusplus


//————————————————-
//
// Dil Class.
//
//    This class encapsulates the
// basic behavior and variables for
// a DIL.
//

    class FAR

DisplayInfoLine
{
    //————- PROTECTED ————-

    protected:
```

```
    HWND    hDilWnd;    // Window handle for our Dil

    BOOL    dilCreated;// Has the Dil been created yet?

    WORD * dilIDs;      // ID of Dils (for mapping)

    LPSTR *dilStrings;// Strings of Dils

WORD * subEntries;// Sub menu ID's—we use this for
                  // drag rights

WORD *  subMap;        // For a given entry in the subEntries
                       // list, this is the ID we should
                       // retrieve to display the right
                       // information

    //————————-

    int GetDILIndex ( WORD id );   // Get index of DIL


//———- PUBLIC ————

public:

    //————————-
    //
    // Constructors and destructors
    //

    DisplayInfoLine();

    ~DisplayInfoLine();

//—————
//
// Manipulation functions
//

//———
//
// InitSelf()
//
//   Creates the Dil window
//
```

continued

Listing 5-1 *continued*

```
//   Call this member function
// in response to the WM_CREATE
// message.
//

    BOOL
InitSelf ( HWND       hWnd,         // Parent window handle
        HINSTANCE     hInst,        // Parent instance
        WORD *        dilIDs,       // ID's of menu entries
        LPSTR *       dilStrings,   // Strings for Dils
        WORD *        mapKeys,      // Values of 1st menu entries
                                    // in drag-rights
        WORD *        mapIDs );     // Values of drag rights

//------------
//
// UpdateDil()
//
//   If a message has come in that
// we need to update the DIL info,
// this routine will do that.
//
// Call this routine in response
// to the WM_MENUSELECT message.
//

    void
UpdateDil ( HWND   hWnd,
        WORD       wParam,
        LONG       lParam );


//------------
//
// MoveDil()
//
//  When the main window
// is moved, then the Dil has to
// be moved also.   This routine
// will do that.
//
// Call this member function in
// response to the WM_SIZE message.
//
```

```
    void

MoveDil (   HWND        hWnd,
            WORD        wParam,
            LONG        lParam );


//————————-
//
// UpdateDisplay()
//
//   Updates the current Dil display
// with the passed-in string.
// Used by the routine UpdateDil()
// for handling when the display has
// changed via a menu, this routine
// can also be used directly by
// a client routine in order to
// provide real-time display
// information.
//

    void

UpdateDisplay ( LPSTR lpDisplayString );


//————————-
//
// UpdateDisplay()
//
//   This version of the UpdateDisplay()
// routine takes an index into our string
// table and uses that to display
// the results.
//

    void
UpdateDisplay ( int    stringIndex );


//————————
//
// GetDilIndex()
```

continued

Listing 5-1 *continued*

```
//
//    Given the array of id values and
// strings, this routine will try and
// match the one to the other.
//
// Returns:
// 0 - n : Index of matching item
//     -1     : No match
//

    int
GetDilIndex ( WORD id );

//────────────────
//
// GetMenuMapIndex()
//
//    This routine takes the menu ID
// of the first entry in a drag-right
// menu, and turns it into the id
// of the pop-up menu itself.  It
// does this using a pair of arrays
// that map one entry to the other
//

    int
GetMenuMapIndex ( WORDmenuID );
};


//────────────────-

#endif // __cplusplus

#endif // __DIL_HPP
```

Listing 5-2, DIL.CPP, gives you the C++ source code for the DisplayInfoLine() class member functions. The member functions were defined in the .hpp file (listing 5-1). Here, we define the actual code that gets used by the **DisplayInfoLine()** class to do the actual work. (By the way, I always break up my C++ object classes like this—first the .hpp file (which contains a class definition), and a .cpp file (which contains the member functions for the class).

Since the class is encapsulating the behavior of a DIL, you'd expect it to be relatively complex, but it's not. It performs three basic behaviors: It creates the window that the DIL will be displayed in, it checks to see if a menu entry has an associated text string to be displayed in the DIL, and it manages what happens when the DIL is moved.

There's no reason that all of this couldn't be straight C code, of course. In fact, the first DIL that I wrote that had this same functionality was written entirely in C. However, by encapsulating it this way, you get rid of a couple of problems—you don't have to have any global variables (besides the single instance of the DIL class), and you don't have to have code that handles only DIL behavior in your app. You simply make a few calls to the DIL, and that's it. This is not the standard view of C++—which is lots of classes, lots of inheritance, but it's the way I tend to use C++ a lot. I simply package a piece of functionality, and then have that functionality ready to go, whenever I need it.

Listing 5-2 DIL.CPP

```
//
// Dil.cpp
//
//   Source code for the Dil (DisplayInfoLine)
// class.
//
// This code provides all the support for the Dil,
// and is completely (well, mostly) modular.
//
// Written by Alex Leavens
// for ShadowCat Technologies
//
//

#include <skeleton.hpp>

//————————————--
```

continued

Listing 5-2 *continued*

```
//
// DisplayInfoLine()
//
//   Constructor
//

DisplayInfoLine::DisplayInfoLine()
{

    hDilWnd = NULL;   // Setup for no window handle yet

    dilCreated = FALSE;   // Dil not yet created

    dilIDs = NULL; // No pointer to dil ID's

    dilStrings = NULL;// No dil strings yet, either.

    subEntries = NULL;

    subMap = NULL;

}

//————————--
//
// ~DisplayInfoLine()
//
//   Destructor
//

DisplayInfoLine::~DisplayInfoLine()
{
}


//————
//
// InitSelf()
//
//   Creates the Dil window
//

    BOOL
DisplayInfoLine::InitSelf ( HWND     hWnd, // Parent window handle
```

```
            HINSTANCE       hInst,          // Parent instance
            WORD * dilIDs,                  // ID's of menu entries
            LPSTR *dilStrings,              // Strings for Dils
            WORD * mapKeys,                 // Values of 1st menu entries
                                            // in drag-rights
            WORD * mapIDs )                 // Values of drag rights
{
    hDilWnd = CreateWindow ( "STATIC",      // Class name
                            "",             // Window name
                WS_BORDER |
                WS_CHILD |
                WS_VISIBLE,         // Window styles
                0,                  // Upper left corner
                0,                  // of window in parent area
                10,                 // Width
                25,                 // Height
                hWnd,               // Parent window handle
                1,                  // Child window ID
                hInst,              // Instance handle
                NULL );             // Extra info (none)

    if ( hDilWnd )
    {
        dilCreated = TRUE;

        //
        // Now copy over the pointers
        //

        DisplayInfoLine::dilIDs = dilIDs;
        DisplayInfoLine::dilStrings = dilStrings;

        subEntries = mapKeys;
        subMap = mapIDs;


    }
}


//————-
//
// UpdateDil()
//
//   If a message has come in that
// we need to update the DIL info,
// this routine will do that
```

continued

Listing 5-2 *continued*

```
//

    void
DisplayInfoLine::UpdateDil ( HWND    hWnd,
              WORD  wParam,
              LONG  lParam )
{
    int    i;

    WORD    menuID;

    //———————-

    //
    // If Dil doesn't exist, bail.
    //

    if ( !dilCreated )
        return;

    //
    // First, check to see if the menu entry
    // being passed in is a pop-up menu entry.
    // If it is, there isn't a valid ID here
    // for us to check, so we have to use
    // the first entry of the pop-up instead.
    //

    if ( LOWORD ( lParam ) & MF_POPUP )
    {
        //
        // Here we check to see if it's
        // a bad menu entry handle.  If
        // it is, it'll crash the system
        // if we try and use it, so punt
        // now.

        if ( ( LOWORD ( lParam ) ) == -1 ||
            ( HIWORD ( lParam ) ) == 0 )
    {
        UpdateDisplay ( -1 );
        return;
    }
```

```
    //
    // Now get the menu item ID of the
    // menu entry, which we'll use
    // to determine the sub-menu
    // entry...
    //

    menuID = GetMenuItemID ( wParam, // Menu item
              0 );        // Entry to get (1st entry)


    //
    // Now test to see what sub-entry this
    // is.  We'll enumerate through
    // our list of Sub ID's to find
    // out which one we need.
    //

    UpdateDisplay ( GetDilIndex ( GetMenuMapIndex ( menuID ) ) );

    }

    //
    // Entry is not a pop-up menu
    // (this means it's a normal menu
    // entry) so go ahead and
    // get it's index
    //

    else
    {
        UpdateDisplay ( GetDilIndex ( wParam ) );
    }
}

//——————--
//
// MoveDil()
//
//  When the main window
// is moved, then the Dil has to
// be moved also.   This routine
// will do that.
//

    void
```

continued

Listing 5-2 *continued*

```
DisplayInfoLine::MoveDil ( HWND              hWnd,
                           WORD              wParam,
                           LONG              lParam )
{
    //————————

    //
    // If Dil doesn't exist, bail.
    //

    if ( !dilCreated )
        return;

    //
    // First, check to see if our Dil
    // window was created.  If it was,
    // then we need to move the window
    // so that it stays glued to the bottom
    // of the screen.
    //

    if ( hDilWnd )
    {
        MoveWindow ( hDilWnd,
                0,
                HIWORD ( lParam ) - 25,
                LOWORD ( lParam ),
                26,
                TRUE );
    }
}

//———————————-
//
// UpdateDisplay()
//
//   Updates the current Dil display
// with the passed-in string.
// Used by the routine UpdateDil()
// for handling when the display has
// changed via a menu, this routine
// can also be used directly by
// a client routine in order to
```

```
// provide real-time display
// information.
//

    void

DisplayInfoLine::UpdateDisplay ( LPSTR        lpDisplayString )
{
    //————-

    //
    // If Dil doesn't exist, bail.
    //

    if ( !dilCreated )
        return;

    //
    // Only update the display if
    // the string pointer is good.
    //

    if ( lpDisplayString )
    {

    SetWindowText ( hDilWnd,
            lpDisplayString );

    InvalidateRect ( hDilWnd,
            NULL,
            TRUE );

    UpdateWindow ( hDilWnd );
    }
}

//———————-
//
// UpdateDisplay()
//
//   This version of the UpdateDisplay()
// routine takes an index into our string
// table and uses that to display
// the results.
```

continued

Listing 5-2 *continued*

```
//

    void

DisplayInfoLine::UpdateDisplay ( int stringIndex )
{
    //————

    //
    // If Dil doesn't exist, bail.
    //

    if ( !dilCreated )
        return;

    //
    // If the index is -1, or the
    // pointer to the string table
    // is bad, just display a
    // blank line.
    //

    if ( stringIndex == -1 ||
         !dilStrings )
    {
        UpdateDisplay ( "                                    " );
    }

    //
    // Ok, we've got a (presumably)
    // good index, so display
    // the string associated with
    // that index
    //

    else
    {
        UpdateDisplay ( dilStrings [ stringIndex ] );
    }
}

//————
//
// GetDilIndex()
```

```
//
//    Given the array of id values and
// strings, this routine will try and
// match the one to the other.
//
// Returns:
//  0 - n : Index of matching item
//    -1      : No match
//

    int
DisplayInfoLine::GetDilIndex ( WORD id )
{
    int i;

    //————-

    //
    // Right away, check for -1.
    // If we've got that for an
    // ID, we don't even need to check...
    //

    if ( id == -1 )
        return -1;

    //
    // Make sure the map pointer is valid,
    // and if it is, search for an ID
    // match.
    //

    if ( dilIDs )
    {
        for ( i = 0; i < MAX_DIL_INDICES; i++ )
        {
        if ( id == dilIDs[i] )
        {
            return i;
        }
        else if ( dilIDs[i] == NULL )
        {
            return -1;
        }
        }
    }
```

continued

Listing 5-2 *continued*

```
    return -1;
}

//————————
//
// GetMenuMapIndex()
//
//   This routine takes the menu ID
// of the first entry in a drag-right
// menu, and turns it into the id
// of the pop-up menu itself.  It
// does this using a pair of arrays
// that map one entry to the other
//

    int
DisplayInfoLine::GetMenuMapIndex ( WORD      menuID )
{
    int    i;

    //————————-

    //
    // Make sure that we've got valid
    // pointers for both sides of the
    // mapping routine...
    //

    if ( !subEntries ||
         !subMap )
    {
        return -1; // At least one invalid pointer,
              // so punt.
    }

    //
    // Ok, now try and map the 1st menu entry
    // in the drag right...
    //

    for ( i = 0; i < MAX_DIL_INDICES; i++ )
    {
    //
```

```
// Did we match the id?
//

    if ( subEntries [ i ] == menuID )
    {
        return subMap [ i ];
    }

    //
    // or are we at the end of the list?
    //

    else if ( subEntries [ i ] == NULL )
    {
        return -1;
    }
}

//
// Dead man switch
//

return -1;
}
```

Listing 5-3 is SKELETON.CPP, which is the basic framework of my skeleton application (I called it Skeleton, because everyone was always talking about how this or that was their programming "skeleton.") is a very straightforward Windows application. It has a **WinMain()**, and a main message loop, called **MainWindowProc()**.

WinMain() is, of course, the startup for every Windows program, and mine does all the basic things you would expect—registering a window class (the "Skeleton" class), creating the window, showing it, handling the message loop, and exiting.

MainWindowProc() handles all the messages that are destined for this instance of the Skeleton app, and it's here that you can add code to deal with different system events such as WM_CREATE, etc.

In addition, this module is the one where all the text strings and ID numbers for the DIL are stored—when we create an instance of the DIL, I use the addresses of these pieces to give the DIL what it needs (see the discussion of the DIL at the end of the listings for more details on how I do this).

Listing 5-3 SKELTON.CPP

```
//
// SKELETON.CPP
//
//    The skeleton application
//
//    This application provides the
// basic framework of a completely
// up and running Windows program.
// You can add code as appropriate.
//
// Written by Alex Leavens
// for ShadowCat Technologies
//
//

#include <skeleton.hpp>


extern WORDdilID[];
extern char * dilStrings[];
extern WORDmenuKey[];
extern WORDmenuMap[];

//————————
//
// WinMain()
//

    int PASCAL
WinMain ( HINSTANCE  hInstance,
          HINSTANCE  hPrevInstance,
          LPSTR      lpCmdLine,
          int        nCmdShow )
{
    MSG    msg;             // Message holder...

    BOOL   returnCode = TRUE; // Return code...

    //————————--
```

```
hInst = hInstance;    // Save instance handle...

//
// Initialize the application as needed
//

if ( !SkeletonInitApplication ( hInstance,
                  hPrevInstance,
                  &nCmdShow,
                  lpCmdLine ) )
{
returnCode = FALSE;
goto Leave;
}

//
// Initialize the class, if necessary...
//

if ( !hPrevInstance )
{
    if ( !SkeletonRegisterClass ( hInstance ) )
    {
    returnCode = FALSE;
    goto Leave;
    }
}

//
// Create the main window...
//

MainhWnd = SkeletonCreateWindow ( hInstance );

if ( !MainhWnd )
{
returnCode = FALSE;
goto Leave;
}

//
// Show the window, so that the message loop gets pumped...
//

ShowWindow ( MainhWnd,
        nCmdShow );
```

continued

Listing 5-3 *continued*

```
    UpdateWindow ( MainhWnd );

    //
    // Now do our message loop
    //

    while ( GetMessage ( &msg,
                0,
                0,
                0 ) )
    {
        TranslateMessage ( &msg );
        DispatchMessage ( &msg );
    }

Leave:

    SkeletonExitApp();    // Cleanup if necessary

    //
    // Give back the proper return code...
    //

    if ( returnCode == TRUE )
    {
        return ( msg.wParam );
    }
    else
    {
        return FALSE;
    }
}

//————
//
// MainWindowProc()
//
//      Main window callback procedure
//

    LONG FAR PASCAL

SkeletonMainWindowProc ( HWND hWnd,
```

```
          UINT    message,
          UINT    wParam,
          LONG    lParam )
{
   //————

   switch ( message )
   {

      case WM_DESTROY:

         PostQuitMessage ( 0 );

      return DefWindowProc ( hWnd,
                  message,
                  wParam,
                  lParam );
         break;

   case WM_COMMAND:

      return DefWindowProc ( hWnd,
                  message,
                  wParam,
                  lParam );
         break;

   case WM_CREATE:

      //
      // First, we'll need to create
      // the DIL so that we can set
      // it up for use.
      //

      dilWind.InitSelf ( hWnd,            // Parent window handle
                  hInst,            // Instance handle
                  dilID,            // Pointer to Dil ID's
                  dilStrings,       // Pointer to dil strings
                  menuKey,          // Pointer to 1st entries
                  menuMap );        // pointer to mapped ids

      //
      // All done, return
      // the default behavior
```

continued

Listing 5-3   *continued*

```
        //

        return DefWindowProc ( hWnd,
                               message,
                               wParam,
                               lParam );
        break;

    case WM_MENUSELECT:

        //
        // Have the display window
        // do it's thing...
        //

        dilWind.UpdateDil ( hWnd,
                 wParam,
                 lParam );

        //
        // All done, return
        // the default behavior
        //

        return DefWindowProc ( hWnd,
                 message,
                 wParam,
                 lParam );

        break;

    case WM_SIZE:

        //
        // In the case of a size message,
        // the window is either being
        // resized or moved.  Therefor,
        // we need to resize or move it.
        //

        dilWind.MoveDil ( hWnd,
                 wParam,
                 lParam );
        //
```

```
        // All done with moving the
        // Dil window, let's move
        // the main window, too....
        //

        return DefWindowProc ( hWnd,
                    message,
                    wParam,
                    lParam );

        break;

case WM_MOUSEMOVE:

        //
        // Here, we're going to crack the mouse
        // position out of the message, and
        // then display that in the DIL.
        //

        char    mouseBuff [ 128 ];

        int     mX;
        int     mY;

        //——————-

        mX = LOWORD ( lParam );
        mY = HIWORD ( lParam );

        //
        // Generate a text string
        // showing the mouse position
        //

        wsprintf ( (LPSTR) mouseBuff,
            "  Mouse position: %d, %d",
            mX,
            mY );

        //
        // Have the DIL display the
        // mouse position
        //
```

continued

Listing 5-3   *continued*

```
        dilWind.UpdateDisplay ( (LPSTR)mouseBuff );

        break;

        default:
        return DefWindowProc ( hWnd,
                    message,
                    wParam,
                    lParam );
        break;
    }

    return FALSE;      // Returns FALSE if processed

}

WORD    dilID[] =
    {
        ID_SkeletonExit,

        IDM_BONES,
        IDM_SKIN,
        IDM_MUSCLES,
        IDM_NERVES,
        IDM_BANDAID,
        IDM_NEURONS,
        IDM_NERVE_HAND,
        IDM_NERVE_FACE,
        IDM_NERVE_LEGS,
        IDM_NERVES,
        NULL
    };

char * dilStrings[] =
    {
        " Exits the skeleton application",
        " Bones are the infrastructure",
        " Skin protects you",
        " Muscles make you move",
        " Nerves are the message system",
        " Makes boo-boos better",
        " Helps you think",
        " Gives your hands the sense of touch",
        " More in your face than anywhere else",
```

```
            " Lets you feel what you're walking on",
            NULL
        };

WORD    menuKey[]=
        {
            IDM_NERVE_HAND,
            NULL
        };

WORD    menuMap[]=
        {
            IDM_NERVES,
            NULL
        };
```

Listing 5-4, SKELINIT.CPP contains all the auxiliary routines for starting and stopping the skeleton application. The first routine, **SkeletonInitApplication()** gets called by **WinMain()** earlier than any other routine—it's here that you can do any specific instance initialization of variables that needs to occur. I typically use this routine to have any instances of **ResBitmap** (my Resource Bitmap class) load themselves out of the instance handle of the program.

The next routine, **SkeletonRegisterClass()**, does exactly what it's name suggests—it registers the class for the Skeleton window, creates a grey background brush, and sets up the various class styles that the window needs to have.

SkeletonCreateWindow() is the routine called a little later by **WinMain()**, and it's responsible for actually creating the Skeleton window and returning the window handle to the main program. It creates a window with the styles that I want the Skeleton to have (these can easily be altered, which is why I put them here).

The final routine in this file, **SkeletonExitApp()**, gets called by **WinMain()** just before that routine returns—in other words, just before the application shuts down. This is a good place to put any cleanup code (such as deleting the background brush, which I do here) that needs doing, such as deleting any instances of a global object class created via a new.

Listing 5-4 SKELINIT.CPP

```cpp
//
// SKELINIT.CPP
//
//    Initialization routines for the skeleton
// application
//
//

#include <skeleton.hpp>


//————————————
//
// SkeletonInitApplication()
//
//    Initialize the application.
//

    BOOL
SkeletonInitApplication ( HINSTANCE   hInst,
                          HINSTANCE   hPrev,
                          int         *pCmdSHow,
                          LPSTR       lpCmd )
{
    return TRUE;
}

//————————————-
//
// SkeletonRegisterClass()
//
//    Registers the skeleton class
//

    BOOL
SkeletonRegisterClass ( HINSTANCE    hInstance )
{
    WNDCLASS WndClass;

    //————————————-

    hMBrush = CreateSolidBrush(RGB(192,192,192));

    WndClass.style       = 0;
```

```
    WndClass.lpfnWndProc   = SkeletonMainWindowProc;
    WndClass.cbClsExtra    = 0;
    WndClass.cbWndExtra    = 0;
    WndClass.hInstance     = hInstance;
    WndClass.hIcon         = LoadIcon ( hInstance,
                                        "SKELETON" );

    WndClass.hCursor       = LoadCursor ( NULL,
                  IDC_ARROW );
    WndClass.hbrBackground = hMBrush;

    WndClass.lpszMenuName  = "SKELETON";

    WndClass.lpszClassName = "SKELETON";

    return RegisterClass(&WndClass);
}

//———————--
//
// SkeletonCreateWindow()
//
//    Creates the main skeleton window
//

    HWND
SkeletonCreateWindow ( HINSTANCE     hInstance )
{
    HWND    hWnd;

    int     coords[4];

    //———————————

    coords [ 0 ] = CW_USEDEFAULT;
    coords [ 1 ] = 0;
    coords [ 2 ] = CW_USEDEFAULT;
    coords [ 3 ] = 0;

    hWnd = CreateWindow (
                "SKELETON",
                "Skeleton Application",
                WS_OVERLAPPED | WS_THICKFRAME | WS_SYSMENU |
                WS_MINIMIZEBOX | WS_MAXIMIZEBOX,
            coords [ 0 ],
```

continued

Listing 5-4 *continued*

```
            coords [ 1 ],
            coords [ 2 ],
            coords [ 3 ],
            0,                   // Parent handle
            0,                   // Child id
            hInstance,           // Instance handle
            (LPSTR)NULL );       // No additional info
    return hWnd;
}


//————————-
//
// SkeletonExitApp()
//
//    Does any final cleanup...
//

    void
SkeletonExitApp( void )
{
    //————————-

    if ( hMBrush )
    {
        DeleteObject ( hMBrush );

        hMBrush = 0;
    }
}
```

Listing 5-5, SKELVARS.cpp, contains definitions for all the global variables used by the application. (Yeah, I know, you shouldn't have any global variables. Show me a way to do without them entirely, and I'll be happy.)

Meanwhile, instead of littering them throughout various files, I put them in one file—here—so that I can at least keep an eye on them, and make sure that they're not off in the corner doing something they shouldn't be.

The first three variables in the file hMBrush, MainhWnd, and hInst, are global to the Skeleton app by itself—any application you base on the Skeleton project needs these three variables. The variables following these three (in this case, there's only one—the instance of the DisplayInfoLine) are variables specific to this particular skeleton app—in other words, variables that are used for the special purpose stuff that this app is going to do.

Listing 5-5   SKELVARS.CPP

```
//
// SKELVARS.CPP
//
//  Global variables for the skeleton application
//
//


#define __SKELETON_GLOBAL_VARS

#include <skeleton.hpp>

//————————————————————-
//
// All the following are standard global
// variables used by the skeleton application
//

HBRUSH      hMBrush;   // Brush for window background

HWND        MainhWnd;  // Main window handle

HINSTANCE   hInst;     // Instance handle that we need


//———————————-
//
// Add custom variables here
//


DisplayInfoLine    dilWind;   // The display info line object
                              // that we'll be using.
```

Listing 5-6   CLASSES.HPP

```
//
// Classes.hpp
//
//    Includes all class library
// references
//
//    Written by Alex Leavens,
//    for ShadowCat Technologies
//
//


#include <dil.hpp>      // Defines our DIL class
```

Listing 5-7, SKELDFNS.HPP contains numerical defines that get used in the program. This allows us to have all the defines that we're going to use in one place, so that both our C++ code and the resource file can use the same set of defines, which ensures that they'll end up with the same numbers. (I once spent two days tracking down a bug which was caused by the resource compiler having one numerical define for a control ID, and the compiled code having another. I was not a happy camper.)

Listing 5-7   SKELDFNS.HPP

```
//
// SKELDFNS.HPP
//
//    Defines used by the skeleton application
//

#ifndef __SKELDFNS_HPP

#define __SKELDFNS_HPP


//————————————-


//
// Maximum number of DIL entries
// (you can change this and make
```

```
// it bigger, but really, are you
// going to have 1000 menu entries??)
//
// This values defines the last position
// in the DIL ID list that will be
// searched.
//

#define    MAX_DIL_INDICES                1000

#define    SKELETON_BASE_ID    4000


//————

//
// This defines the values
// for all the menu entries.
// We'll use these values to
// look up in a table what
// the DIL string should be.
//

#define    ID_SkeletonExit                SKELETON_BASE_ID + 0

#define    IDM_BONES        SKELETON_BASE_ID + 1
#define    IDM_SKIN         SKELETON_BASE_ID + 2
#define    IDM_MUSCLES      SKELETON_BASE_ID + 3
#define    IDM_NERVES       SKELETON_BASE_ID + 4
#define    IDM_BANDAID      SKELETON_BASE_ID + 5
#define    IDM_NEURONS      SKELETON_BASE_ID + 6
#define    IDM_NERVE_HAND     SKELETON_BASE_ID + 7
#define    IDM_NERVE_FACE     SKELETON_BASE_ID + 8
#define    IDM_NERVE_LEGS     SKELETON_BASE_ID + 9

//————————————-

#endif  // __SKELDFNS_HPP
```

Listing 5-8 is SKELETON.HPP, which is the single include file which gets
included in all my C++ files. If you've chanced to see a copy of my previous book, *Visual C++: A Developer's Guide*, you know that this is the way
that I recommend doing it—by having one big include file that *all* source
files must include. There are a number of reasons for this, but the primary
one is that by having *one* file, you make sure that all the source files are

talking the same language—all the defines are consistent across files, as well as all included definitions, function prototypes, and so on. Some of the most insidious bugs can arise from two files which have slightly different versions of the include files that define the world for them. This file scheme eliminates that avenue as a source of potential bugs.

Listing 5-8   SKELETON.HPP

```
//
// SKELETON.HPP
//
//    Mondo include file for
// the skeleton app.
//
//   __EVERYTHING__ gets included here, ONCE.
//
// That's it.
//

#ifndef __SKELETON_HPP

#define __SKELETON_HPP

//————————————--


#include <WINDOWS.H>

#include <classes.hpp>    // Class library definitions

#include <skelextn.hpp>   // Externs for the global variables

#include <skelprot.hpp>   // Prototypes for all functions in skeleton

#include <skelincs.hpp>   // Includes which define things


//————————————--


#endif // __SKELETON_HPP
```

Listing 5-9, SKELEXTN.HPP, contains external definitions for all the
global variables in the Skeleton program. This header file gets included
in all source files, so that all files have access to these variables.

Listing 5-9   SKELTON.HPP

```
//
// SKELEXTN.HPP
//
//    External define file for the skeleton app
//
//

#ifndef __SKELETON_GLOBAL_VARS

#define __SKELETON_GLOBAL_VARS

//——————————

extern HBRUSH     hMBrush;   // Brush for window background

extern HWND       MainhWnd;  // Main window handle

extern HINSTANCE  hInst;     // Instance handle that we need


//————————————-

//———————————-
//
// Add custom variables here
//

extern DisplayInfoLine   dilWind;   // The display info line object
                  // that we'll be using.

//——————————

#endif // __SKELETON_GLOBAL_VARS
```

Listing 5-10, SKELINICS.HPP is a file which packages up Windows.h
and skeldfns.hpp. This file exists so that both the resource compiler and

the C++ source code can have access to the definitions file (skeldfns.hpp), which holds all our #defines.

Listing 5-10 SKELINCS.HPP

```
//
// SKELINCS.HPP
//
//    Skeleton includes.
//
//    Packaged this way so that both the
// .cpp files and the .rc files can
// use them.
//

#ifndef __SKELINCS_HPP

#define __SKELINCS_HPP

//————————

#include <WINDOWS.H>

#include <skeldfns.hpp>        // Resource and other ID defines


//————————

#endif // __SKELINCS_HPP
```

Listing 5-11, SKELPROT.HPP, is the file which contains all the prototypes for all of the functions in the Skeleton program. Again, it's packaged this way so that all files will get the same function prototypes, and we can be sure that there aren't any random discontinuities between files. Note that this file does *not* contain function definitions for class member functions—those occur in the .hpp file for each class.

Listing 5-11 SKELPROT.HPP

```
//
// SKELPROT.HPP
//
```

```
//      Prototype file
//

#ifndef __SKELETON_PROTOTYPES_HPP

#define __SKELETON_PROTOTYPES_HPP

//————————————-

//————————————-
//
// Extern C wrappers
//

#ifdef __cplusplus

extern "C" {

#endif

//————————————————-

    int PASCAL
WinMain (   HINSTANCE   hInstance,
            HINSTANCE       hPrevInstance,
            LPSTR           lpCmdLine,
            int             nCmdShow );

    LONG FAR PASCAL
SkeletonMainWindowProc ( HWND        hWnd,
                         UINT        message,
                         UINT        wParam,
                         LONG        lParam );
    BOOL
SkeletonInitApplication ( HINSTANCE          hInst,
                          HINSTANCE          hPrev,
                          int                *pCmdSHow,
                          LPSTR              lpCmd );
    BOOL
SkeletonRegisterClass ( HINSTANCE    hInstance );

    HWND
SkeletonCreateWindow ( HINSTANCE     hInstance );
```

continued

Listing 5-11 *continued*

```
    void
SkeletonExitApp( void );

//——————————-

//——————————-
//
// Extern C wrappers
//

#ifdef __cplusplus

};

#endif


//——————————-

#endif  // __SKELETON_PROTOTYPES__HPP
```

And that's a wrap. Here's the screen shot of the DIL application in action:

Although a DIL *looks* hard, it really isn't, especially if you use the class I've built, the **DisplayInfoLine** class. What?? You're not using C++ yet? Pardon me while I get out my pocket mini-rant: If you're not using C++ yet, you're working too hard, too long, and with too little reward. Modern Windows C++ compilers make it practically painless to develop really killer applications in almost no time at all. Yes, you can do it by hand, but believe me, you'll be wasting your time. Not only that, but even if you insist on doing it by hand, there are lots of other people who are perfectly willing to use the tools available to them. Guess who's lunch they're going to be eating? Right—yours. So go ahead—learn C++, and learn it *now*. (Ok, rant over).

Since I've just boxed you about the head and ears about making your development life simpler, you've probably noticed my skeleton application looks like a framework application. It is—it's called the skeleton application because I use it as a skeleton—every time I need an application, I just clone this whole directory structure, and boom! I've got a working Windows application. Total elapsed time—about 30 seconds. Aha! you may be thinking to yourself, his skeleton application isn't based on anybody's framework class—it looks more like C code than C++ code. He's telling us to learn C++, but this thing's written in C.

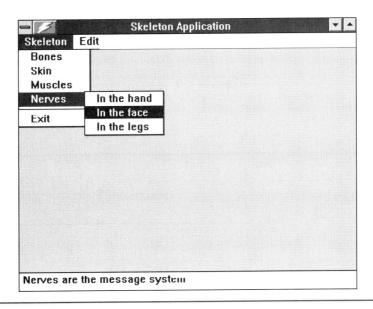

FIGURE 5-6   THE DIL APPLICATION IN ACTION. NOTICE HOW THE DISPLAY INFORMATION LINE SHOWS INFORMATION ABOUT EACH MENU ENTRY AS THE MOUSE PASSES OVER IT.]

Very true, but notice what the extension of all my source files is: CPP for C++ source code, not .C for C source. Although my skeleton application itself doesn't take advantage of any of the features of C++, the code *compiles* under the C++ compiler as C++ code. I can just plug my C++ objects in—just as I did with the **DisplayInfoLine** class, which literally took about 20 minutes to hook up to my application. I'll say it again: C++ provides packaged functionality you can take advantage of *right now*. And if you're not using C++, there are plenty of people who will—and you don't want them to beat you to market, do you? (Ok, rant *really* over.)

Anyway, before I got off on that tangent about C++ (don't start *that* again!), I was mentioning how easy **DisplayInfoLine** allows you to build a DIL. Let's look at what's going on behind the scenes to make this so.

Probably the most important piece of the DIL is understanding *why* it works. How do we know what text string to put up? It's actually quite straightforward. When you create your menu structures, one of the things you'll do is assign each menu entry a unique ID. It's possible to assign them non-unique IDs, of course, but it would be bad. Anyway, this unique ID is one of the values passed to our program via the WM_MENUSELECT message. When we receive the WM_MENUSE-LECT message, one of the fields it contains is the (hopefully) unique ID of the menu that's been selected.

So how does this help us? Easy. We've just gotten a unique ID—or key—we can use to generate a unique text string. In some sense, it's like a very simple database with only one field per key. We use the key value (the menu ID) to look up the corresponding entry (the text string to be displayed).

Of course, for something like this we don't really need a database; a much simpler mapping function will do the trick. In fact, this mapping is one of the things you must provide the **DisplayInfoLine** class when you create it, like so:

```
    BOOL
InitSelf (
        HWND        hWnd,           // Parent window handle
        HINSTANCE   hInst,          // Parent instance
        WORD *      dilIDs,         // ID's of menu entries
        LPSTR *     dilStrings,     // Strings for Dils
        WORD *      mapKeys,        // Values of 1st menu entries
                                    // in drag-rights
        WORD *      mapIDs );       // Values of drag rights
```

The first two items you pass to the **DisplayInfoClass** are merely the window handle of your application, and its instance handle. These are nothing out of the ordinary. The next four parameters you pass are the key to making the DIL work properly. They are the arrays of information that define the mapping the DIL will make.

The third and fourth options, dilIDs and dilStrings are a matched pair. The first one, dilIDs, is an array of WORDs (or, more properly, a WORD *), which is simply a list of the menu IDs of the menu options in your program. DilStrings is an array of char *s; that is, it's an array of strings. This array of strings are the strings displayed by the DIL. Here's the key to making it work: The position in which a menu ID occurs in the array dilIDs must be the *same* as the position in which a string that should be displayed for that menu occurs in the array dilStrings. In other words, there's a one-to-one correspondence between the position of a menu ID in the dilIDs array, and the position of a string in the array dilStrings.

For example, assume your first menu option was Open, and it had a menu ID of 1001, and you wanted to have the DIL line "Opens a file" be displayed for it. Then you'd have something like this:

```
WORD    dilID[] =
    {
        1001,       // 'Open' menu entry ID
        1002,       // 'New' menu entry ID
        1003        // 'Save' menu entry ID
    };

char * dilStrings[] =
    {
    " Opens a file",            // 'Open' menu string
    " Creates a new file",      // 'New' menu string
    " Saves the current file"   // 'Save' menu string
    };
```

Of course, you wouldn't have just one entry in each table—you'd have one entry for each of the menu items in your program. The point here is the position in the first table of your menu ID corresponds to the position in the second table for the display line for that menu option. Thus, 1001 (the ID of the Open menu) corresponds to "Opens a file" (the string to be displayed for the Open menu). The ID 1002 corresponds to

"Creates a new file," and 1003 corresponds to "Saves the current file." The code that handles this mapping is in the member function **GetDilIndex()**. It takes the passed-in menu ID, and returns the index of the string that should be displayed for that menu ID. If it can't find the ID, it returns a -1. **GetDilIndex()** is a member function that's only called from within other member functions of the **DisplayInfoLine** class; you should never need to call it yourself.

A similar mapping scheme is at work for the final two entries of the **InitSelf()** routine:

```
WORD *      mapKeys,    // Values of 1st menu entries
                        // in drag-rights
WORD *      mapIDs );   // Values of drag rights
```

Just as with the previous two options, these two tables provide a mapping from one value to another. In this case, the first table contains the value of the first item in a submenu (a drag-right menu). The second table contains the corresponding ID value that should be searched for in the "ID value to string" mapping table pair (remember, this mapping is handled by the routine **GetDilIndex()**). At first glance, this seems extremely odd—why do you need such a mapping?

Here's why: Although menu options have an ID associated with them, pop-up menus do not, and the top level of a drag-right menu is itself a pop-up menu (see figure 5-7).

However, each pop-up menu has some menu options in it. Each of these menu options (unless they are themselves pop-up menus) have a menu ID. The trick I use here is to find the ID of the first menu entry of the pop-up menu. You then compare it to the ID of the menu option you know is the first entry in the pop-up menu. If they match, then users must be on the pop-up menu option, in which case we can display an information line for that item.

Our two tables provide you with a one-to-one correspondence between the ID of the first menu option in our pop-up, and an ID you can use to look up a string for display with. Here's how it works: The member function **GetMenuMapIndex()** looks through the list of menu

IDs pointed to by mapKeys. If it finds a match, it uses the index of the match to look in the table mapIDs. It takes this value and returns it to the calling routine. This value is an ID that can be looked up using the routine **GetDilIndex()**. From this point, the process works the same way as if the pop-up menu really did have an ID. All you have done is turn the ID of the first option of the pop-up menu into an ID for the pop-up menu itself. (You can distinguish between the pop-up menu and it's first option by the fact that pop-up menus have the MF_POPUP bit of LOWORD (lParam) set.)

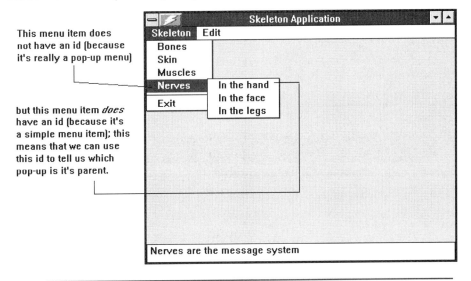

FIGURE 5-7   An illustration of a menu option that has a drag-right menu associated with it. The menu entry Nerves does not have an ID, because it's a pop-up menu. The options in the drag-right menu all do have menu IDs, and we can use this fact to determine what the pop-up menu is.

Putting it together: The DIL in action

Now that you have created the tables that you need for the DIL to work properly, and initialed the DIL itself, it's time to make it do it's magic. There are a couple of messages you need to handle for the DIL to function. The first of these is the WM_SIZE message. This message is generated whenever the parent window has been moved or resized. When this occurs, you need to move the DIL window so it will stay "glued" to the bottom of the screen. D this by calling the member function **MoveDil()**. This routine simply finds the new size of the parent window (contained in lParam), and moves the DIL window just slightly above the bottom of the parent window. The DIL is only 1 line of text high, so that's how far up in the parent window you need to move it.

Once you have dealt with the WM_SIZE and WM_CREATE messages, the only other message you need to handle is WM_MENUSELECT. This message lets you know the user has moved the mouse over a menu option. Pass this information along to the member function **UpdateDil()**, which handles all of the processing of this message.

Although **UpdateDil()** looks pretty complex, it really isn't. The basic algorithm at work here can be described this way:

1. Is the menu item in question a pop-up menu? If yes, go to Step 3.
2. Get the menu ID of the item in question, and match it to a string index, using **GetDilIndex()**. If there was a match, display the text string, and exit.
3. The item was a pop-up menu. Validate it as a pop-up, then get the menu ID of the first item in the pop-up (if it was the first item itself, you would have branched to Step 2). Using the member function **GetMenuMapIndex()**, turn the menu ID into one that matches the pop-up menu. Then go to Step 2.

And that's it! There's more going on inside the routine, of course, but it deals primarily with parameter validation, and making sure you don't blow up under various degenerate conditions.

The **DisplayInfoLine()** class is ready to use in your program as it stands right now, and it'll provide great functionality. However, you can also use it for additional tasks—if you run the sample program on the disk, you'll see in addition to showing information about the menu entries, the DIL also displays the current mouse position as you move it around the client area of the main window.

This additional functionality comes as a result of the member function **UpdateDisplay**, which lets you pass in a string to the DIL and have it be immediately displayed. Normally, this routine is only used by other DIL member functions (which use it to display the menu entry strings), but you can access it directly at any time, simply by passing it a non-NULL string pointer. In this case, I've passed in a string that shows the current mouse positions (which I crack from the WM_MOUSEMOVE message), but you can put *any* valid string in there, and have it be displayed.

Other things to do with menus

Menus can provide a useful level of feedback for users. By using checked menu entries, for example users can see if a particular feature is on or off (see Figure 5-8).

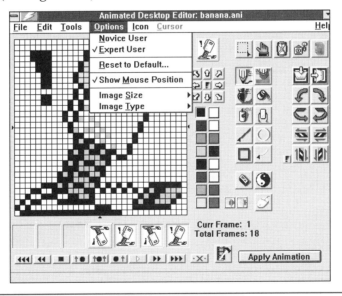

FIGURE 5-8   A MENU FROM MY ICE/WORKS PROGRAM SHOWING THE USE OF A CHECKED MENU ITEM. THE MENU OPTION SHOW MOUSE POSITION IS CHECKED, INDICATING THE MOUSE POSITION SHOWS UP IN THE DIL AT THE BOTTOM OF THE WINDOW. IT ALSO SHOWS AT A GLANCE WHICH MODE THE USER IS CURRENTLY IN, NOVICE OR EXPERT.

As you can see in the figure, the user can instantly tell whether they are in novice or expert mode, as well as whether the mouse position is going to be displayed in the DIL. Now, since we can see that being able to check menu items is a useful thing, how do you go about doing it?

It's easy, really. Here's a code fragment that'll do it for you:

```
HMENU   hMenu; // Menu handle

hMenu = GetMenu ( hWnd ); // Get the menu handle
                          // of our program. Use
                          // the main window handle
                          // here.
CheckMenuItem ( hMenu,
                ID_MENU_ITEM_TO_CHECK,
                MF_BYCOMMAND | MF_CHECKED );
```

And that does the trick. Obviously, you'll need to substitute the actual ID of the menu entry that you want to have a check mark for the second parameter, ID_MENU_ITEM_TO_CHECK. The flags MF_BYCOMMAND and MF_CHECKED tell Windows, respectively, you are specifying a menu entry by it's numeric identifier (as opposed to MF_BYPOSITION, which specifies the menu entry by absolute position). It also tells Windows you want the menu item to be checked (MF_UNCHECKED clears a check mark from a menu item).

Undo and Redo, how do you do?

(That's a really awful section heading, isn't it?) Another common menu behavior I mentioned earlier is the Undo/Redo pairing some applications have. When you undo an action, the menu entry changes to Redo, to let you know you can undo the undo. Here's a code fragment that shows you how to accomplish this:

```
//
// The variable 'undoFlag' indicates whether
// the user can currently undo an action.  If
// undoFlag = 0, then the user can undo an action;
// if undoFlag = 1, then the user can redo the action.
```

```
//
// The value 'ID_Undo_Menu' is a #define value in your
// program which defines the id of the menu entry which
// is the 'Undo' entry.
//

HMENU   hMenu;  // Menu handle so that
                // we can manipulate the menu

char        undoLabel [ 20 ];  // Text label for
                               // undo message

hMenu = GetMenu ( hWnd ); // Main window handle,
                          // remember?

if ( undoFlag == 0 )
{
    _lstrcpy ( undoLabel,
            "Undo" );
}
else
{
    _lstrcpy ( undoLabel,
            "Redo" );
}

ModifyMenu ( hMenu,
             ID_Undo_Menu,
             MF_BYCOMMAND | MF_STRING,
             ID_Undo_Menu,
```

As you can see, changing the text of a menu item is really a trivial task—it's simply a matter of getting the menu handle, and then performing a **ModifyMenu()** call to make the appropriate change.

Graying a menu entry

Another thing you can do with menu entries is gray them out. This means that the menu entry in question is not currently valid, or is an action which cannot be currently taken. One thing I use this for is to let users know an action doesn't make sense or isn't needed. For example, when users save a file in ICE/Works, I gray out the menu entry that says Save. After all, they've just saved it, haven't they? They certainly don't need to do it again. The Save menu entry stays gray until an action occurs (such as painting) that causes a change to the image. At that point, I ungray the menu entry (I turn it black) again, because it's now an action that makes sense—they've changed the image, and they might want to save it.

Here's how you gray a menu entry:

```
HMENU   hMenu;

hMenu = GetMenu ( hWnd ); // Main window handle,
                          // or else it won't work.

EnableMenuItem ( hMenu,
                 ID_MenuEntry,
                 MF_GRAYED );
```

Pretty simple. Making a menu entry black, or enabling it, consists of changing the last parameter in the **EnableMenuItem()** call from MF_GRAYED to MF_ENABLED. Also note that when a menu item is grayed out, it's *really* out. Windows won't send you any command messages from the menu entry (users can't select it), although you'll still get the WM_MENUSELECT message (so that your DIL still works on grayed entries).

Summary

In this chapter, I've shown you how you can use menus to your program's best advantage—make the layout make sense, and follow some basic guidelines for menu structures. Although menu interactions such as graying and checking seem fairly basic, they provide a good level of information and feedback to users. Also, don't forget many users browse menu structures to get a feel for the program's layout and capabilities. Make sure your menus communicate the proper information to your users.

Now that we've talked about menus, it's time to discuss the next important Windows interface object—the button. It's the subject of the next chapter. See you there!

CHAPTER 6

BUTTONS

Next to menus, buttons are one of the most often used controls in Windows—open up any commercial application, and chances are you'll see a palette of buttons representing the tools of the application. (See figure 6-1).

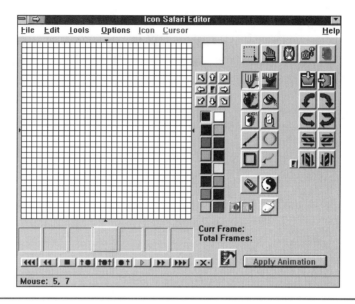

FIGURE 6-1   A SCREEN SHOT SHOWING THE TOOL BUTTONS FOR THE PRODUCT ICE/WORKS. NOTICE
THAT THERE ARE MORE TOOL BUTTONS THAN THERE ARE MAIN MENU ENTRIES.

TEXT BUTTONS, GRAPHIC BUTTONS

There are two types of buttons—text buttons, which have one or more words in them (the most common one, of course, is the button in many dialog boxes labeled "OK"), and graphic buttons, which have pictures (and sometimes small amounts of text) in them. Text buttons tend to mostly populate dialog boxes, with the vast majority of buttons being labeled either "OK" or "Cancel." Graphic buttons, on the other hand, tend to inhabit tool bars and tool palettes, and appear to be most used as tool markers—select a button and get a tool.

The common thinking, of course, is that text buttons just aren't appropriate for toolbars, and that graphic buttons aren't appropriate for anything else. Like all common wisdom, there is a kernel of truth and a hull of falsehood to this thinking. There's an underlying assumption behind this thinking—an assumption which is almost never questioned because it's almost never thought about. The assumption is this:

People understand pictures better than words. (Also known as the "one picture is worth a thousand words maxim). Like many maxims, this one seems self-obvious. Let's think about it, however. Take a look at figure 6-2, which shows several graphic buttons from several applications. Without looking at the answers (no cheating, now!) can you determine what functions they provide?

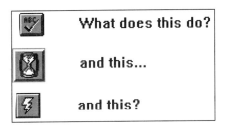

FIGURE 6-2   THREE TOOL BUTTONS FROM POPULAR COMMERCIAL APPLICATIONS. CAN YOU DETERMINE WHAT THE THREE BUTTONS DO JUST BY LOOKING AT THEIR GRAPHICS?

I'm burying the answers to all three of these graphics here in the text so that your eye won't automatically pick them out; the first button is from Word for Windows, and activates the spelling checker. The second button is from ICE/Works, and performs an "Undo." The third button is from Borland's C++ compiler (version 4.0)—clicking on this button runs the application that you are currently developing.

If you use these applications on your machine, then you probably know what each button means—but if you don't, then I'd wager that you missed at least one of them. You didn't miss any? Good for you! But most people do miss at least one of them—the Undo, from ICE/Works. I have to admit it—I'm the one responsible for the Undo button. In case you haven't figured out what the button is, it's an hourglass with the sand running upwards—indicating a reversed flow of time. In other words, it takes the user back to a previous version of the image. Presto, an Undo button!

Okay, I'll admit that this is a little strained—really, it's a visual pun, (I'm notorious for making puns) and it's understandable only when you know what the button does. This brings me to my point (you knew I was going to get there sooner or later) which is this:

Not every graphic button is intuitive. Some are obvious, some are obscure, some make jokes, and some just plain don't work.

I know, your boss and her boss are breathing down your necks, demanding a newer, prettier interface for the product. People are visually oriented, everyone likes pretty pictures, and when are the buttons going to look better?

Stand firm, stand tall, show 'em figure 6-2, and ask them how many *they* can figure out. That ought to humble them a little bit.

Not that I'm against graphic buttons, mind you—in many cases, a well-designed graphic button can communicate what it does more effectively than a text button. It's just that many graphic buttons out there look like they were drawn by four year-olds with blunt crayons (nothing against four year-olds, I own one myself) instead of highly paid graphic artists. Maybe what we need is more highly paid four year-olds.

The point of all this is that graphic buttons are not *inherently* more understandable than text buttons, any more than Egyptian hieroglyphs are more understandable than English text. Pictures, especially pictures that are supposed to convey a specific meaning, must be understood in the framework of context. Without this context, a picture on a graphic button cannot convey the specific piece of information that it is designed to communicate.

THE THREE KINDS OF GRAPHIC BUTTONS

Understanding, then, that graphic buttons must be designed with the context in which they will be used in mind, let's take a look at the three levels of graphic buttons that can be made.

✦ Level 1 [best] Graphic buttons which are obvious.

(I'm going to dodge the bullet about what's "obvious" and what isn't.). This means buttons whose purpose and function are clear and discernible to an average user. In other words, you've got to be able to look at the button and figure out what it does. Take a look at figure 6-3. You can immediately make a very good guess at what each button does, just by the picture on it.

Many of the best graphic buttons come from analogous relationships to real-world objects which perform much the same function. A pencil tool, for example, allows the user to draw a thin line on the editing screen, much the way a real pencil allows someone to draw a real line on real paper. This points up the fact that the best graphics buttons are extremely context sensitive—a pencil tool in a check-book balancing program, for example, would be a lot less obvious about what function it performed than it would be in a drawing program.

✦ Level 2 [second best] Graphic buttons which aren't obvious, but become so after you use them.

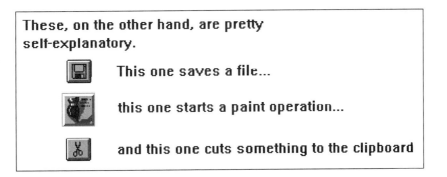

FIGURE 6-3   THREE BUTTONS THAT ARE PRETTY DARN OBVIOUS. A DISK BUTTON SAVES SOMETHING TO THE DISK (ALTHOUGH IT MIGHT LOAD SOMETHING FROM DISK), A PAINT BRUSH STARTS A PAINT OPERATION, AND A PAIR OF SCISSORS CUTS SOMETHING.

This includes one of my favorite categories of button, the visual pun button. Why do I name them this? Because a well-designed button of this category will allow the user to remember what the button does after only one or two uses. Take a look at figure 6-4, which shows several buttons of this category. One of my favorites is the yin/yang button, which shows the yin/yang symbol on it.

This button has no obvious meaning for the new user of the program. However, once they start using the program, they discover (by pressing the button) that the yin/yang button *inverts* the current image. In other words, it converts black pixels to white pixels and vice versa; dark red pixels to light blue pixels and vice versa; and so on. In this context, the use of the yin/yang symbol becomes clear (or at least I hope it does). The symbol itself is a symmetrical representation of an image and it's inverse—just the functionality that the button performs!

FIGURE 6-4   SOME GRAPHIC BUTTONS HAVE A MEANING ONLY AFTER ONE HAS USED THEM.
THIS ONE INVERTS THE COLORS OF AN IMAGE.

This is really one step removed from the ideal type of graphic button, which is the first kind (i.e., a self-obvious pictograph). It represents a compromise on the part of the designer, which is this—how do you communicate with a picture an idea which may not be readily communicable in this fashion?

Let's examine how I arrived at my yin/yang button in a little more detail. In the original version of my icon editor, I had a function which would let you invert the image. The button was labeled "Invert". For reasons that had to do with the "look and feel" of the product, our publisher asked me to change the button from a text button to a graphic button (in other words, they wanted something that looked prettier). At this point, I became pretty hard pressed for a graphic that would intuitively mean "Invert the current image."

I thought about it—a picture of a film negative? Maybe. But the image of a piece of film is not directly related to the process of creating and editing graphical images (unlike a pencil, which is). In cases where the pictograph being used is ambiguous, the user must resort to guessing which attribute of the pictograph is supposed to be important. Would it be the film itself, (suggesting plasticity), the fact that it was film (suggesting a snap-shot), or the fact that there was an image *on* the film?

Other possibilities were just as fraught with the potential for misinterpretation: A black and white television couldn't be clearly shown as being black and white only. A picture of a half positive and half-negative image didn't suggest much of anything, and others I considered were worse.

I finally settled on the yin/yang symbol for two reasons:

1. Although it was difficult to interpret it correctly without knowing what it did, it was even more difficult to interpret it incorrectly. After all, I figured that most users would know that pressing on the button was not going to bring spiritual balance to their lives. (Although two of the ones who did interpret it that way later wrote me that it had been a major positive influence in their lives).

2. The yin/yang symbol did give a very good visual representation of what the function actually did—perform a perfectly symmetrical transformation of an image from one set of colors to it's exact opposite. In that sense, the yin/yang symbol fit extremely well with what I wanted to communicate to the user.

As you can see, I had to compromise. I had to create a button which was visually distinctive, and whose meaning would become clear once the button was used, instead of being clear just upon inspection. I think that I accomplished this, but it's hard to know. There is no direct mapping between what the button looks like and what it does. The mapping between the two gets created as the user uses the product, and not before.

Probably my favorite button in this category comes from a program that's not even a Windows program—the DOS game Lemmings has as one of its buttons a pictograph of two lemming paw prints and the button function is "Pause" (Paws)! Truly a terrible pun, but an extremely easy button for users to remember. The one drawback of this button is, of course, that it only works for English speaking players.

◆ Level 3) [worst] Buttons which have no apparent relationship to the task being performed.

These are the most difficult kind of button to use, because the picture on the button has no bearing on the task or function that the button performs. You've seen lots of buttons like this. A lightning bolt button means "Run program." A button with a sheet of paper on it means "Create new database." You've seen these—you may even have written some of these (no finger pointing, please).

You may be thinking to yourself, what's the big deal? People can very quickly learn that a lightning bolt means "Run program," after all.

Indeed, that's true. People are very adaptable (much more so than computers), so users can eventually learn that the lightning bolt button means "Run program." The problem with that, of course, is that it requires the user to learn how the program works. This is not what good user interface design is all about. The program should work the way the user expects it to—the user should not have to learn the way the program works.

Recently, many programs have started adding a text string to the bottom of their graphic buttons—a tacit admission that many graphic buttons simply aren't very good at communicating what it is they do to the user.

By the way, don't get me wrong. I love graphic buttons—when they make sense. A good Type 1 or 2 button can be much quicker to understand and use than parsing out a text button; and, done right, they can be a significant enhancement to user productivity. But you have to make absolutely sure that the user can understand the pictographs in your buttons. If you don't, then you might as well make them text buttons. At least the user can read (and understand) those.

USING BUTTONS

Text button examples

We're going to look at several different ways that you can use buttons in your programs. The first way, using a text button in a dialog box, is probably the simplest method of all.

Here's how you create a text button in a dialog box: Go into your compiler's resource editor, open up the dialog box, and add a text button. That was easy, wasn't it? Sure was. The resource editor takes care of generating all the positional information about the button, based on where you placed it and what text you put into it.

When the dialog box is displayed on the screen, the text button is also automatically put on the screen. All you have to do in your dialog procedure is provide some code to respond to your button. Here's a code fragment for how that would look:

```
switch ( message )
{
    case WM_COMMAND:

        switch ( wParam )
        {
            case ID_MY_BUTTON:

                // Do my button stuff here
                // ....
```

As you can see, it's quite easy to respond to the button—all you have to do is add a case in your dialog procedure's WM_COMMAND handler, and look for the ID of the text button that you've created.

Creating and using a text button in a dialog box is really simplicity itself, since much of the work has been handled for you. Suppose, however, that you want to be able to create a text button in the client area of your main window. How do you go about doing that?

There are two parts to this problem: the first part is creating the button, and the second part is handling messages from it. Unlike a dialog box, where the button is created automatically for you, a text button in a main window has to be created by hand. Here's some code that shows how you do that:

```
HWND        buttonWnd;
int         buttonHeight;

HWND        deskhWnd;
HDC         deskhDC;

TEXTMETRIC sysText;

int     gl_hchar;
int     gl_wchar;

//————————-

//
// In order to ensure that the buttons are
// created so that the text string appears in them
// properly (regardless of the default font being
// used) we need to figure out the 'average' size
// of a text cell. We do this by talking to the
// desktop window.

deskhWnd = GetDesktopWindow();
deskhDC = GetDC(deskhWnd);

//
// Now get the size of a character cell...
//

GetTextMetrics ( deskhDC,
            (LPTEXTMETRIC)&sysText );

// Get the average cell width and height here
```

```
gl_wchar = sysText.tmAveCharWidth;
gl_hchar = sysText.tmHeight;

//
// Give the DC back...
//

ReleaseDC ( deskhWnd,
            deskhDC );


//
// Calculate a button height
// that will hold the text fully
//

buttonHeight = gl_hchar + gl_hchar / 3 + 1;

//
// Now create a text button window in
// the client area of our main window.
//

 buttonWnd = CreateWindow (
        "BUTTON",           // Standard text button class
        "My Button",        // String to display in the button
        BS_PUSHBUTTON |     // Standard pushbutton type,
        WS_CHILD |          // Child window, and visible
        WS_VISIBLE,         // at creation time
        50,                 // X position of the button
        50                  // Y position of the button
        11 * gl_wchar,      // Width of the button
        buttonHeight,       // Height of the button
        hWnd,               // Parent window
        1001,               // ID of the button
        hInst,              // Instance of app
                            // creating the button
        NULL);              // No extra data
```

As you can see, there's quite a bit more here than simply creating a text button in a dialog box. Since a button is just another kind of control, you have to create it by hand, using the **CreateWindow()** call. As with any call to **CreateWindow()**, you're going to need to know a bunch of things about the window in order to create it. Here's a list of the things you'll need to know:

1. The class name. In this case, it's "BUTTON," which will create a standard Windows button for us.

2. The text string that's going to appear in the button. This, of course, is going to be governed by what you intend the button to do. In the example above, I've created a button named "My Button."

3. The style flags for this window. Since we're creating a pushbutton, we need to use the BS_PUSHBUTTON style, as well as the WS_CHILD style, indicating that it's a child window of the parent (our main window), and the WS_VISIBLE style (which indicates that we want the button to be shown when we show our parent window).

4. The position of the button. In this case, I've positioned the button at the pixel location (50, 50) in the client area of the parent window. This has the effect of placing the text button 50 pixels down and 50 pixels from the left of the client area of the parent window.

5. The size of the button. Here's where some tricky stuff is going on. In order to properly create the button, we have to know how big the text font that we're going to be using is going to be. In a dialog box, this is all taken care of for you—if the user decides that they want Helvetica Frankenstein Bold 40 point as the default system font, the dialog box procedure will automatically resize the dialog box and all its controls to properly take this into account. In this case, however, there is no dialog box procedure to handle this for us—we're going to have to do it ourselves. This is what the code prior to the **CreateWindow()** call is doing.

   In order for us to properly determine how big to make our text button, we're going to have to figure out how big an "average" character of the default font is. Doing this is quite straightforward—we simply need to get the handle to the desktop window, and get a device context for that window. Then, by using the call

```
GetTextMetrics ( deskhDC,
          (LPTEXTMETRIC)&sysText );
```

we can retrieve the metrics of the default font of the desktop. Among other things, this structure will return to us the width and height of an "average" character cell of this font. We retrieve these two pieces of information like so:

```
gl_wchar = sysText.tmAveCharWidth;
gl_hchar = sysText.tmHeight;
```

and finally we can use this information to figure out the height of a text button that will hold the text of the button, as well as having some extra "whitespace" above and below the button, so that it doesn't look crowded when it gets drawn. Here's the calculation that does that:

```
buttonHeight = gl_hchar + gl_hchar / 3 + 1;
```

This is the value that we use in the call to **CreateWindow()** for the height of the button that we're creating. The value that we use for the width of the button window is even easier. We simply take the value of gl_wchar (the width of an average character cell), and multiply it by 2 more than the length of the text string of the button. In this case, since my button text string is 9 characters long, I'm multiplying gl_wchar by 11. In a real-world application, you'd probably be loading this text string from a resource file, so you wouldn't know the value beforehand. In this case, you could use the **_lstrlen()** function on the button text string, and add 2 to the value returned, like this:

```
buttonWidth = gl_wchar * ( _lstrlen ( myString ) + 2 );
```

6. You need to know the window handle of the parent window. Of course, if you're creating a button to fit in the client area of a parent, you already know the window handle of the parent, so you can simply fill that in here.

7. You need to create a unique ID for this button. In this case I've used the value 1001 (decimal) as the ID, but if you're building a commercial application, you need to ensure that the button ID values are unique. The best solution that I've found is to create a header file, such as button.h, and have a series of #defines in it for each of the button ID's, something like this:

```
#define    BASE_BUTTON_ID              0x3000

#define    ID_PENCIL                   BASE_BUTTON_ID + 1
#define    ID_PAINTBRUSH               BASE_BUTTON_ID + 2
#define    ID_BUCKET                   BASE_BUTTON_ID + 3
```

You can also include this file in your resource header. This has two advantages: One, you can refer to all your buttons by a mnemonic identifier in your code, like so:

```
case ID_BUCKET:

        // Do bucket stuff
```

which is infinitely better than something like this:

```
case 0x3003:           // Bucket button

        // Do bucket stuff
```

because in the former case you can change the value of the ID without worrying that your code is going to break, and in the latter case you cannot. The second advantage to doing it this way is that it's easy to ensure that your buttons get unique identifiers, simply by adding new ones on at the end.

8. You need to know the instance handle of your application. This is simply the instance handle that gets passed into your **WinMain()** procedure.

Whew. As you can see, creating buttons this way takes a bit of work. However, if you need to be able to have text buttons in your main window, this is what you're going to have to do.

Fortunately, handling the messages from buttons created in this fashion is no harder than handling messages from buttons in a dialog box. You simply have to look for them in your WM_COMMAND message handler in the same way you did before, ie, like this:

```
case WM_COMMAND:

    switch ( wParam )

        case ID_BUCKET:

            // Do bucket stuff
.
.
.
```

Graphic buttons: An example

The next level of complexity is the graphic button, which, as we've already discussed, is a button with a graphic in it. Graphic buttons have all the wrinkles associated with hand-created text buttons, and they throw in quite a few new ones on top of it. Fortunately, I've created an object class in C++ which will let you handle graphic buttons with aplomb. To get an idea of how easy it is to use graphic buttons, let's create a sample application which creates two graphic buttons in the client area of our main window. After I show you the source code, and a screen shot of our application in action, I'll discuss with you the interesting bits of the program, what they do, and why they do it.

First, let's look at the code for our sample application. Listings 6-1 through 6-10 show you the source.

Listing 6-1   Skeleton.cpp

```
//
// SKELETON.CPP
//
//    The skeleton application...
//
//

#include <skeleton.hpp>

//————————
//
// WinMain()
//

    int PASCAL
WinMain ( HINSTANCE    hInstance,
          HINSTANCE    hPrevInstance,
          LPSTR        lpCmdLine,
          int          nCmdShow )
{
    MSG    msg;            // Message holder...

    BOOL   returnCode = TRUE; // Return code...

    //————————————-

    hInst = hInstance;    // Save instance handle...

    //
    // Initialize the application as needed
    //

    if ( !SkeletonInitApplication ( hInstance,
                    hPrevInstance,
                    &nCmdShow,
                    lpCmdLine ) )
    {
        returnCode = FALSE;
        goto Leave;
    }

    //
    // Initialize the class, if necessary...
    //
```

```
if ( !hPrevInstance )
{
    if ( !SkeletonRegisterClass ( hInstance ) )
    {
        returnCode = FALSE;
        goto Leave;
    }
}

//
// Create the main window...
//

MainhWnd = SkeletonCreateWindow ( hInstance );

if ( !MainhWnd )
{
    returnCode = FALSE;
    goto Leave;
}

//
// Now create the child button windows that
// we're going to be using...
//

CreateGraphicButtons ( MainhWnd );

//
// Show the window, so that the message loop gets pumped...
//

ShowWindow ( MainhWnd,
             nCmdShow );

UpdateWindow ( MainhWnd );

//
// Now do our message loop
//

while ( GetMessage ( &msg,
                     0,
                     0,
```

continued

Listing 6-1 *continued*

```
                            0 ) )
    {
        TranslateMessage ( &msg );
        DispatchMessage ( &msg );
    }

Leave:

    SkeletonExitApp();     // Cleanup if necessary

    //
    // Give back the proper return code...
    //

    if ( returnCode == TRUE )
    {
        return ( msg.wParam );
    }
    else
    {
        return FALSE;
    }
}

//————————
//
// MainWindowProc()
//
//      Main window callback procedure
//

    LONG FAR PASCAL

SkeletonMainWindowProc ( HWND hWnd,
                         UINT  message,
                         UINT  wParam,
                         LONG  lParam )
{

    int    i;

    LPDRAWITEMSTRUCT   lpDis;

    //————————
```

```
switch ( message )
{

    case WM_DESTROY:

        PostQuitMessage ( 0 );

        return DefWindowProc ( hWnd,
                               message,
                               wParam,
                               lParam );
        break;

    case WM_COMMAND:

        //
        // Here's where we check to see
        // if one of our graphic buttons
        // generated a command. If it did,
        // the button is responsible for
        // dispatching the appropriate action.
        //

        for ( i = 0; i < ID_NumberOfButtons; i++ )
        {
            if ( buttons [ i ].GetID() == ( HMENU ) LOWORD ( wParam )
)
            {
                //
                // Set parent window back in focus
                //

                SetActiveWindow ( MainhWnd );
                SetFocus ( MainhWnd );

                buttons [ i ].PerformActionIfID ( (HMENU) wParam,
                                                  hWnd,
                                                  message,
                                                  wParam,
                                                  lParam );

                return FALSE;
            }
        }
```

continued

Listing 6-1   *continued*

```
        return DefWindowProc ( hWnd,
                               message,
                               wParam,
                               lParam );
      break;

  case WM_CREATE:

        return DefWindowProc ( hWnd,
                               message,
                               wParam,
                               lParam );
      break;

  //
  // The case of WM_DRAWITEM is the only
  // special thing we have to handle.
  // Because we've assumed the responsibility
  // for drawing these buttons, we need
  // to manage that. The WM_DRAWITEM
  // message lets us do this by informing
  // us that something needs to be drawn.
  //

  case WM_DRAWITEM:

      //
      // Get the drawitemstruct, which
      // contains important information
      // on how we need to draw this
      // object.
      //

      lpDis = ( LPDRAWITEMSTRUCT ) lParam;

      //
      // Now ask each button to render itself
      // if appropriate. By pushing this
      // responsibility off on the object
      // class, we make it much simpler
      // for our main procedure code here.
      //
```

```
        for ( i = 0; i < ID_NumberOfButtons; i++ )
        {
            if ( buttons [ i ].RenderSelfIfID ( (HMENU) lpDis->
                                              CtlID, lParam ) )
            {
                return TRUE;
            }
        }

        return DefWindowProc ( hWnd,
                               message,
                               wParam,
                               lParam );
        break;

    default:

        return DefWindowProc ( hWnd,
                               message,
                               wParam,
                               lParam );
        break;
    }

    return FALSE;      // Returns FALSE if processed

}
```

Listing 6-2   Skelinit.cpp

```
//
// SKELINIT.CPP
//
//    Initialization routines for the skeleton
// application
//
//

#include <skeleton.hpp>


//──────────────────
//
```

continued

Listing 6-2   *continued*

```
// SkeletonInitApplication()
//
//    Initialize the application.
//

    BOOL
SkeletonInitApplication ( HINSTANCE  hInst,
                          HINSTANCE  hPrev,
                          int        *pCmdSHow,
                          LPSTR      lpCmd )
{
    return TRUE;
}


//————————-
//
// SkeletonRegisterClass()
//
//    Registers the skeleton class
//

    BOOL
SkeletonRegisterClass ( HINSTANCE    hInstance )
{
    WNDCLASS WndClass;

    //————————-

    hMBrush = CreateSolidBrush(RGB(192,192,192));

    WndClass.style        = 0;
    WndClass.lpfnWndProc  = SkeletonMainWindowProc;
    WndClass.cbClsExtra   = 0;
    WndClass.cbWndExtra   = 0;
    WndClass.hInstance    = hInstance;
    WndClass.hIcon        = LoadIcon ( hInstance, "SKELETON" );

    WndClass.hCursor      = LoadCursor ( NULL, IDC_ARROW );
    WndClass.hbrBackground = hMBrush;

    WndClass.lpszMenuName  = "SKELETON";

    WndClass.lpszClassName = "SKELETON";
```

```
    return RegisterClass(&WndClass);
}

//——————-
//
// SkeletonCreateWindow()
//
//    Creates the main skeleton window
//

    HWND
SkeletonCreateWindow ( HINSTANCE    hInstance )
{
    HWND    hWnd;

    int     coords[4];

    //——————

    coords [ 0 ] = CW_USEDEFAULT;
    coords [ 1 ] = 0;
    coords [ 2 ] = CW_USEDEFAULT;
    coords [ 3 ] = 0;

    hWnd = CreateWindow (
                "SKELETON",
                "Skeleton Application",
                WS_OVERLAPPED |
                  WS_THICKFRAME |
                  WS_SYSMENU |
                  WS_MINIMIZEBOX |
                  WS_MAXIMIZEBOX,
                coords [ 0 ],
                coords [ 1 ],
                coords [ 2 ],
                coords [ 3 ],
                0,                  // Parent handle
                0,                  // Child id
                hInstance,          // Instance handle
                (LPSTR)NULL );      // No additional info
    return hWnd;
}

//——————-
//
```

continued

Listing 6-2   *continued*

```
/ SkeletonExitApp()
//
//   Does any final cleanup...
//

    void
SkeletonExitApp( void )
{
    //—————-

    if ( hMBrush )
    {
        DeleteObject ( hMBrush );

        hMBrush = 0;
    }
}

//—————
//
// CreateGraphicButtons()
//
//   Creates the graphic buttons
// that we're going to be
// displaying.
//

    void FAR PASCAL

CreateGraphicButtons ( HWND   hWnd )
{

    //—————

    buttons[0].BuildSelf ( hInst,          // Instance handle
                    hWnd,                   // Parent window
                    1001,                   // Button id
                    28,                     // x position
                    19,                     // y position
                    (LPSTR)"BT1U",          // Button up
                    (LPSTR)"BT1D",          // Button down
                    NULL,                   // Button grey
                    NULL,                   // Button selected
                    Button1SCAction,        // Single click
```

```
                                              // callback
                         Button1DCAction ); // double click
                                              // callback


    buttons[1].BuildSelf ( hInst,            // Instance handle
                           hWnd,             // Parent window
                           1002,             // Button id
                           28,               // x position
                           55,               // y position
                           (LPSTR)"BT2U",    // Button up
                           (LPSTR)"BT2D",    // Button down
                           NULL,             // Button grey
                           NULL,             // Button selected
                           Button2SCAction,  // Single click
                                              // callback
                           Button2DCAction ); // double click
                                              // callback

}
```

Listing 6-3   Skelvars.cpp

```
//
// SKELVARS.CPP
//
//  Global variables for the skeleton application
//
//

#define __SKELETON_GLOBAL_VARS

#include <skeleton.hpp>

//——————————————————-
//
// All the following are standard global
// variables used by the skeleton application
//

HBRUSH     hMBrush;   // Brush for window background

HWND       MainhWnd;  // Main window handle
```

continued

Listing 6-3 *continued*

```
HINSTANCE  hInst;      // Instance handle that we need


//——————————-
//
// Add custom variables here
//

//
// These are our bitmap button
// object classes. They contain
// all the functionality of
// our bitmap buttons.
//

BmButton   buttons [ ID_NumberOfButtons ];   // We have two buttons...
```

Listing 6-4 Callback.cpp

```
//
// CALLBACK.CPP
//
//    Callbacks...
//
#include <skeleton.hpp>


//———————————

#ifdef STUB_CALL

//——————————-
//
// Action()
//
//    Placeholder for a callback

    PMorphRoutine

Action ( HWND  hWnd,
    UINT  message,
```

```
      UINT    wParam,
      LONG    lParam )
{
      //——————————
}

#endif

//——————————-
//
// Button1SCAction()
//
//  Button 1's single click callback
//

      PMorphRoutine

Button1SCAction ( HWND hWnd,
                  UINT message,
                  UINT wParam,
                  LONG lParam )
{
      //——————————

      MessageBox ( hWnd,
                  " Single click action from button 1",
                  "",
                  MB_OK );
}

//——————————-
//
// Button1DCAction()
//
//  Button 1's double click callback
//

      PMorphRoutine

Button1DCAction ( HWND hWnd,
                  UINT message,
                  UINT wParam,
                  LONG lParam )
{
      //——————————
```

continued

Listing 6-4 *continued*

```
    MessageBox ( hWnd,
              " Double click action from button 1",
              "",
              MB_OK );
}
//——————————-
//
// Button2SCAction()
//
//   Button 2's single click callback
//

    PMorphRoutine

Button2SCAction ( HWND hWnd,
              UINT message,
              UINT wParam,
              LONG lParam )
{
    //——————————

    MessageBox ( hWnd,
              " Single click action from button 2",
              "",
              MB_OK );
}
//——————————-
//
// Button2DCAction()
//
//   Button 2's double click callback
//

    PMorphRoutine

Button2DCAction ( HWND hWnd,
              UINT message,
              UINT wParam,
              LONG lParam )
{
    //——————————
```

```
    MessageBox ( hWnd,
              " Double click action from button 2",
              "",
              MB_OK );
}
```

Listing 6- 5   Skeleton.hpp

```
//
// SKELETON.HPP
//
//    Mondo include file for
// the skeleton app.
//
//    __EVERYTHING__ gets included here, ONCE.
//
// That's it.
//

#ifndef __SKELETON_HPP

#define __SKELETON_HPP

//———————————--

#include <WINDOWS.H>

#include <gocl.hpp>        // Class library definitions

#include <skelincs.hpp>    // Packaged #defines

#include <skelextn.hpp>    // Externs for the global variables

#include <skelprot.hpp>    // Prototypes for all functions in skeleton


//———————————--


#endif  // __SKELETON_HPP
```

Listing 6-6   Skelincs.hpp

```
//
// SKELINCS.HPP
//
//   Skeleton includes.
//
//   Packaged this way so that both the
// .cpp files and the .rc files can
// use them.
//

#ifndef __SKELINCS_HPP

#define __SKELINCS_HPP

//————————————

#include <WINDOWS.H>

#include <skeldfns.hpp>        // Resource and other ID defines

//————————————

#endif // __SKELINCS_HPP
```

Listing 6-7   Skeldfns.hpp

```
//
// SKELDFNS.HPP
//
//   Defines used by the skeleton application
//

#ifndef __SKELDFNS_HPP

#define __SKELDFNS_HPP

//————————————-

#define    SKELETON_BASE_ID   4000

#define    ID_NumberOfButtons 2
```

```
//———
```

```
#define    ID_SkeletonExit              SKELETON_BASE_ID + 0
```

```
//————————-
```

```
#endif // __SKELDFNS_HPP
```

Listing 6-8   Skelextn.hpp

```
//
// SKELEXTN.HPP
//
//    External define file for the skeleton app
//
//

#ifndef __SKELETON_GLOBAL_VARS

#define __SKELETON_GLOBAL_VARS

//————————


extern HBRUSH      hMBrush;    // Brush for window background

extern HWND        MainhWnd;   // Main window handle

extern HINSTANCE   hInst;      // Instance handle that we need


//———————-
//
// Add custom variables here
//

//
// These are our bitmap button
// object classes. They contain
// all the functionality of
// our bitmap buttons.
//
```

continued

Listing 6-8   *continued*

```
extern BmButton buttons [ ID_NumberOfButtons ];    // We have four buttons

//————————————

#endif // __SKELETON_GLOBAL_VARS
```

Listing 6-9   Skelprot.hpp

```
//
// SKELPROT.HPP
//
//     Prototype file
//

#ifndef __SKELETON_PROTOTYPES_HPP

#define __SKELETON_PROTOTYPES_HPP

//————————————-

//————————————--
//
// Extern C wrappers
//

#ifdef __cplusplus

extern "C" {

#endif

//————————————--

    int PASCAL
WinMain ( HINSTANCE    hInstance,
         HINSTANCE    hPrevInstance,
         LPSTR        lpCmdLine,
         int          nCmdShow );

    LONG FAR PASCAL
SkeletonMainWindowProc ( HWND        hWnd,
```

```
                        UINT        message,
                        UINT        wParam,
                        LONG        lParam );
    BOOL
SkeletonInitApplication ( HINSTANCE  hInst,
                          HINSTANCE  hPrev,
                          int        *pCmdSHow,
                          LPSTR      lpCmd );
    BOOL
SkeletonRegisterClass ( HINSTANCE    hInstance );

    HWND
SkeletonCreateWindow ( HINSTANCE     hInstance );

    void
SkeletonExitApp( void );


    void FAR PASCAL
CreateGraphicButtons ( HWND   hWnd );

    PMorphRoutine
Button1SCAction ( HWND hWnd,
                UINT message,
                UINT wParam,
                LONG lParam );
    PMorphRoutine
Button1DCAction ( HWND hWnd,
                UINT message,
                UINT wParam,
                LONG lParam );
    PMorphRoutine
Button2SCAction ( HWND hWnd,
                UINT message,
                UINT wParam,
                LONG lParam );
    PMorphRoutine
Button2DCAction ( HWND hWnd,
                UINT message,
                UINT wParam,
                LONG lParam );

//————————————--

//————————————--
```

continued

Listing 6-9   *continued*

```
//
// Extern C wrappers
//

#ifdef __cplusplus

};

#endif


//————————————-

#endif  //  __SKELETON_PROTOTYPES__HPP
```

Listing 6-10   Skeleton.rc

```
//
// Skeleton.rc
//

#include <skelincs.hpp>

#include <cppres.rc>

//#include <skeleton.dlg>

//————————-
//
// Bitmaps, icons, cursors
//

SKELETON    ICON       SKELETON.ICO

BT1U        BITMAP     BT1U.BMP
BT1D        BITMAP     BT1D.BMP
BT2U        BITMAP     BT2U.BMP
BT2D        BITMAP     BT2D.BMP

//————————--
//
// Menus
```

```
//
SKELETON MENU
    BEGIN
    POPUP "Skeleton"
        BEGIN
        MENUITEM "Exit",    ID_SkeletonExit
        END
    END
```

LOOKING AT THE GRAPHIC EXAMPLE

You can find all the source code for this application, as well as the project and make files (this app was created under Borland C++ 4.0) on the disk, in case you want to make it yourself.

As you can see, there are two graphic buttons in the client area of our main window. Clicking on either button brings up a dialog box indicating which button was clicked.

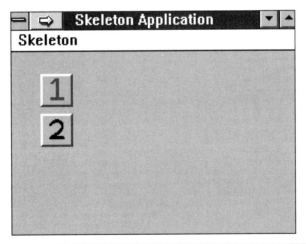

FIGURE 6-5   THE GRAPHIC BUTTON APPLICATION IN ACTION. THESE TWO BUTTONS WERE DRAWN IN THE MAIN CLIENT AREA OF OUR WINDOW

Creating the buttons

From our application's standpoint, there are a couple of important pieces in using graphic buttons. The first is the declaration of an instance of the graphic button object class, **BmButton**. This occurs in the file skelvars.cpp, like so:

```
BmButton    buttons [ ID_NumberOfButtons ];   // We have two
                                              // buttons...
```

This creates two instances of a **BmButton** class (the value ID_NumberOfButtons has been #defined to be 2). Next, in our startup code for our application, we make a call to **CreateGraphicButtons(),** which creates the buttons for us. The code inside **CreateGraphicButtons()** looks like this:

```
CreateGraphicButtons ( HWND   hWnd )
{

    //————————

buttons[0].BuildSelf ( hInst,          // Instance handle
           hWnd,                        // Parent window
           1001,                        // Button id
           28,                          // x position
           19,                          // y position
           (LPSTR)"BT1U",               // Button up
           (LPSTR)"BT1D",               // Button down
           NULL,                        // Button grey
           NULL,                        // Button selected
           Button1SCAction,             // Single click
                                        // callback
           Button1DCAction );           // double click
                                        // callback
```

This call to the member function **BuildSelf()** is the piece of code that's responsible for having the button set itself up properly. (I'll discuss what goes on internally in this function in just a minute). The things to notice here are:

1. The first five parameters are ones that correspond directly to the parameters we needed for the **CreateWindow()** call when we were creating a text button; we need the instance handle, parent window handle, button id, and x and y position for our graphic button.

2. The next four parameters are the names of the button resources that we intend to use for each of the four button states—up, down, greyed, and selected. In this case, we don't have a greyed or selected state, so we simply pass NULL values, which lets our button class know not to attempt to load these bitmaps.

3. The final two parameters are the callback actions that we want to occur when a single click or a double click action occurs, respectively. This allows us to define the action that should be taken for each button, and then have the button be responsible for carrying out that action when necessary.

Handling the buttons

Now that we've got the buttons created, we only need to worry about two things:

1. Drawing the buttons, and
2. responding to the WM_COMMAND message for the buttons.

Our first concern is making sure the buttons get drawn. Since these are graphic buttons, and not text buttons, Windows itself has no idea of how the buttons need to be drawn. In order to be able to handle this case, Windows provides an extra class style for buttons, called WS_OWNERDRAW. This flag value, passed in the class style parameter of the **CreateWindow()** call, acts just like the other flag values (WS_CHILD, etc.). However, this value tells Windows that we, not Windows, are going to be handling the drawing of this button.

That's all very well, you may be thinking to yourself, but just what does that get us? What it gets us is the WM_DRAWITEM message. This message is passed to the parent of a WS_OWNERDRAW control any time the control needs to be redrawn. In essence, whenever Windows needs to redisplay the control, it comes back to our program, and asks us to draw it.

Of course, if we just ignore this message, then nothing at all will get drawn; in our case, we'd just have big white holes where our buttons were supposed to be. However, if we pass this message on to our button's member function **RenderSelfIfID(),** each button will take care of drawing itself into our main window. (The mechanics of how this works is coming up in just a little bit).

Now that we've gotten the buttons drawn, we need to be able to respond to them. This is handled in the WM_COMMAND message, and again, we simply pass of the responsibility of determining what to do to the buttons themselves, via the member function **PerformActionIfID().**

How the button class works internally

From the standpoint of our application, using a graphic button is pretty darned simple (if you use the **BmButton()** class). You create one, using some standardly available parameters, and in your main window procedure you make sure that two messages are handled. That's it!

Having seen how the **BmButton** class works from the outside, now let's take a look at it from the inside. This view will show us all of the gory details about how graphic buttons work. As you might expect, they're a lot like text buttons.

Here's the source listings for the **BmButton** class; let's talk more about it after you look over the code.

Listing 6-11   BmButton.hpp

```
/*
 * BMBUTTON.H
 *
 *    Defines the class for a bitmap button, which
 * knows how to do all sorts of buttony things.
 *
 *


 *
 * (C) Copyright 1991 by ShadowCat Technologies
 * All Rights Reserved
 *
 * This software is a copyrighted work of software, and
 * is protected by domestic and international copyright laws.
 * Some parts of this software may constitute trade secrets
 * and/or intellectual property rights of ShadowCat Technologies.
 * This software, or any portion thereof, may not be copied, stored,
 * transmitted, reproduced or otherwise used in any form without the
 * express written consent of ShadowCat Technologies.
 *
 * Written by Alex Leavens

 *
 *
 *_____-
 *
 *
 * History: $Log: $
 *
 *
 *
 *
 *_____
 */

#ifndef __BMBUTTON_H

#define __BMBUTTON_H

#ifdef __cplusplus

//———————————————————
```

continued

Listing 6-11   *continued*

```
/*****************************
 *
 * Class: BmButton
 *
 *   Bitmap button class, which uses the ResBitmap class
 * to build it's objects with.
 *
 */

    class

BmButton
{

    // ————— PROTECTED —————

    protected:

    int     xSavePos;   // Desired x position (used for
                        // deferred button creation)
    int     ySavePos;

    Boolean   internalsBuilt;

    HANDLE    saveInst;

    Boolean   btEnabled;  // Will button respond to actions?

    ButtonStyle btStyle;    // Button style

    //—————
    //
    // BuildInternals() sets up all the internal stuff
    // that we need to have happen in order for a button
    // to work.
    //

        void
    BuildInternals(HANDLE   hInst,
            HMENU       windID,
            int         xPos,
            int         yPos,
            LPSTR       upName,
```

```
            LPSTR        dnName,
            LPSTR        greyName,
            LPSTR        selectName,
            PMorphCall   sCall,
            PMorphCall   dCall);

//─────────────────────────-

ResBitmap   imageUp;         // Up image
ResBitmap   imageDown;       // Down image
ResBitmap   imageGrey;       // Image state if tool is unavailable
ResBitmap   imageSelect;     // Button pressed, but not released

BtnState    btnState;        // Current setting of the button image

HWND        btnWnd;          // Window handle of button

HMENU       selfID;          // Id of object

PMorphCall  singleClick;     // Single click callback for the button

PMorphCall  doubleClick;     // Double click callback

// ───────── PUBLIC ─────────-

public:

    /*─────────────-
     *
     * BmButton() - DEFAULT constructor
     *
     */

    BmButton( void );

    /*─────────────-
     *
     * BmButton() - Constructor
     *
     */

    BmButton(HANDLE hInst,   // Instance of application
        HWND        hWnd,        // Parent window handle
        HMENU       windID,      // ID for the button
        int         xPos,        // x position for button
```

continued

Listing 6-11 *continued*

```
            int         yPos,           // y position for button
            LPSTR       upName,         // name of up image
            LPSTR       dnName,         // name of down image
            LPSTR       greyName,       // name of grey image
            LPSTR       selectName,     // name of selected image
            PMorphCall sCall,           // single click callback
            PMorphCall dCall);              // double click callback

/*-------------
 *
 * ~BmButton() - Destructor
 *
 */

    ~BmButton( void );

    //------------------------------
    //----------- Information retrieval routines ---
    //------------------------------

/*-------------
 *
 * GetWndHand() returns the window handle
 * of the button image.
 *
 */

    HWND
GetWndHand( void )
{
    return btnWnd;
}

    HWND
GetHandle ( void )
{
    return btnWnd;
}

/*-------------
 *
 * GetButtonState() returns the current state
 * of the button image.
 *
```

```
*/

    BtnState
GetButtonState( void )
{
    return btnState;
}

/*———————--
 *
 * GetID() returns the value of the ID associated with
 * this button control's window.
 */

    HMENU
GetID( void )
{
    return selfID;
}

/*———————
 *
 * GetButtonSize()
 *
 *     Returns the size of the button image
 * (based on the up image)
 *
 */

    POINT
GetButtonSize ( void )
{
    return imageUp.GetSize();
}

//———————
//
// DetermineRequestedDisplayState()
//
//     Detemines the display state that the button is being
// asked to be drawn in, but does not change any of the
// internal states of the button itself.
//

    BtnState
```

continued

Listing 6-11   *continued*

```
DetermineRequestedDisplayState ( LPDRAWITEMSTRUCT lpDis );

/*————————————-
 *
 * MatchSelfID()
 *
 *    This routine returns a boolean, indicating
 * whether or not the ID passed in matches the ID
 * of this control.
 *
 */

    Boolean
MatchSelfID ( HMENU testID )
{
    if (testID == GetID())
        return true;
    else
        return false;
}

/*————————————-
 *
 * MatchSelfWindow()
 *
 *    Same idea as MatchSelfID, this routine returns a
 * boolean, indicating whether or not the Window handle
 * passed in matches the window handle of this control.
 *
 */

    Boolean
MatchSelfWindow ( HWND testWnd )
{
    if ( testWnd == GetWndHand() )
        return true;
    else
        return false;
}

/*————————————-
 *
 * ButtonEnabled()
 *
```

```
*    Returns the state of the enabled flag:
*
*   true - button is active
*   false - button is inactive
*
*/

    Boolean
ButtonEnabled ( void ) { return    btEnabled; }

//****************************************************

    //————————————————————————
    //—————————- Data alteration routines ——-
    //————————————————————————


/*——————————-
 *
 * EnableButton()
 *
 *   Enables or disables the button
 *
 *
 */

    void

EnableButton ( HWND parentWnd,
          Boolean  enState );


/*——————————-
 *
 * SetButtonState() sets the button state.
 *
 */

SetButtonState( BtnState newState )
{
    btnState = newState;
    return NULL;
}

//****************************************************
```

continued

Listing 6-11 *continued*

```
//————————————————————
//——————————-- Construction routines ——-
//————————————————————

//————————————————-
//
// BuildButtonWindow()  actually creates the button's window
// for us. This call can be made immediately after the BuildInternals()
// call (as in the case of BuildSelf()), or it can occur at a later time,
// (as in the case of BuildSelfDeferred()). IT MUST OCCURR
// AFTER a call to BuildInternals().
//

    void
BuildButtonWindow(HWND      hWnd);

/*————————————-
 *
 * BmButton::BuildSelfDeferred()
 *
 * Creates a bitmap button, BUT WITHOUT CREATING THE WINDOW FOR IT.
 * This allows us to come back at a later point in time, and
 * perform a createwindow call on the button, at which point it will
 * create itself in a window.
 *
 */

    void
BuildSelfDeferred(HANDLE   hInst,          // Instance of application
         HMENU        windID,         // ID for the button
         int          xPos,           // x position for button
         int          yPos,           // y position for button
         LPSTR        upName,         // Up name
         LPSTR        dnName,         // Down name
         LPSTR        greyName,       // Grey name
         LPSTR        selectName,     // Selected name
         PMorphCall   sCall,          // Single click callback
         PMorphCall   dCall);

    /*————————————-
     *
     * BuildSelf()
     *    Does the same thing as the constructor
     *
```

```
        */

            void
        BuildSelf(HANDLE    hInst,
                HWND        hWnd,         // Parent window handle
                HMENU       windID,       // ID for the button
                int         xPos,         // x position for button
                int         yPos,         // y position for button
                LPSTR       upName,       // name of up image
                LPSTR       dnName,       // name of down image
                LPSTR       greyName,     // name of grey image
                LPSTR       selectName,   // Name of selected image
                PMorphCall  sCall,        // single click callback
                PMorphCall  dCall);       // Double click callback


/*————————————
 *
 * RenderSelfIfID()
 *
 *    Causes the button to check and see
 * if the control ID being passed in
 * matches it's own ID. If it does,
 * then it displays itself in its window
 * in its current state.
 *
 */

    Boolean
RenderSelfIfID( HMENU   testID,
        LONG    lParam );

/*————————————
 *
 * RenderSelfInWindow()
 *
 *    Causes the button to render itself into its
 * own window.
 *
 */

RenderSelfInWindow( void );

//————————————
//
```

continued

Listing 6-11   *continued*

```
// RenderSelfAsDialogControl()
//
//    This function assumes that the bitmap button is a child window
// control of some parent window (typically a toolbar or toolpalette),
// and will render itself in its current state into that parent window.
//

RenderSelfAsDialogControl ( HWND   parentWnd );

/*—————————
 *
 * RenderSelf() causes the button to
 * display itself in its current state in the
 * requested DC.
 *
 */

    void
RenderSelf(HDC     hDC,
      short   x,
      short   y);

/*—————————
 *
 * RenderSelfRequested()
 *
 *    Renders the button in the requested state
 *
 */

    void
RenderSelfRequested(BtnState        requestState,
         HDC     hDC,
         short   x,
         short   y);

/*—————————
 *
 * DetermineDisplayState()
 *
 *    Determines if the button is up or down, according
 * to the itemState field of the DrawItemStruct that is
 * passed in.
 *
```

```
    */

    BtnState
DetermineDisplayState(LPDRAWITEMSTRUCT    lpDis);

/*—————————
 *
 * SingleClickAction()
 *
 *   Performs the function associated with this button
 * (which is a user supplied routine that must be passed in
 * at creation time).
 */

    void
SingleClickAction(HWND      hWnd,
        unsigned  message,
        WORD      wParam,
        LONG      lParam);


/*—————————
 *
 * DoubleClickAction()
 *
 *   Performs the function associated with this button
 * (which is a user supplied routine that must be passed in
 * at creation time).
 */

    void
DoubleClickAction(HWND      hWnd,
        unsigned  message,
        WORD      wParam,
        LONG      lParam);

/*———————--
 *
 * PerformActionIfID()
 *
 *   Checks to see if the ID passed in matches
 * the ID of the control (which is a values supplied
 * by the user), and if it is, executes the
 * callback function for this tool.
 *
```

continued

Listing 6-11 *continued*

```
    */

        Boolean
    PerformActionIfID(HMENU      testID,
            HWND       hWnd,
            unsigned   message,
            WORD       wParam,
            LONG       lParam);

};


//——————————————————————————

#endif // __cplusplus

#endif // __BMBUTTON_H
```

Listing 6-12 BmButton.cpp

```
/*
 * BMBUTTON.CPP
 *
 *    Routines for handling bitmap button class
 *
 *

 *
 * (C) Copyright 1991 by ShadowCat Technologies
 * All Rights Reserved
 *
 * This software is a copyrighted work of software, and
 * is protected by domestic and international copyright laws.
 * Some parts of this software may constitute trade secrets
 * and/or intellectual property rights of ShadowCat Technologies.
 * This software, or any portion thereof, may not be copied, stored,
 * transmitted, reproduced or otherwise used in any form without the
 * express written consent of ShadowCat Technologies.
 *
 * Written by Alex Leavens
 *
 *
```

```
 *
 *———————————————-
 *
 *
 * History: $Log: $
 *
 *
 *
 *
 *————————————————————
 */


#include "cplus.hpp"


//————————
//
// BuildInternals() sets up all the internal stuff
// that we need to have happen in order for a button
// to work.
//

    void
BmButton::BuildInternals(HANDLE              hInst,
            HMENU       windID,
            int         xPos,
            int         yPos,
            LPSTR       upName,
            LPSTR       dnName,
            LPSTR       greyName,
            LPSTR       selectName,
            PMorphCall  sCall,
            PMorphCall  dCall)
{

    /*———————————-*/

    internalsBuilt = true;

    saveInst = hInst;

    imageUp.LoadSelf ( hInst,        // Load up image     upName );

    imageDown.LoadSelf ( hInst,
```

continued

Listing 6-12 *continued*

```
                dnName ); // Load down image

    imageGrey.LoadSelf ( hInst,
            greyName );   // Load grey image (if there)

    imageSelect.LoadSelf ( hInst,    // Load selected image ( if there )
            selectName );

    singleClick = sCall;      // Set callback routines
    doubleClick = dCall;

    xSavePos = xPos;          // X position of button in parent
    ySavePos = yPos;          // Y position of button in parent

    btnState = invalid;       // Set initial button state

    btEnabled = true;         // Button initially enabled

    btnWnd = NULL;            // No button window handle

    selfID = windID;          // ID of button when created

    btStyle = bitmap;         // Define the type of button
                              // being created...
}

//———————————-
//
// BuildButtonWindow()  actually creates the button's window
// for us. This call can be made immediately after the BuildInternals()
// call (as in the case of BuildSelf()), or it can occur at a later time,
// (as in the case of BuildSelfDeferred()). IT MUST OCCURR
// AFTER a call to BuildInternals().
//

    void
BmButton::BuildButtonWindow(HWND        hWnd)
{
    POINT   ptSize;         // Size of bitmap image

    /*———————————-*/

    if (btnWnd == NULL && internalsBuilt == true)
    {
```

```
        ptSize = imageUp.GetSize();            // Get image size

        btnWnd = CreateWindow("BUTTON",        // Button class
                    NULL,      // No text string
                    BS_OWNERDRAW | WS_CHILD | WS_VISIBLE,  // styles
                    xSavePos,       // x position of button
                    ySavePos,       // y position of button,
                    ptSize.x,       // image size, x
                    ptSize.y,       // image size, y
                    hWnd,           // Parent window handle
                    selfID,         // Child window id
                    saveInst,       // Module instance
                    NULL);          // extra data
    }

    else if (btnWnd && internalsBuilt == true)
    {
        ShowWindow(btnWnd,
            SW_SHOW);
    }
}

/*——————————-
 *
 * BmButton::BmButton() - DEFAULT Constructor
 *
 *   For creating BmButton classes inside other classes.
 *
 */

BmButton::BmButton(void)
{
    /*————————-*/

    internalsBuilt = false;
}

/*——————————-
 *
 * BmButton::BuildSelfDeferred()
 *
 *    Creates a bitmap button, BUT WITHOUT CREATING THE WINDOW FOR IT.
 *  This allows us to come back at a later point in time, and
 *  perform a createwindow call on the button, at which point it will
 *  create itself in a window.
```

continued

Listing 6-12 *continued*

```
 *
 */

    void
BmButton::BuildSelfDeferred(HANDLE    hInst,   // Instance of application
                HMENU   windID,               // ID for the button
                int     xPos,                 // x position for button
                int     yPos,                 // y position for button
                LPSTR   upName,               // Up name
                LPSTR   dnName,               // Down name
                LPSTR   greyName,             // Grey name
                LPSTR   selectName    ,       // selected name
                    PMorphCall sCall,         // Single click callback
                    PMorphCall dCall)
{
    /*——————*/

    BuildInternals(hInst,
            windID,      // Build internal structures that
            xPos,        // don't rely on having a window
            yPos,        // built.
            upName,
            dnName,
            greyName,
            selectName,
            sCall,
            dCall);
}

/*—————————-
 *
 * BmButton::BuildSelf()
 *
 *    Builds itself. Wrapper function so that we
 * can initialize arrays of BmButton types.
 *
 */

    void
BmButton::BuildSelf(HANDLEhInst,     // Instance of application
            HWND        hWnd,         // Parent window handle
            HMENU       windID,       // ID for the button
            int         xPos,         // x position for button
            int         yPos,         // y position for button
```

```
            LPSTR     upName,        // Up name
            LPSTR     dnName,        // Down name
            LPSTR     greyName,      // Grey name
            LPSTR     selectName,    // Selected name
            PMorphCall sCall,        // Single click callback
            PMorphCall dCall)
{
    BuildInternals(hInst,
            windID,      // Build internal structures that
            xPos,        // don't rely on having a window
            yPos,        // built.
            upName,
            dnName,
            greyName,
            selectName,
            sCall,
            dCall);

    BuildButtonWindow(hWnd);
}

/*————
 *
 * BmButton::BmButton() - Constructor
 *
 * Returns: Nothing
 *
 *
 */

BmButton::BmButton(HANDLE hInst,     // Instance of application
            HWND     hWnd,           // Parent window handle
            HMENU    windID,         // ID for the button
            int      xPos,           // x position for button
            int      yPos,           // y position for button
            LPSTR    upName,         // Up name
            LPSTR    dnName,         // Down name
            LPSTR    greyName,       // greyed image
            LPSTR    selectName,     // selected image
            PMorphCall  sCall,       // single click callback
            PMorphCall  dCall)
{
    BuildSelf(hInst,
        hWnd,
        windID,
```

continued

Listing 6-12 *continued*

```
            xPos,
            yPos,
            upName,
            dnName,
            greyName,
            selectName,
            sCall,
            dCall);
}

/*——————————
 *
 * ~BmButton() - Destructor
 *
 */

BmButton::~BmButton( void )
{
    /*————————*/

    imageUp.DeleteSelf();
    imageDown.DeleteSelf();
    imageGrey.DeleteSelf();
    imageSelect.DeleteSelf();
}

/*——————————
 *
 * RenderSelfIfID()
 *
 *    Causes the button to check and see
 * if the control ID being passed in
 * matches it's own ID. If it does,
 * then it displays itself in its window
 * in its current state.
 *
 */

    Boolean
BmButton::RenderSelfIfID( HMENU        testID,
            LONG  lParam)
{
    BtnState        cState;
```

```
    LPDRAWITEMSTRUCT   lpDis;

    /*————*/

    if ( testID == GetID() )
    {
        lpDis = (LPDRAWITEMSTRUCT)lParam;

    cState = DetermineDisplayState(lpDis);    // Figure out requested
                                              // button state

    switch(cState)
    {
        case up:
        case down:
        case grey:
        case selected:

        RenderSelfRequested(cState,
                    lpDis->hDC,           // hDC to draw into...
                    0,
                    0);
            break;

        case invalid:
        default:
            return false;
    }

        return true;
    }
    else
        return false;
}

/*————
 *
 * RenderSelfInWindow()
 *
 *    Causes the button to render itself into its
 * own window.
 *
 */

BmButton::RenderSelfInWindow( void )
```

continued

Listing 6-12 *continued*

```
{
    HDC hDC;

    /*————————*/

    hDC = GetDC(btnWnd);

    if (hDC)
    {
    RenderSelf(hDC,
            0,
            0);

    ReleaseDC(btnWnd,
            hDC);
    }

    return NULL;
}
//————————
//
// RenderSelfAsDialogControl()
//
//    This function assumes that the bitmap button is a child window
// control of some parent window (typically a toolbar or toolpalette),
// and will render itself in its current state into that parent window.
//

BmButton::RenderSelfAsDialogControl ( HWND    parentWnd )
{
    HWND    toolWnd;   // Window handle of this button as a child control

    HDC     toolDC;

    //————————

    toolWnd = GetDlgItem ( parentWnd, // Window handle of parent (dialog)
                (int)selfID );

    if ( toolWnd )
    {
        toolDC = GetDC ( toolWnd );

        if ( toolDC )
```

```
    {
        RenderSelf ( toolDC,
                0,
                0 );

        ReleaseDC ( toolWnd,
            toolDC );
    }
}

    return NULL;
}
/*————————
 *
 * RenderSelfRequested()
 *
 *   Renders the button in the requested state
 *
 */

    void
BmButton::RenderSelfRequested(BtnState        requestState,
            HDC     hDC,
            short   x,
            short   y)
{
    /*————————*/

    switch(requestState)
    {
        case down:
            imageDown.DisplaySelf(hDC,
                        x,
                        y);
        break;

        case grey:
            imageGrey.DisplaySelf(hDC,
                        x,
                        y);
        break;

    case selected:

        if ( imageSelect.GetBitmapHandle() )
```

continued

Listing 6-12 *continued*

```
        {
            imageSelect.DisplaySelf ( hDC,
                        x,
                        y );
        }
        else
        {
            imageDown.DisplaySelf ( hDC,
                        x,
                        y );
        }
        break;

        case up:
        case focus:
        default:

            imageUp.DisplaySelf( hDC,
                        x,
                        y );
        break;
    }
}

/*——————————
 *
 * RenderSelf() causes the button to
 * display itself in it's current state.
 *
 */

    void
BmButton::RenderSelf(HDC   hDC,
            short x,
            short y)
{
    BtnState    currentState;

    /*————————-*/

    currentState = GetButtonState();

    RenderSelfRequested(currentState,
            hDC,
```

```
            x,
            y );
}

//————————————————
//
// DetermineRequestedDisplayState()
//
//  itemAction  itemState    Action
//  ——————————————————-
//   ODA_SELECT    ODS_FOCUS  Mouse down, moved OFF of button
//   ODA_SELECT    FOCUS | SELECT     Mouse down, moved ON to button,
//                 or new mouse down on button
//   ODA_FOCUS ODS_SELECT Mouse up while on button
//

    BtnState

BmButton::DetermineRequestedDisplayState ( LPDRAWITEMSTRUCT lpDis )
{
    //
    // If not an owner draw button, punt.
    //

    if ( lpDis->CtlType != ODT_BUTTON )
        return invalid;

    //
    // If button disabled, the only thing it can be is grey.
    //

    if ( ButtonEnabled() != true )
        return grey;

    //
    // If drawing the entire button, and the button state is valid, go
    // ahead and return current button state.
    //

    if ( lpDis->itemAction & ODA_DRAWENTIRE )
    {
        switch ( GetButtonState() )
        {
            case down:
```

continued

Listing 6-12 *continued*

```
            case grey:
                return GetButtonState();
                break;

            default:
                break;
        }
    }

    //
    // Only a portion of the button is being redrawn
    // (due to some form of state change). Do that...
    //

    if (lpDis->itemState & ODS_SELECTED)      // Button down
    {
        if ( lpDis->itemAction & ODA_SELECT )
        return selected;
    else
        return down;
    }
    else if (lpDis->itemState & ODS_DISABLED)
    {
        return grey;
    }
    else
    {
        return up;
    }

    return invalid;    // Should never reach here.
}

/*————————————
 *
 * DetermineDisplayState()
 *
 *    Determines if the button is up or down, according
 * to the itemState field of the DrawItemStruct that is
 * passed in.
 *
 */

    BtnState
```

```
BmButton::DetermineDisplayState(LPDRAWITEMSTRUCT     lpDis)
{
    BtnState    requestedState;

    /*————*/

    requestedState = DetermineRequestedDisplayState ( lpDis );

    switch ( requestedState )
    {
        case down:
        case grey:
        case up:
        case selected:

            SetButtonState ( requestedState );
        return requestedState;
        break;

        case invalid:
        default:
            return requestedState;
            break;
    }

    return invalid;

}

/*——————
 *
 * SingleClickAction()
 *
 *   Performs the function associated with this button
 * (which is a user supplied routine that must be passed in
 * at creation time).
 */

    void
BmButton::SingleClickAction(HWND     hWnd,
            unsigned    message,
            WORD    wParam,
            LONG    lParam)
{
    /*————*/
```

continued

Listing 6-12 *continued*

```
    if ( ( singleClick != NULL ) && ( ButtonEnabled() == true ) )
    {
        (*singleClick)(hWnd,
            message,
            wParam,
            lParam);
    }
}

/*————————
 *
 * DoubleClickAction()
 *
 *    Performs the function associated with this button
 * (which is a user supplied routine that must be passed in
 * at creation time).
 */

    void
BmButton::DoubleClickAction(HWND      hWnd,
                unsigned    message,
                WORD    wParam,
                LONG    lParam)
{
    /*————*/

    if ( ( doubleClick != NULL ) && ( ButtonEnabled() == true ) )
    {
        (*doubleClick)(hWnd,
            message,
            wParam,
            lParam);
    }
}

/*————————-
 *
 * PerformActionIfID()
 *
 *    Checks to see if the ID passed in matches
 * the ID of the control (which is a values supplied
 * by the user), and if it is, executes the
 * callback function for this tool.
```

```
    *
  */

    Boolean

BmButton::PerformActionIfID(HMENU      testID,
                HWND    hWnd,
                unsigned   message,
                WORD    wParam,
                LONG    lParam)
{
    WORD    noteCode = HIWORD (lParam);      // Double click code

    /*————*/

    if ( testID == GetID() )
    {
        switch ( noteCode )
        {
            case BN_DOUBLECLICKED:

                DoubleClickAction(hWnd,
                        message,
                        wParam,
                        lParam);
        break;

            default:

                SingleClickAction(hWnd,
                        message,
                        wParam,
                        lParam);
        break;

        }
    return true;
    }

    return false;
}

/*——————--
 *
 * EnableButton()
 *
```

continued

Listing 6-12 *continued*

```
*    Enables or disables the button
*
*
*/

    void

BmButton::EnableButton ( HWND           parentWnd,
          Boolean   enState )
{
    //————————

    //
    // If requested new state is the same as the current
    // one, then we're done, so return.
    //

    if ( btEnabled == enState )
    return;

    //
    // Set new window state...
    //

    btEnabled = enState;   // Set new window state

    //
    // Set the new button image according to the desired button state...
    //

    switch ( enState )
    {
        case true:

            SetButtonState ( up );

            break;

        case false:

            SetButtonState ( grey );

            break;
    }
```

```
        RenderSelfAsDialogControl ( parentWnd ); // Redraw self
}
```

Although there's an enormous amount of housekeeping that's going on inside the **BmButton** class, conceptually it's pretty simple. It works like this:

1. An instance of the **BmButton** class is simply a BUTTON control that was created with the WS_OWNERDRAW style flag set.

2. An instance of the **BmButton** class contains up to four bitmaps for the button: An up image, a down image, a grey image, and a selected image. The first two are required, the second two are optional. If the second two are present, they will be used when appropriate. The **BmButton** class knows exactly how the WM_OWNERDRAW message works, and can draw itself in the requested state when asked to do so by the parent application.

3. An instance of the **BmButton** class can contain callbacks for single and double clicks. When the parent application passes a WM_COMMAND message to **BmButton**, the button knows how to determine if the WM_COMMAND message is directed towards itself, and if it is, whether it is a single or a double click. Based on this, the button will then execute either the single or the double click action (if it was given one).

And that's pretty much it. All the rest of the code in the class is devoted to housekeeping and internal details, most of which you don't need to know about.

The things you do need to know about, of course, are the three things we've just talked about:

1. How does it create itself?
2. How does it draw itself?
3. How does it respond to WM_COMMAND?

Starting with the first question, let's take a look. The important member function here is **BuildButtonWindow()**, and internally it looks much like this:

```
btnWnd = CreateWindow("BUTTON",  // Button class
            NULL,                // No text string
            BS_OWNERDRAW | WS_CHILD | WS_VISIBLE, // styles
            xSavePos,            // x position of button
            ySavePos,            // y position of button,
            ptSize.x,            // image size, x
            ptSize.y,            // image size, y
            hWnd,                // Parent window handle
            selfID,              // Child window id
            saveInst,            // Module instance
            NULL);               // extra data
```

In other words, all this function is doing is a **CreateWindow()** call with a bunch of member variables (these member variables have been set with the values that we passed in to the externally used member function **CreateSelf()**), and the important class style BS_OWNERDRAW. Otherwise, it looks just like any other **CreateWindow()** call that you've seen, and in particular, it looks like the **CreateWindow()** call that we used to build our text button. This is because fundamentally it is the same call—it works just the same way. It's just that we've buried it in here in order to encapsulate the behavior of our button class, and hide it from our application, which has very little need to know how this stuff works.

The third question, how does it respond to WM_COMMAND, is also quite simple. The member function **PerformActionIfID()** is responsible for that, and it looks like this:

```
BmButton::PerformActionIfID(HMENU    testID,
            HWND     hWnd,
            unsigned  message,
            WORD     wParam,
            LONG     lParam)
{
    WORD    noteCode = HIWORD (lParam);    // Double click code

    /*————*/
```

```
    if ( testID == GetID() )
    {
        switch ( noteCode )
        {
            case BN_DOUBLECLICKED:

                DoubleClickAction(hWnd,
                        message,
                        wParam,
                        lParam);
        break;

            default:

                SingleClickAction(hWnd,
                        message,
                        wParam,
                        lParam);
        break;

        }
    return true;
    }

    return false;
}
```

Really, this is pretty simple stuff. We check the ID of the control that is specified in the WM_COMMAND message against our own internal ID (which we passed in via the **CreateSelf()** call, and which can be retrieved by the **GetID()** member function). If the two ID's match, then this command message is for us. From there we simply determine whether it's a single or a double click, and then go execute the function that was passed to us.

The member functions **SingleClickAction()** and **DoubleClickAction()** wrapper this for us—they ensure that there is, in fact, a function callback before attempting to call it (calling a NULL function pointer is considered bad form, especially since doing so will cause a General Protection Fault.)

You'll notice that I've saved the toughest question for last—that is, how does our button draw itself. Although this is more complex than the other two things our button has to do, it's still pretty simple—at least conceptually. Our button does the following things:

1. Just as in its response to the WM_COMMAND message, the first thing our button does in response to the WM_DRAWITEM message is to determine whether or not the message refers to itself. Again, it does this by comparing the ID of the control specified by the WM_DRAWITEM message and it's own internal ID. If the two match, then it proceeds to the next step.

2. It determines in what state it should be drawn. This is probably the worst part of this whole control—how the button should be drawn is specified in two flags in the DRAWITEMSTRUCT, and the documentation on the flags is somewhat misleading. However, that's why it's buried in here. Once I got it working, I never wanted to have to look at it again!

3. In any case, after the button determines how it's supposed to be drawn, it simply has the appropriate bitmap render itself into the drawing space provided by the WM_DRAWITEM message.

That's it. Now let's take a look at the actual code for the two most important pieces of this rigamarole, **RenderSelfIfID(),** which is the member function called by the parent application to determine whether or not this button should be drawn, and if so, how to draw it, and **DetermineDisplayState(),** which does the actual figuring out of how the button is now supposed to look.

```
/*————————
 *
 * RenderSelfIfID()
 *
 *    Causes the button to check and see
 * if the control ID being passed in
 * matches it's own ID. If it does,
 * then it displays itself in its window
 * in its current state.
 *
 */
```

```
     Boolean
BmButton::RenderSelfIfID( HMENU          testID,
          LONG lParam)
{
    BtnState          cState;

    LPDRAWITEMSTRUCT  lpDis;

    /*————*/
```

Here's where I check to see if the ID of the control in question matches the ID of this button (returned by the member function **GetID()**). Only if these two match is the code in the middle of this routine executed, and a true returned. If the ID's don't match, then this routine does nothing, and returns a false.

```
    if ( testID == GetID() )
    {
        lpDis = (LPDRAWITEMSTRUCT)lParam;

    cState = DetermineDisplayState(lpDis);   // Figure out requested
                                             // button state

    switch(cState)
    {
        case up:
        case down:
        case grey:
        case selected:

        RenderSelfRequested(cState,
                lpDis->hDC,          // hDC to draw into...
                0,
                0);
            break;

        case invalid:
        default:
            return false;
    }

        return true;
    }
```

```
    else
        return false;
}
```

The big internal piece of magic here is the following routine:

```
//————————————————
//
// DetermineRequestedDisplayState()
//
// itemAction itemState          Action
// ——————————————————-
//   ODA_SELECT  ODS_FOCUS       Mouse down,
//                               moved OFF of button.
//                               Button needs to be
//                               displayed in the
//                               'Up' state
//
//   ODA_SELECT  FOCUS | SELECT
//                               Mouse down, moved ON
//                               to button,
//                               or new mouse down
//                               on button. Button
//                               needs to be displayed
//                               in the 'Down' state
//                               (for FOCUS), or the
//                               'Selected' state (if
//                               itemState == ODS_SELECT)
//
//   ODA_FOCUS   ODS_SELECT      Mouse up while on button
//                               Button needs to be
//                               displayed in the 'Up'
//                               state
//
```

The truth table above says it all. The two flags in question, itemAction and itemState, are both part of the DRAWITEMSTRUCT, a long pointer to which is passed in as the lParam of the WM_DRAWITEM message. This is the key—the code in **DetermineRequestedDisplayState()** is merely an algorithmic expression of this truth table that I've shown you above. Trust me—it works.

[You can find the **BmButton** object class, and many others, (including the **ResourceBitmap** class, upon which **BmButton** relies) in the GOCL subdirectory of your source disc.]

SUMMARY

In this chapter we've looked at how you can use buttons in your application, how graphic buttons work (and sometimes, how they don't work), when it's appropriate to use text buttons versus graphic buttons, and we've look at code that actually implements both kinds of buttons.

In the next chapter, we're going to look at one of the most common elements of Windows programming, the dialog box. We'll talk about what to do (and what not to do) in dialogs, and I'll show you some examples of how you can create dialogs to handle specific tasks.

CHAPTER 7

DIALOG BOXES

INTRODUCTION

There are lots of things you shouldn't do in dialog boxes, and this chapter tells you some of them. (There are lots more that you'll have to discover on your own, not because I refuse to tell you what they are, but because they are case-specific. You can't know in advance some kinds of problems with dialog boxes, but believe me, they're there.)

Before we get into an extensive discussion of what you shouldn't be doing in dialog boxes let's take a look at what you *should* be doing in dialog boxes—in other words, what are dialog boxes good for?

In general, dialog boxes are good for a number of things:

✦ Showing the user a set of options and letting him/her choose one or several. (See figure 7-1).

✦ Displaying information to the user that needs to be acted on. ("Caution! Pressing OK means having your mouth filled with cement! OK | Cancel "). (See figure 7-2).

✦ Showing the user some information (such as an "About" box). (See figure 7-3).

✦ To perform some sort of data interaction with the user, such as letting the user select a sound to be associated with a particular text button. (See figure 7-4).

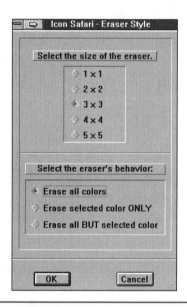

FIGURE 7-1   SCREEN SHOT OF THE ERASER TOOL DIALOG BOX THAT LETS YOU SET OPTIONS FOR THE ERASER TOOL. FROM ICE/WORKS.

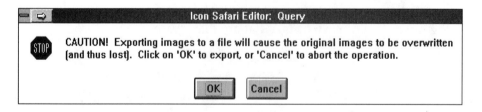

FIGURE 7-2   SCREEN SHOT OF THE DIALOG BOX FROM ICE/WORKS THAT YOU GET WHEN YOU'RE ABOUT TO OVERWRITE AN EXECUTABLE FILE. THIS IS THE SORT OF DIRE WARNING THAT'S APPROPRIATE FOR THIS KIND OF OPERATION.

FIGURE 7-3   THE ABOUT BOX FROM ICE/WORKS.

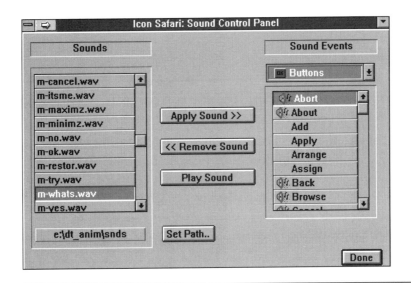

FIGURE 7-4   THE SOUND CONTROL PANEL FROM A PRODUCT THAT I WROTE. THIS DIALOG ALLOWS THE USER TO PREVIEW .WAV (SOUND) FILES, AND OPTIONALLY ATTACH THEM TO VARIOUS SYSTEM EVENTS AND WINDOW ACTIONS. THIS BOX DIFFERS FROM THE FIRST TYPE (SHOWN IN FIGURE 7-1) IN THAT IT ALLOWS MORE OPTIONS FOR USER INTERACTION.

Of course, these are just general categories of dialog boxes. There are obviously some dialogs that fit into more than one of these categories, as well as dialogs that don't fit into any of them. The trick in all of this is to figure out what kind of tasks you want the dialog to accomplish.

THE GOOD, THE BAD, AND THE UGLY

Before we get too much farther into dialog box mechanics, and specifics of responses, I want to take a few minutes and talk about the really pathetic state of dialog box design. Take a look at any commercial application (some are worse than others), and you'll find dialog boxes that suffer from one or more of the following fatal flaws:

✦ They're too busy. Busy dialogs are ones that have about a zillion controls in them, none of which are aligned with each other or anything else. They practically scream. "I was too busy coding this to worry about how the dialogs look!" These are seen most often in shareware programs—written by developers with Visual Basic and a large tube of crazy glue.

✦ They're too cute. Someone just discovered the exciting world of Visual Basic custom controls (which are really great if you're writing VB apps, but are an insane nightmare if you're using C, C++, and the SDK), and they are going to share with you all these really fabulous controls that they've found. All at once. In the same dialog.

They have lots of colors. Buttons which go ZING! when you press them. Combo boxes that don't just roll up, they roll up like an old window shade. Chartreuse list boxes. You get the idea.

Basically, the programmers of these misbegotten monstrosities have forgotten something very basic—form should follow function, not dictate it. In other words, your dialog box should be as effective and good looking if you stripped all of the excessive garbage out and used just the built-in Windows controls.

If you do that, and everything works, it's in the right place (I can't define it for you, but you'll know it when you see it. If your users like it, they just wish it were a little fancier, then you can whip out the cool 3-D looking, metal edge, techno-hip controls and give your dialog box a makeover that'll make Dolly Parton drool with envy. But only then.

◆ They're not organized. Disorganized dialog boxes lack a critical piece of information—a control structure that will tell the user how the contents of the dialog are organized. Remember, when you're designing a dialog box, you're not only giving the user the ability to manipulate something, but you are also defining for the user the underlying structure of how the controls (and hence the information they manipulate) fit together.

Was that too big a mouthful for you? (Me, too.) In English, I simply mean this: users will gain an understanding of what your dialog box does and why simply by the way the controls are laid out. Of course, if your controls are laid out badly, the user won't get this information.

Take a look at figure 7-5. This is a screen shot of a product that I wrote that allows users to animate their mouse cursor. One of the features of the program was its ability to play a different animation based on which direction the user was moving the mouse. Users loved hearing about this feature (although in practice it was insanely difficult to use—one animation for all directions worked a lot better). Better still, when they saw the dialog box, they immediately understood which animation went with which mouse motion. They understood this not only because of the little graphic that I had in the center of all the animation spaces, but also because I'd spaced out the animations to match the intuitive way the user thought about moving the mouse. Thus, the space that played the animation when the mouse moved up and left was in the upper left corner of a rectangular grid—the grid being centered around the image of a mouse.

This is harder to describe in words than it is in pictures—you simply look at the dialog box, and you know which animation goes with which mouse direction. Why? Because it looks like it goes with the proper mouse direction.

Now suppose that I hadn't done this—that instead, I'd simply placed the animation slots in a vertical column, along with a little description of the mouse motion that would trigger that animation. Would this dialog be as easy to use and understand? Of course not. Why? Because I've removed the structure of the relationship between the direction of the mouse movement and the corresponding animation image.

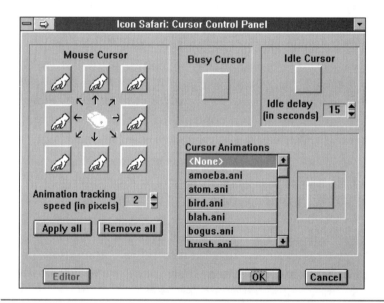

FIGURE 7-5   SCREEN SHOT OF MY CURSOR ANIMATION DIALOG BOX. THE DIRECTION THAT YOU MOVE THE CURSOR IN DETERMINES WHICH ANIMATION SEQUENCE GETS PLAYED BACK. THE DIRECTION OF MOTION CORRESPONDS WITH THE ANIMATION SPACES CLUSTERED AROUND THE MOUSE CURSOR IMAGE. THE USER UNDERSTANDS INTUITIVELY WHICH ANIMATION WILL BE PLAYED IN ANY GIVEN SITUATION.

Of course, this applies to the general case; that's why, it's important to group related pieces of information together (for example, parity settings on a modem: Odd, even, or none). It's also important to not group together things which aren't related—don't create a false relationship where none really exists.

This grouping of related items is extremely important—so important that I'm going to risk boring you by repeating it—things which are related should be visually grouped, and things which are not related should not be. See figure 7-6 for some examples of visual grouping and non-grouping. Remember, you're communicating information about your product when you group things properly. Doing so lets the user understand the causal relationships between objects and actions.

Information which is related is grouped together (ie, when you have one fill style chosen, you can't have the other one chosen). Information that is not related (make default) is not visually associated.

FIGURE 7-6   VISUALLY GROUPING RELATED ITEMS GIVES THE USER IMPORTANT INFORMATION ABOUT HOW YOUR PRODUCT WORKS. DON'T NEGLECT TO DO THIS.

✦ They're just plain ugly. Some dialog boxes (and you know the ones I mean) have all the sex appeal of a traffic accident. They look like they were designed by Quasimodo with a hangover. Their controls are misshapen, they have no particular organization to anything, and they are confusing to boot. In short, they are bad, they know it, and they just don't care.

How can you avoid this awful fate? Simple, take some time, look at how you're laying the dialog box out, and ask yourself if you could do it any better. If you're really hopeless at this kind of stuff, go hire a graphic artist. Or, if you can't afford one, find someone with a good eye for interior decorating. (No, I'm not kidding). Get them to lay out the dialog for you or at least provide you with suggestions.

This might seem like a violation of the "stay away from cute" rule that I talked about above, but it really isn't. Just because form follows function doesn't mean that you should leave form out of the equation entirely.

If all else fails, remember KISS—Keep It Simple, Stupid. If you find that your dialogs are becoming overly complex, maybe it's time to start thinking about breaking the information down into several smaller, more manageable dialogs.

One of the coolest things to come down the pipe in quite a while are tabbed dialogs (see figure 7-7). They allow you the ability to break the information into smaller chunks, yet still show the user how the information is related. If you're having problems with dialog box bloat, you might want to give tabs a try.

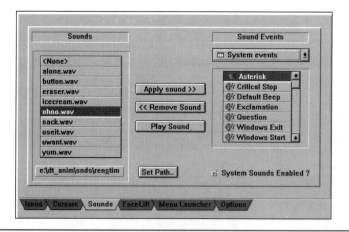

FIGURE 7-7 A TABBED DIALOG. TABBED DIALOGS ARE VERY EXCITING, BECAUSE THEY ALLOW YOU (AS A PROGRAMMER) THE ABILITY TO LAY OUT THE INFORMATION IN THE DIALOG IN A MORE HIERARCHICAL FASHION. THIS REVEALS EVEN MORE OF THE STRUCTURE TO THE USER, AS WELL AS SIMPLIFYING HIS OR HER LIFE. THERE ARE LOTS OF GOOD TAB CONTROLS ON THE MARKET, SO PICK ONE UP AND TRY IT OUT.

NOW WHAT?

Once you've figured out where you're going with your dialog, it's time to design it. This is going to lead you into a couple of different areas. The first of these is how information is going to be presented to the user. This means, primarily, custom controls—such as list boxes, combo boxes, check boxes, and more. There are the standard Windows controls, the list box, combo box, check box, radio button, text edit field, and text button. (We talked about text buttons last chapter, and I'll talk about some of the others in the next chapters).

There are also a dizzying profusion of third-party, add-on custom controls that do such specialized things as provide a tab control, display a histogram, create a chart, and so on. (One of the most popular third-party controls appears to be the spreadsheet control—last time I checked there were at least six different spreadsheet controls, all of which did pretty much the same thing—encapsulate an entire spreadsheet for you).

In any case, you have to figure out what the appropriate control for the job is. This can be a lot harder than it sounds, because it isn't always obvious how to use the controls. In this chapter we'll touch briefly on the issue of custom controls in dialog boxes. The next two chapters will focus on that topic in much more detail.

To begin with, let's look at some general rules of thumb for dialog box. Remember, these are rules of thumb, so each one may or may not be applicable to a given situation.

RULES OF THUMB: THINGS TO DO, THINGS NOT TO DO

A big problem with dialog boxes that you don't see very often (because it's obviously ridiculous) is one in which the program asks the user some very important question, such as "Format your hard disk?" but provides no way out of the dialog box other than pressing "OK."

Don't laugh—I've really seen a product that had this in it. All right, I'll admit it—I *wrote* a product with this in it. The dialog box looked very much like the one in figure 7-8, complete with scary "Writing this file will permanently alter it's contents!" a cheery "OK" button, and nary a "Cancel" button to be found.

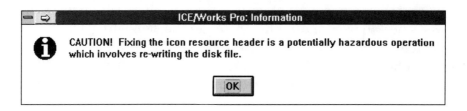

FIGURE 7-8: THE SCARY DIALOG BOX THAT WON'T LET YOU GET AWAY. AFTER WARNING YOU OF THE DIRE CONSEQUENCES AHEAD, THERE'S NO WAY TO CANCEL OUT! WHAT WAS I THINKING THAT DAY, ANYWAY??]

Whenever you present the user with a choice, and particularly when it's a choice with grave ramifications, you should *always* make sure that the user can bail out (generally, via a "Cancel" button). Also please note the following points:

✦ Do not make the choice ambiguous or contrary to what the user is expecting. Most users don't read very closely, and if your dialog box is such that "OK" actually means "Don't do whatever it is you just asked me," you'll be courting disaster. "OK" should always mean that the user is accepting the choice presented in the dialog, and "Cancel" should always mean that the user is declining the choice. Most users have already learned this very clearly: OK = Yes, and Cancel = No. Phrase your dialog box messages accordingly.

✦ Do not make the dialog box overly complex. "Format hard disk? All data will be ERASED!" is infinitely preferable to "It appears that you want to format your hard disk. Please think about this action very carefully, as it involves the potential loss of a great deal of information which is potentially very valuable to you (and possibly to other people as well), so before you say "OK" please think about it."

✦ Buttons with odd or ambiguous words on them should be avoided. "Go ahead" is a better button title than "Proceed with caution." "OK" is better still, and it's clear in the user's mind what's supposed to happen.

✦ If the user presses "Cancel" then nothing should happen. Any changes that were made in the dialog box should be unrolled or undone. There are several ways to go about this. One is to make local copies of variables for manipulation within the dialog box. Only when the user clicks on "OK" will the changes be propagated back to the parent variables. That way, when the user is manipulating values in the dialog box (for example, the number of pixels to track), the change is not occurring in the main program, just in the dialog box's copy of the variable. When the user is finished and clicks "OK", then the program can copy the new value of the dialog box variable back into the parent variable. Another method is to simply set the values of the controls that the user will manipulate, and then read those values out only if the user clicks on "OK."

✦ If the user can make changes in the dialog box that cannot be undone, then there should not be a "Cancel" button in the dialog box. Substitute another word, such as "Done" or "Finished," in order to indicate that the choices made in the dialog box are permanent. Do not use the word "OK," because that has come to mean that the user has a choice about the results of the dialog— and in this case, they don't.

DIALOG BOXES—FROM SIMPLE TO COMPLEX

Let's take a look at the different kinds of dialog boxes that you can create. We'll start out simple, and work into more complex kinds as we go. Along the way, we'll explore just what each kind is good for, and how you can go about using it.

The simplest kind of dialog box you can create is the message box. Surprised? Don't be—the message box can be extremely useful for querying the user about a binary or tertiary set of conditions, and it sure beats going into Resource Workshop and hand-creating the conditions. If your program is a medium-to large-size one, you can have dozens (even hundreds) of these kind of informational queries scattered throughout your program. The last thing you want to have to do is create a dialog for each one, along with a corresponding dialog box procedure and custom code.

THE MESSAGE BOX: CARE AND FEEDING THEREOF

The first thing you're going to want to do if you use a lot of message boxes is create a wrapper for them. Why? Because if you use them a lot, you end up with code that looks a lot like the code below:

```
retValue = MessageBox ( hWnd,
              "Aren't you done yet?",
              "Mom's message box",
              MB_YESNO );

if ( retValue == IDYES )
{
    // Do something
}
else
{
    // Do something else
}
```

and you may be thinking to yourself What's the problem with that? The answer, of course, is nothing at all—if this is the only message box you've got. However, when you've got dozens of message boxes, and dozens (maybe hundreds) of source modules that they exist in, then trying to find this *particular* message box is going to be an exercise in frustration.

I forgot to mention the other reason you shouldn't do this—it isn't very easy to change the text strings for this message box (assuming you can even *find* the darn thing amongst all the others). That's okay, you may be thinking, I don't intend to change the little bugger. You may not be, but what about when it comes time to port the application to another language?

What's that? You don't intend to ever port this thing to another language? Dollars to donuts someone does, even if it's only that guy over in marketing. (Nothing against marketing guys, I've met plenty that I like. Two, as I recall.) Seriously, if you're not loading all of your text resources out of a resource file (and I mean *all* of them), you're hurting yourself in a couple of ways:

✦ Your program can't be easily ported to other languages. (This is more important than you may think—the international market has become an integral part of many company's revenue streams).

✦ It's a lot harder to find text strings that are scattered throughout your code, as opposed to being in a single file. (When you create a string table, all of the strings go in one place—the file that contains the string table.)

✦ Static text strings take up precious space in your DGROUP segment. This alone should convince you to put those strings into a string table. Remember—when you've got a static string in your program (like in our example above), that sucker is just lying around in your DGROUP segment, doing nothing but occupying space—you can't modify the darn thing, 'cause you never know when you'll need it. (Actually, I know programmers who do this—modify static strings in their DGROUP because they need the space. Some people will do anything.) If you have enough of these static strings, you can start making a pretty significant dent in the amount of variable space you have. Now I mean—really—do you need this things lying around in memory, using up your precious variable space? Of course not. Load them from a resource, and then, when you're done, punt them. No muss, no fuss, no space wasted.

Have you gotten the idea that I don't want you using static text strings in your program, regardless of the circumstance? Subtle I ain't.

Anyway, before I got off on that long tangent, I was telling you why you wanted to wrapper your calls to MessageBox. The reason is because of all the stuff you go through to load a string resource (come to think of it, it wasn't such a tangent after all). Here's what the code looks like when you factor all of that stuff in:

```
char    messageBuff [ 256 ];
char    titleBuff [ 256 ];

//————————

LoadString ( hInst,
             ID_MYTITLE,
             (LPSTR) titleBuff,
             255 );

LoadString ( hInst,
             ID_MYMESSAGE,
             (LPSTR) messageBuff,
             255 );

MessageBox ( hWnd,
             messageBuff,
             titleBuff,
             MB_ICONINFORMATION | MB_OK );
```

This is still pretty simple—you get both the title of the message box, and the text string for the message box out of a resource file via the *LoadResource()* call, and then you display the message box. Of course, in this case we're ignoring the return value, because it's always going to be the OK button (that's all we're giving them!).

If we want to make this a little more general purpose, however, we're going to need to pay attention to several additional things: what kind of message box we want to be displaying, what the id's of the text strings are, and what the return value of the message was. Here's the more general purpose version of the routine:

```
//—————————-
//
// AlertBox()
//
//    General purpose wrapper around
// the MessageBox() function, this routine
// hides the fact that we're loading text
// strings out of a resource file in
// order to save DGROUP space (not to
// mention making it more portable).
//
//
    int FAR PASCAL

AlertBox ( HANDLE  hInst,     // Instance handle to
                             // load text strings from
          HWND    hWnd,      // Parent window handle
                             // (can be NULL)
          int     sID,       // ID of text string to
                             // be displayed as the
                             // message
          int     tID,       // ID of text string to
                             // be displayed as the
                             // title of this message
                             // box
          UINT    mbStyle )  // Message box
                             // style flags
{
    char       messageBuff [ 256 ];
    char       titleBuff [ 256 ];

    //—————————

    LoadString ( hInst,
                 sID,
                 messageBuff,
                 255 );

    LoadString ( hInst,
                 tID,
                 titleBuff,
                 255 );

    return MessageBox ( hWnd,
                        messageBuff,
```

```
                           titleBuff,
                           mbStyle );

}
```

What are the changes? First off, we've given our routine, **AlertBox()** the capacity to have different **MessageBox()** flags passed in, and the return code passed back out. This gives us the ability to specify whether we're creating an information box (i.e., "Copy done | OK") versus a query box (i.e., "Do you want to quit now? OK | Cancel"). Just in case you've forgotten what those flags are (or are, like me, far too lazy to look them up every time), here they are:

FLAGS	DESCRIPTION
MB_ABORTRETRYIGNORE	The message box contains three push buttons, Abort, Retry, and Ignore
MB_APPLMODAL	The message box is a parent window modal dialog, meaning that this dialog box locks up the parent window (the user can't go on until /he responds to this message). Depending upon who the parent was, this might lock up the entire application, or only part of it.
MB_DEFBUTTON1	The first button is the default. Note that this is the default (i.e., the first button is by default the default button), unless one of the next two flags is specified.
MB_DEFBUTTON2	The second button is the default.
MB_DEFBUTTON3	The third button is the default

MB_ICONASTERISK	Equivalent to MB_ICONINFORMA-TION
MB_ICONEXCLAMATION	The message box displays the system exclamation point icon
MB_ICONHAND	Same as MB_ICONSTOP
MB_ICONINFORMATION	The message box displays the system information icon (by default, a circle with an "i" in the middle)
MB_ICONQUESTION	The message box displays the system question mark icon
MB_ICONSTOP	The message box displays the system stop sign icon
MB_OK	The message box contains one push-button: OK.
MB_OKCANCEL	The message box contains two push-buttons: OK and Cancel
MB_RETRYCANCEL	The message box contains two push-buttons: Retry and Cancel
MB_SYSTEMMODAL	All applications are suspended until the user responds to the message box. Used for serious errors (like General Protection Faults).
MB_TASKMODAL	Same as MB_APPLMODAL, except that all top-level windows belonging to the current task are disabled if the hWndParent parameter is NULL.
MB_YESNO	The message box contains two push-buttons: Yes and No.
MB_YESNOCANCEL	The message box contains three pushbuttons: Yes, No, and Cancel.

You've got to admit—doing it this way beats the pants off of having static strings in your source code. Now an informational message box might look something like this:

```
[In the header file]

#define ID_ERROR_TITLE      0x1000
#define ID_BAD_ERROR        0x1001

[In the resource file]

STRINGTABLE

    BEGIN
        ID_ERROR_TITLE,        "Major System Error"
        ID_BAD_ERROR,      "Holy Toledo!   The processor's on fire!"
    END

[In your source file]

.
.
.
AlertBox ( hInst,
       hWnd,
       ID_BAD_ERROR,
       ID_ERROR_TITLE,
       MB_OK | MB_ICONHAND );
```

I'll admit—this is more difficult initially than simply slamming a call to **MessageBox()** in your code. You've got three files that you have to hit if you add a new error or information string, instead of only one file. On the other hand, when a change has to be made, it's always being made to the *same* files—your resource file that contains the string table, your include file that defines the string constants, and your source file. Now you don't have to play the game of "Message box, message box, who's got the message box?" if you need to change something. You simply change the text string in the resource file, and it automatically gets changed in your program. You don't even need to know where the message box call is occurring.

Looking at it this way, it's easy to see why I like doing this. I know exactly where every single text string is, and I don't have to go searching all over the place for it. (Believe me, when your projects start pushing 90 or 100 .cpp files, each well over 1000 lines long, doing this is no longer optional—it's *required*!)

MORE COMPLEX DIALOG BOXES

Of course, message boxes are the easiest types of dialog boxes to build—they just require a single line of code. Real dialog boxes, however, are a little more complex. "Real," in this case, means a dialog box that you create either with **CreateDialog()** [for a modeless dialog box] or **DialogBox()** [for a modal dialog].

I'm assuming here, of course, that you already know how to write a basic dialog box, and handler (although a little later on I'll give you a couple of object classes that make this much simpler), so I'm not going to go into a long, detailed explanation of how that's done. Instead, I'm going to show you the more interesting bits of dealing with dialog boxes—how to set up controls, how to monitor them, and how to change a control's state in response to a user action. This is where many dialogs do a less than stellar job. Really, though, it's not hard to do, it just requires a little thought.

Dialog boxes can be quite complex, (as I'll get to in just a minute), but at their heart, they are quite simple—they are simply another form of window. They have their own window procedure that gets called, and they handle messages in much the same way as any other window does. This means, for example, that they have an initialization message the way a window does. For a window, this message is WM_CREATE; for a dialog, the corresponding message is WM_INITDIALOG. WM_INITDIALOG is a very important message, because it's in the initialization stages of the dialog box that you're going to do all your setup for your controls. This is because the WM_INITDIALOG message gets called (and finishes processing) *before* the dialog box gets shown. If you set it up here, then it will be properly shown once this message returns.

DEALING WITH DIALOGS (AND THEIR CONTROLS)

What sort of setup might you want to do in the WM_INITDIALOG section of your dialog box's window procedure? Let's take a look at a couple of examples. Figure 7-9 shows you a dialog box with several sets of controls. There is a group of three radio buttons, two check boxes, and an edit control.

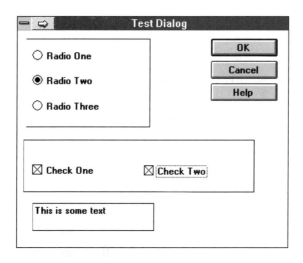

FIGURE 7-9   A SAMPLE DIALOG BOX SHOWING SEVERAL SETS OF CONTROLS. EACH OF THESE CONTROLS NEEDS TO BE INITIALED WITH SOME VALUE. BY USING WM_INITDIALOG, WE CAN ENSURE THAT THE CONTROLS ARE PROPERLY SET

Listings 7-1 through 7-11 give you all the source to our sample dialog box app; take a look at the code, and I'll discuss it with you afterwards.

Listing 7-1   Skeleton.cpp

```
//
// SKELETON.CPP
//
//    The skeleton application...
//
//

#include <skeleton.hpp>

//————————
//
// WinMain()
//

    int PASCAL
WinMain ( HINSTANCE    hInstance,
     HINSTANCEhPrevInstance,
     LPSTR     lpCmdLine,
     int       nCmdShow )
{
    MSG    msg;            // Message holder...

    BOOL    returnCode = TRUE; // Return code...

    //————————-

    hInst = hInstance;    // Save instance handle...

    //
    // Initialize the application as needed
    //

    if ( !SkeletonInitApplication ( hInstance,
                    hPrevInstance,
                    &nCmdShow,
                    lpCmdLine ) )
    {
        returnCode = FALSE;
        goto Leave;
    }

    //
    // Initialize the class, if necessary...
```

continued

Listing 7-1   *continued*

```
//

if ( !hPrevInstance )
{
    if ( !SkeletonRegisterClass ( hInstance ) )
    {
        returnCode = FALSE;
        goto Leave;
    }
}

//
// Create the main window...
//

MainhWnd = SkeletonCreateWindow ( hInstance );

if ( !MainhWnd )
{
    returnCode = FALSE;
    goto Leave;
}

//
// Show the window, so that the message loop gets pumped...
//

ShowWindow ( MainhWnd,
             nCmdShow );

UpdateWindow ( MainhWnd );

//
// Now do our message loop
//

while ( GetMessage ( &msg,
             0,
             0,
             0 ) )
{
    TranslateMessage ( &msg );
    DispatchMessage ( &msg );
}
```

```
Leave:

    SkeletonExitApp();    // Cleanup if necessary

    //
    // Give back the proper return code...
    //

    if ( returnCode == TRUE )
    {
        return ( msg.wParam );
    }
    else
    {
        return FALSE;
    }
}

//————————
//
// MainWindowProc()
//
//     Main window callback procedure
//

    LONG FAR PASCAL

SkeletonMainWindowProc ( HWND hWnd,
                         UINT  message,
                         UINT  wParam,
                         LONG  lParam )
{
    //————————

    switch ( message )
    {

        case WM_DESTROY:

            PostQuitMessage ( 0 );

            return DefWindowProc ( hWnd,
                                   message,
                                   wParam,
```

continued

Listing 7-1 *continued*

```
                                    lParam );
          break;

      case WM_COMMAND:
          {
              ModalDialogHandler     modalBox;

              //———————-
              //
              // Have the modal dialog box
              // handler create the modal
              // dialog box
              //

              modalBox.CreateSelf ( hWnd,
                                    "TestDialog",
                                    (FARPROC)SkeletonDlgProc,
                                    hInst );

              return DefWindowProc ( hWnd,
                                     message,
                                     wParam,
                                     lParam );
          }

          break;


      case WM_CREATE:

          return DefWindowProc ( hWnd,
                                 message,
                                 wParam,
                                 lParam );
          break;

      default:

          return DefWindowProc ( hWnd,
                                 message,
                                 wParam,
                                 lParam );
          break;
```

```
    }

    return FALSE;      // Returns FALSE if processed
}
```

Listing 7-2 Skelinit.cpp

```
//
// SKELINIT.CPP
//
//    Initialization routines for the skeleton
//    application
//
//

#include <skeleton.hpp>


//————————————
//
// SkeletonInitApplication()
//
//    Initialize the application.
//

    BOOL
SkeletonInitApplication ( HINSTANCE  hInst,
                  HINSTANCE hPrev,
                  int            *pCmdSHow,
                   LPSTR    lpCmd )
{
    return TRUE;
}

//————————————-
//
// SkeletonRegisterClass()
//
//    Registers the skeleton class
//

    BOOL
SkeletonRegisterClass ( HINSTANCE    hInstance )
{
```

continued

Listing 7-2 *continued*

```
WNDCLASS WndClass;

//——————————-

hMBrush = CreateSolidBrush(RGB(192,192,192));

WndClass.style          = 0;
WndClass.lpfnWndProc    = SkeletonMainWindowProc;
WndClass.cbClsExtra     = 0;
WndClass.cbWndExtra     = 0;
WndClass.hInstance      = hInstance;
WndClass.hIcon          = LoadIcon ( hInstance,
                          " SKELETON" );

WndClass.hCursor        = LoadCursor ( NULL,
                    IDC_ARROW );
WndClass.hbrBackground = hMBrush;

WndClass.lpszMenuName   = "SKELETON";

WndClass.lpszClassName = "SKELETON";

return RegisterClass(&WndClass);
}

//——————————-
//
// SkeletonCreateWindow()
//
//    Creates the main skeleton window
//

    HWND
SkeletonCreateWindow ( HINSTANCE      hInstance )
{
    HWND    hWnd;

    int     coords[4];

    //——————————

    coords [ 0 ] = CW_USEDEFAULT;
    coords [ 1 ] = 0;
    coords [ 2 ] = CW_USEDEFAULT;
```

```
    coords [ 3 ] = 0;

    hWnd = CreateWindow (
                "SKELETON",
                "Skeleton Application",
                WS_OVERLAPPED | WS_THICKFRAME | WS_SYSMENU |
WS_MINIMIZEBOX | WS_MAXIMIZEBOX,
                coords [ 0 ],
                coords [ 1 ],
                coords [ 2 ],
                coords [ 3 ],
                0,              // Parent handle
                0,              // Child id
                hInstance,      // Instance handle
                (LPSTR)NULL );  // No additional info
    return hWnd;
}


//——————————-
//
// SkeletonExitApp()
//
//   Does any final cleanup...
//

    void
SkeletonExitApp( void )
{
    //——————————-

    if ( hMBrush )
    {
        DeleteObject ( hMBrush );

        hMBrush = 0;
    }
}
```

Listing 7-3   Skelvars.cpp

```
//
// SKELVARS.CPP
//
// Global variables for the skeleton application
```

continued

Listing 7-3   *continued*

```
//
//

#define __SKELETON_GLOBAL_VARS

#include <skeleton.hpp>

//————————————————————-
//
// All the following are standard global
// variables used by the skeleton application
//

HBRUSH      hMBrush;   // Brush for window background

HWND        MainhWnd;  // Main window handle

HINSTANCE   hInst;     // Instance handle that we need


//————————————————-
//
// Add custom variables here
//
```

Listing 7-4   Skeldlg.cpp

```
//
// Skeldlg.cpp
//
//    Skeleton dialog procedure code
//

#include <skeleton.hpp>

//——————————
//
// SkeletonDlgProc()
//
//    Dialog box procedure for the cursor control panel
//
//
```

```
    BOOL FAR PASCAL
SkeletonDlgProc ( HWND hDlg,
                UINT message,
                UINT wParam,
                LONG lParam )
{

    WORD    screenWidth;
    WORD    screenHeight;

    int     i;

    RECT    rectal;

    char    windowText [ 128 ];
    char    soundText [ 128 ];
    char    fullAniName [ 128 ];
    char    iniFile [ 128 ];

    //——————————

    switch ( message )
    {
        case WM_INITDIALOG:

            //
            // This code here allows us to center
            // the dialog in the middle of the
            // screen, regardless of resolution
            //

            screenWidth = GetSystemMetrics ( SM_CXSCREEN );

            screenHeight = GetSystemMetrics ( SM_CYSCREEN );

            GetWindowRect ( hDlg,
                        &rectal );

            screenWidth -= ( rectal.right - rectal.left );

            screenHeight -= ( rectal.bottom - rectal.top );

            screenWidth /= 2;

            screenHeight /= 2;
```

continued

Listing 7-4 *continued*

```
            MoveWindow ( hDlg,
                         screenWidth,
                         screenHeight,
                         rectal.right - rectal.left,
                         rectal.bottom - rectal.top,
                         TRUE );

        //
        // All done with moving the screen,
        // now let's setup our buttons
        //

        return TRUE;   // TRUE means Windows will continue processing

        break;

    case WM_COMMAND:

        switch ( LOWORD ( wParam ) )
        {
            case IDOK: // All done, cleanup and go home...

                EndDialog ( hDlg,
                            IDOK );
                break;

            case IDCANCEL:

                EndDialog ( hDlg,
                            IDCANCEL );
                break;

            default:
                return FALSE;       // Didn't process message
        }

        break;

    default:

        return FALSE; // Didn't process message...
        break;
    }
```

```
    return TRUE;
}
```

Listing 7-5   Skeleton.hpp

```
//
// SKELETON.HPP
//
//    Mondo include file for
// the skeleton app.
//
//   __EVERYTHING__ gets included here, ONCE.
//
// That's it.
//

#ifndef __SKELETON_HPP

#define __SKELETON_HPP

//——————————————-

#include <WINDOWS.H>

#include <gocl.hpp>        // GOCL definitions

#include <skelextn.hpp>    // Externs for the global variables

#include <skelprot.hpp>    // Prototypes for all functions in skeleton

#include <skelincs.hpp>


//——————————————-


#endif // __SKELETON_HPP
```

Listing 7-6 : Skelextn.hpp

```
//
// SKELEXTN.HPP
//
```

continued

Listing 7-6 *continued*

```
//     External define file for the skeleton app
//
//

#ifndef __SKELETON_GLOBAL_VARS

#define __SKELETON_GLOBAL_VARS

//————————————


extern  HBRUSH      hMBrush;   // Brush for window background

extern  HWND        MainhWnd;  // Main window handle

extern  HINSTANCE   hInst;     // Instance handle that we need


//————————————————-


//————————————

#endif // __SKELETON_GLOBAL_VARS
```

Listing 7-7 Skelprot.hpp

```
//
// SKELPROT.HPP
//
//     Prototype file
//

#ifndef __SKELETON_PROTOTYPES_HPP

#define __SKELETON_PROTOTYPES_HPP

//————————————-

//————————--
//
// Extern C wrappers
//
```

```
#ifdef __cplusplus

extern "C" {

#endif

//——————————————-

    int PASCAL
WinMain ( HINSTANCE    hInstance,
     HINSTANCEhPrevInstance,
     LPSTR     lpCmdLine,
     int       nCmdShow );

    LONG FAR PASCAL
SkeletonMainWindowProc ( HWND hWnd,
          UINT   message,
          UINT   wParam,
          LONG   lParam );
    BOOL
SkeletonInitApplication ( HINSTANCE   hInst,
          HINSTANCEhPrev,
          int       *pCmdSHow,
          LPSTR     lpCmd );
    BOOL
SkeletonRegisterClass ( HINSTANCE    hInstance );

    HWND
SkeletonCreateWindow ( HINSTANCE     hInstance );

    void
SkeletonExitApp( void );

    BOOL FAR PASCAL
SkeletonDlgProc ( HWNDhDlg,
             UINT message,
             UINT wParam,
             LONG lParam );


//——————————————-

//——————————-
//
```

continued

Listing 7-7   *continued*

```
// Extern C wrappers
//

#ifdef __cplusplus

};

#endif


//————————————-

#endif // __SKELETON_PROTOTYPES__HPP
```

Listing 7-8 : Skelincs.hpp

```
//
// SKELINCS.HPP
//
//    Skeleton includes.
//
//    Packaged this way so that both the
//    .cpp files and the .rc files can
//    use them.
//

#ifndef __SKELINCS_HPP

#define __SKELINCS_HPP

//————————————

#include <WINDOWS.H>

#include <skeldfns.hpp>        // Resource and other ID defines


//————————————

#endif // __SKELINCS_HPP
```

Listing 7-9   Skeldfns.hpp

```
//
// SKELDFNS.HPP
//
//   Defines used by the skeleton application
//

#ifndef __SKELDFNS_HPP

#define __SKELDFNS_HPP

//————————————-

#define     SKELETON_BASE_ID   4000

#define     DIALOG_1    1
#define     IDC_EDIT1   106
#define     ID_Check2   104
#define     ID_Check1   105
#define     ID_Radio3   103
#define     ID_Radio2   102
#define     ID_Radio1   101


//———————

#define     ID_SkeletonExit          SKELETON_BASE_ID + 0


//————————————-

#endif // __SKELDFNS_HPP
```

Listing 7-10   Skeleton.rc

```
//
// Skeleton.rc
//

#include <skelincs.hpp>

#include <cppres.rc>
```

continued

Listing 7-10 *continued*

```
#include <skeleton.dlg>

//——————————-
//
// Bitmaps, icons, cursors
//

SKELETON    ICON        SKELETON.ICO


//——————————-
//
// Menus
//

SKELETON MENU
{
 POPUP "Skeleton"
  {
   MENUITEM "Dialog Box", ID_SkeletonExit
  }

}
```

Listing 7-11 Skeleton.dlg

```
//
// Skeleton.dlg
//
//  File which holds the
// dialog definition for
// our standard dialog box.
//

TestDialog DIALOG 6, 15, 207, 179
STYLE DS_MODALFRAME | WS_POPUP | WS_VISIBLE | WS_CAPTION | WS_SYSMENU
CAPTION "Test Dialog"
FONT 8, "MS Sans Serif"
{
 CONTROL "Radio One", ID_Radio1, "BUTTON", BS_AUTORADIOBUTTON, 12, 12,
84, 15
 CONTROL "Radio Two", ID_Radio2, "BUTTON", BS_AUTORADIOBUTTON, 12, 32,
70, 15
```

```
CONTROL "Radio Three", ID_Radio3, "BUTTON", BS_AUTORADIOBUTTON, 12, 52,
74, 15
CONTROL "", -1, "static", SS_BLACKFRAME | WS_CHILD | WS_VISIBLE |
WS_GROUP, 7, 6, 95, 71
CHECKBOX "Check Two", ID_Check2, 97, 103, 77, 17, BS_AUTOCHECKBOX |
WS_TABSTOP
CHECKBOX "Check One", ID_Check1, 12, 102, 83, 17, BS_AUTOCHECKBOX |
WS_TABSTOP
CONTROL "", -1, "static", SS_BLACKFRAME | WS_CHILD | WS_VISIBLE |
WS_GROUP, 5, 87, 176, 42
DEFPUSHBUTTON "OK", IDOK, 148, 6, 50, 14
PUSHBUTTON "Cancel", IDCANCEL, 148, 24, 50, 14
PUSHBUTTON "Help", IDHELP, 148, 42, 50, 14
EDITTEXT IDC_EDIT1, 12, 137, 93, 22
}
```

All of these source files, plus all the other files that you need to make this project are on the accompanying disk—I built this application using Borland C++ v. 4.0, but it should compile just as well under Microsoft Visual C++.

One of the most interesting chunks of code here is in the main window procedure, under the WM_COMMAND message handler:

```
case WM_COMMAND:
    {
        ModalDialogHandler modalBox;

        //——————————-

        //
        // Have the modal dialog box
        // handler create the modal
        // dialog box
        //

        modalBox.CreateSelf ( hWnd,
                    "TestDialog",
                    (FARPROC)SkeletonDlgProc,
                    hInst );

        return DefWindowProc ( hWnd,
                    message,
                    wParam,
                    lParam );
```

```
     }

   break;
```

What's a **ModalDialogHandler(),** and where can I get one? To answer the second question first, you'll find this object class (and a bunch of others) in the subdirectory marked GOCL, which is short for Graphics Object Class Library. It's a very useful collection of classes that I've built over the past several years in order to make my own programming life much simpler under Windows.

To answer the first question, a **ModalDialogHandler()** is just what it sounds like—it encapsulates all the startup code needed to create a modal dialog box. Simply pass it the parent window handle, dialog name, dialog box procedure, and instance handle of the application that contains the dialog box, and it handles the rest. You'll find that this greatly simplifies the task of creating a dialog box, without having to resort to a huge class library in order to instantiate one.

The next bit of interesting stuff is in the dialog box handler code itself. If you take a look at the WM_INITDIALOG message, you'll see that I'm using that message to center the dialog box. This is the perfect place to do it, since the dialog box hasn't yet been shown. This centering code allows us to center the dialog in the middle of the screen, regardless of what shape the dialog is, or what resolution the user is currently running in.

```
//
// This code here allows us to center
// the dialog in the middle of the
// screen, regardless of resolution
//

screenWidth = GetSystemMetrics ( SM_CXSCREEN );

screenHeight = GetSystemMetrics ( SM_CYSCREEN );

GetWindowRect ( hDlg,
          &rectal );

screenWidth -= ( rectal.right - rectal.left );
```

```
screenHeight -= ( rectal.bottom - rectal.top );

screenWidth /= 2;

screenHeight /= 2;

MoveWindow ( hDlg,
        screenWidth,
        screenHeight,
        rectal.right - rectal.left,
        rectal.bottom - rectal.top,
        TRUE );
```

Handling the controls

Each of the controls in our dialog needs to be initialized with some reasonable value. In a real-world application, which radio button (for example) was selected would probably depend on something that the user had done earlier (for example, selected one of three different sizes of object). We'll need to make sure that the earlier selection is reflected via the proper radio button being pressed.

As it stands in the initial version, none of the controls remembers it's state from one session to another (go in and out of the dialog a few times, and you'll see what I mean). In order to rectify this, we'll have to learn how to handle each of the controls in the button—more importantly, we'll learn *why* we would want to do so.

Handling the radio buttons

If you edit the resource file for this dialog box with Resource Workshop, one thing you'll notice is that the three radio buttons are a group. They are also *auto* radio buttons—which means that when one is turned on, the other two are turned off. This is an incredible help, because otherwise you have to do that nonsense by hand, like so:

```
case WM_COMMAND:

    switch ( wParam )
```

```
{
    case ID_Radio1:
    case ID_Radio2:
    case ID_Radio3:

        //
        // First, we have to turn all
        // three radio buttons OFF...
        //

        CheckDlgButton ( hDlg,
                    ID_Radio1,
                    FALSE );

        CheckDlgButton ( hDlg,
                    ID_Radio2,
                    FALSE );

        CheckDlgButton ( hDlg,
                    ID_Radio3,
                    FALSE );

        //
        // Ok, now we have to turn
        // back on the one that
        // got checked.
        //

        CheckDlgButton ( hDlg,
                    wParam,
                    TRUE );

        //
        // ...and all of that was just
        // to figure out which button
        // to turn on. The real work
        // to handle what the button
        // actually does has to go
        // here.
    }

    break;
```

As you can see, we have to monitor the WM_COMMAND message for the ID's of our three buttons—and once we get a message to one of them, we have to turn all of them off, and then turn the one on that we got the message for.

Really, is this necessary? Of course not—simply make your set of radio buttons a group, and set the auto radio button property of each button control, and the buttons will handle all of this nonsense for themselves.

A couple of things you must make sure of:

✦ Only the radio buttons that you want grouped should be in the same group, and no others. This means that if you have two sets of radio buttons, you'll need two sets of groups. If you don't do this, then when you click one radio button, all the others will go out—in both sets! The best way to ensure that your radio buttons are in a group all by themselves is to make sure the control before the radio buttons has the group style set, and the control after the radio buttons has the group style set. None of the radio buttons themselves should have the group style set.

✦ All of the radio buttons must have the BS_AUTORADIOBUT-TON style set in order for this to work. If any button is missing, then it won't work with the others.

I'll talk more about what you actually do in response to a radio button next chapter (which covers radio buttons and check boxes (which are really another kind of button). Right now, the important thing for us to deal with is how the radio buttons get set up. As you can probably guess, we need to first turn all the buttons off, and then turn the right one on. The code for that is in the new version of our skeleton dialog window proc, which I'll now show you:

Listing 7-12 Skeldlg.cpp (the new version)

```
//
// Skeldlg.cpp
//
```

continued

Listing 7-12 *continued*

```
//    Skeleton dialog procedure code
//

#include <skeleton.hpp>

//————————
//
// SkeletonDlgProc()
//
//    Dialog box procedure for the cursor control panel
//
//

    BOOL FAR PASCAL
SkeletonDlgProc ( HWND hDlg,
                  UINT message,
                  UINT wParam,
                  LONG lParam )
{

    WORD    screenWidth;
    WORD    screenHeight;

    int    i;

    RECT    rectal;

    //————————————

    switch ( message )
    {
        case WM_INITDIALOG:

            //
            // Set up the radio buttons and
            // czech boxes
            //

            CheckRadioButtons ( hDlg );

            CheckCheckBoxes ( hDlg );

            //
            // This code here allows us to center
```

```
// the dialog in the middle of the
// screen, regardless of resolution
//

screenWidth = GetSystemMetrics ( SM_CXSCREEN );

screenHeight = GetSystemMetrics ( SM_CYSCREEN );

GetWindowRect ( hDlg,
                &rectal );

screenWidth -= ( rectal.right - rectal.left );

screenHeight -= ( rectal.bottom - rectal.top );

screenWidth /= 2;

screenHeight /= 2;

MoveWindow ( hDlg,
             screenWidth,
             screenHeight,
             rectal.right - rectal.left,
             rectal.bottom - rectal.top,
             TRUE );

//
// Disable the OK button,
// until the user types something...
//

EnableWindow ( GetDlgItem ( hDlg,
                                   IDOK ),
               FALSE );

//
// All done with moving the screen,
// now let's setup our buttons
//

return TRUE;   // TRUE means Windows will continue processing

break;

case WM_COMMAND:
```

continued

Listing 7-12 *continued*

```
switch ( LOWORD ( wParam ) )
{
    case IDC_EDIT1:
        {
            int     textLen;
            char    editText [ 128 ];

            //————————

            //
            // The user has to have at least
            // one character in the edit box
            // in order to be able to exit
            // the dialog box via OK.
            //

            textLen = GetDlgItemText ( hDlg,
                                       IDC_EDIT1,
                                       editText,
                                       127 );
            if ( textLen != 0 )
            {
                EnableWindow ( GetDlgItem ( hDlg, IDOK ),
                                            TRUE );
            }
            else
            {
                EnableWindow ( GetDlgItem ( hDlg,IDOK ),
                                            FALSE );
            }
        }

        break;

    case IDOK: // All done, cleanup and go home...

        //
        // Since we're leaving on the OK
        // button, the new states of our
        // radio and check boxes has to
        // be determined.
        //
```

```
                    DetermineRadioButtonState ( hDlg );

                    DetermineCheckBoxState ( hDlg );

                    //
                    // Ok, all done, punt...
                    //

                    EndDialog ( hDlg,
                                IDOK );
                    break;

                case IDCANCEL:

                    EndDialog ( hDlg,
                                IDCANCEL );
                    break;

                default:
                    return FALSE;       // Didn't process message
            }

            break;

        default:

            return FALSE; // Didn't process message...
            break;
    }

    return TRUE;
}

//————————
//
// CheckRadioButtons()
//
//   This routine sets up our
// radio buttons properly
//

    void WINAPI
CheckRadioButtons ( HWND  hDlg )
{
    //
```

continued

Listing 7-12 *continued*

```
// First, let's set up our three radio buttons
//

CheckDlgButton ( hDlg,
                 ID_Radio1,
                 FALSE );

CheckDlgButton ( hDlg,
                 ID_Radio2,
                 FALSE );

CheckDlgButton ( hDlg,
                 ID_Radio3,
                 FALSE );
//
// Now we have to turn on
// the right one (which is
// based on the flag value
// rbSetting).
//

switch ( rbSetting )
{

    case 0:

        CheckDlgButton ( hDlg,
                         ID_Radio1,
                         TRUE );
        break;

    case 1:

        CheckDlgButton ( hDlg,
                         ID_Radio2,
                         TRUE );
        break;

    case 2:

        CheckDlgButton ( hDlg,
                         ID_Radio3,
                         TRUE );
        break;
```

```
        default:

            //
            // Put in protection to
            // prevent runaway train
            // errors...
            //

            rbSetting = 0;

            CheckDlgButton ( hDlg,
                             ID_Radio1,
                             TRUE );
            break;
    }

}

//——————————
//
// CheckCheckBoxes()
//
//

    void WINAPI
CheckCheckBoxes ( HWND hDlg )
{

    //
    // Now check each of the
    // check box settings,
    // and check (or not check)
    // each of the boxes accordingly
    //

    //
    // Czech box #1...
    //

    if ( cbSetting & CB_ONE )
    {
        CheckDlgButton ( hDlg,
                         ID_Check1,
                         TRUE );
```

continued

229

Listing 7-12 *continued*

```
    }
    else
    {
        CheckDlgButton ( hDlg,
                         ID_Check1,
                         FALSE );
    }

    //
    // Czech box #2...
    //

    if ( cbSetting & CB_TWO )
    {
        CheckDlgButton ( hDlg,
                         ID_Check2,
                         TRUE );
    }
    else
    {
        CheckDlgButton ( hDlg,
                         ID_Check2,
                         FALSE );
    }
}

//————————
//
// DetermineRadioButtonState()
//
//   This routine determines the
// current radio button state,
// and sets the rbSetting flag
// based on it.
//

    void WINAPI
DetermineRadioButtonState ( HWND      hDlg )
{
    int     check1;
    int     check2;
    int     check3;

    //—————————-
```

```
//
// Get the status of each of
// our three buttons
//

check1 = SendDlgItemMessage ( hDlg,
                              ID_Radio1,
                              BM_GETCHECK,
                              0,
                              0 );

check2 = SendDlgItemMessage ( hDlg,
                              ID_Radio2,
                              BM_GETCHECK,
                              0,
                              0 );

check3 = SendDlgItemMessage ( hDlg,
                              ID_Radio3,
                              BM_GETCHECK,
                              0,
                              0 );

//
// Now, let's figure out which
// one is checked, and set
// rbSetting accordingly.
//

if ( check1 )
{
    rbSetting = 0;
}
else if ( check2 )
{
    rbSetting = 1;
}
else
{
    rbSetting = 2;
}
}


//————————————
```

continued

Listing 7-12 *continued*

```
//
// DetermineCheckBoxState()
//
//   This routine determines the
// current check box states, and
// sets the cbSetting flag based
// on the results.
//

    void WINAPI
DetermineCheckBoxState ( HWND         hDlg )
{
    int    check1;
    int    check2;

    //———————--

    //
    // Set the settings flag to
    // neither check box checked
    //

    cbSetting = 0;

    //
    // Get the status of each of
    // the two check boxes.
    //

    check1 = SendDlgItemMessage ( hDlg,
                                  ID_Check1,
                                  BM_GETCHECK,
                                  0,
                                  0 );

    check2 = SendDlgItemMessage ( hDlg,
                                  ID_Check2,
                                  BM_GETCHECK,
                                  0,
                                  0 );

    //
    // Now check each
    // box, and set the value
```

```
// accordingly.
//

if ( check1 )
{
    cbSetting |= CB_ONE;
}

if ( check2 )
{
    cbSetting |= CB_TWO;
}

}
```

The important routine here is *CheckRadioButtons()*, which simply turns all three buttons off, and then, based on the value of the flag *rbSetting*, turns one of the three buttons on.

Handling the Czech boxes

(And isn't that an awful pun?) Similar to the function *CheckRadioButtons()* is *CheckCheckBoxes()*, which checks to see if either (or both) check boxes should be checked, and if so, checks them. The function we use in this case is also *CheckDlgButton()*, because it works not only on radio buttons and auto radio buttons, but on check boxes (and auto check boxes) as well.

The interesting thing about both the radio buttons and check boxes is how we preserve the state of the buttons once the user has exited the dialog. Just before the user leaves, we check the current state of each of the controls, and save that state. This is done in the two routines *DetermineRadioButtonState()* and *DetermineCheckBoxState()*. Each of these routines sends a BM_GETCHECK message to each of the corresponding controls (the BM_GETCHECK message also works for both radio buttons and check boxes). This message returns to us the current state of the button—if checked, the return is 1, and if unchecked, the return is 0.

The reason we send a message to each of the controls to find out their check status, instead of using a Windows function to do the same thing, is simple—there *isn't* a Windows function to determine the current button state. So,if you're browsing through the SDK, trying to find *GetDlgButtonState()*, you won't find it—it isn't there. Interestingly, we could also use the *SendMessage()* function to *set* the button's state—all we need to do is use the BM_SETCHECK message.

Keeping the user around

The final bit of interesting new technology in our updated version of the dialog box handler is the bit that prevents the user from leaving via the OK button unless there's at least one text character in the edit box.

When you first fire up the new version of the dialog box, you'll notice that the OK button is greyed out—that is, it's disabled. The user cannot leave by pressing the OK button until at least one character has been typed in the edit box. As soon as the user types a character, the OK button becomes selectable.

This is a really neat feature, and it's applicable to not just edit fields, but any field where the user must fill in (or respond to) required information. They haven't filled out all the pieces? They can't leave—at least not via OK, which would mean "I'm done, go ahead and perform this action." The user can always exit via Cancel, which merely means "Do nothing."

How do we achieve this enabling and disabling of the OK button? Easy as pie. In the WM_INITDIALOG message, have the following:

```
//
// Disable the OK button,
// until the user types something...
//

EnableWindow ( GetDlgItem ( hDlg,
                    IDOK ),
        FALSE );
```

This disables the OK button right from the start. Now, to enable the button, we need to check the edit box. Here's how we do that:

```
case WM_COMMAND:

    switch ( LOWORD ( wParam ) )
    {
        case IDC_EDIT1:
            {
                int     textLen;
                char    editText [ 128 ];

                //————————

                //
                // The user has to have at least
                // one character in the edit box
                // in order to be able to exit
                // the dialog box via OK.
                //

                textLen = GetDlgItemText ( hDlg,
                                           IDC_EDIT1,
                                           editText,
                                           127 );
                if ( textLen != 0 )
                {
                    EnableWindow ( GetDlgItem ( hDlg,
                                                IDOK ),
                                                TRUE );
                }
                else
                {
                    EnableWindow ( GetDlgItem ( hDlg,
                                                IDOK ),
                                                FALSE );
                }
```

All we do is each time we get a command message for the edit control, we check to see how long the text string in the edit control is. If it's non-zero, we enable the OK button, and if it's zero we disable the OK button.

Of course, in a real application, you might also check for acceptable words, or other things.

SUMMARY

In this chapter I've talked about a number of important things that you need to do when designing dialog boxes. These things will make your dialog boxes easier for customers of your software to use. In addition, you can guide the user in how your software works, as well as what choices to make, by laying out your dialog boxes in a sensible fashion.

Once inside a dialog box, the user is going to encounter lots of controls. Although we've discussed controls a little bit in this chapter (it's inevitable, of course—a dialog box without controls would be pretty useless), it's time to examine them in more detail. The next chapter takes a look at two important dialog controls—check boxes and radio buttons.

CHAPTER 8

RADIO BUTTONS AND CHECK BOXES

BUTTONS AND BOXES: AN INTRODUCTION

Last chapter we looked at dialog boxes, and some of the basics of using dialog boxes. One of the things we covered a little bit was the use of radio buttons and check boxes in dialogs. I promised then that we'd give the subject a closer look—that's what this chapter is about.

The first thing to understand about radio buttons and check boxes is that they are, in many ways, exactly the same thing. They can both be checked, unchecked, or greyed; and the user selects them in the same way—by clicking on them.

The difference between a radio button and a check box is this: A check box represents a single selection of something which may or may not be selected, while a set of radio buttons represents a choice between several options, one of which *must* be selected.

I see a few puzzled looks out there, so I'll put it another way: A check box gives the user the ability to turn on or off some feature, and see that selection visually represented. Take a look at figure 8-1, which shows a dialog with a single check box that has the caption: Always use selected color when drawing? If the box is checked, then the question is answered in the affirmative (yes, always use the selected color), otherwise it's answered in the negative (no, don't always use the selected color).

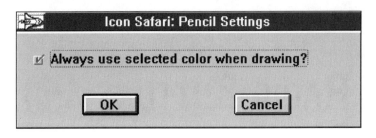

FIGURE 8-1   A SCREEN SHOT OF A DIALOG BOX WITH A SINGLE CHECK BOX IN IT.
THE CHECK BOX CAN EITHER BE ON OR OFF.

Check buttons, then, can be seen as toggles. They are either on or off, and correspondingly they turn on or off some functionality in your product.

Radio buttons, on the other hand, provide the user a set of mutually incompatible choices, one of which is always on. This is in contrast to a check box, where the behavior can be either on or off. Take a look at figure 8-2, which shows a dialog box with five radio buttons—one of which is on at any given time.

Another thing to notice is that we could simulate the behavior of one check box with two radio buttons: Have one radio button for the "unselected" state of the check box, and one radio button for the "selected" state.

Of course, most times this is a silly thing to do—if you've got a condition that can be expressed this way, you might as well use a check box, not two radio buttons. In some instances, however, it won't be possible for the user to infer the inverse of a check box function. Take a look back at figure 7-6, which shows the control panel for the fill tool from ICE/Works. As you can see, it's got a pair of radio buttons which determine which fill mode gets used—either flood fill, or replace fill. I could have used a single check box, like this:

[ ] Replace fill

but then it wouldn't have been clear what would happen if the "Replace fill" box weren't checked. This is because a flood fill isn't the opposite of a replace fill. They are two different fill modes, but they don't bear any relationship to each other—other than the fact that when one is selected, the other one can't be.

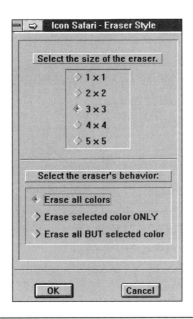

FIGURE 8-2   A SCREEN SHOT FROM THE ERASER TOOL OF ICE/WORKS. NOTICE THAT ALTHOUGH THE USER CAN SELECT FROM ANY OF 5 SIZES OF ERASER, THERE WILL ALWAYS BE ONE (AND ONLY ONE) SIZE IN USE AT ANY GIVEN TIME.

Here's a quick rundown of how you use these controls:

✦ Use a check box when you have a single piece of information that has two states which are easily inferred: "Allow fast save?" for example, is a good candidate for a check box, because we can easily figure out what both states of the button mean—check means "Yes, allow fast saves," and unchecked means "No, don't allow fast saves."

✦ Use a pair of radio buttons when you have a single piece of information that has two states which are *not* easily inferred: "Quicksort" and "Shellsort" would be a good candidate for this, because a quicksort is not the opposite of a shellsort—they are merely both sorts, only one of which can be used for any given sorting operation

✦ Use a set of radio buttons when you have a single piece of information that can attain many (up to 10) states, one of which must always be in force at any given time.

What to do with check boxes and radio buttons is important, but just as important (maybe more important) is what *not* to do with them. Here's a list of things you shouldn't do:

✦ Don't use a check box where you need to use a text (or graphic) button. What does this mean? It's the difference between a state change and a transition change. In other words, a check box (or radio button) implies that the program has entered a new *state* that is now permanent until changed—thus, the user may have turned "Fast saves" on (or off). A text (or graphic) button, on the other hand, implies an immediate *action* that takes place—for example, resetting all the selections to "Default." A check box labeled "Default" would make no sense, because the user wouldn't be in the 'default' state, they would merely want to restore the original set of conditions.

✦ Don't group disparate check box items together if they aren't related. This means that if you have several check boxes in a dialog, they should be grouped together *only* if they relate to each other—otherwise they should be separated (this goes back to our earlier rule that you shouldn't imply a connection between items where none exists).

✦ If you have 20 or 30 items, only one of which can be selected at one time, *please* don't use radio buttons! Use something else, such as a list box or combo box (which I'll discuss in more detail in the next chapter).

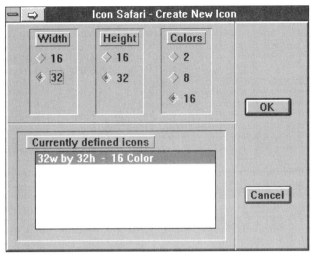

Some check boxes in action...

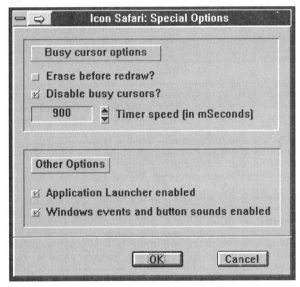

...and some check boxes

FIGURE 8-3   A SCREEN SHOT OF A DIALOG BOX WITH SEVERAL SETS OF CONTROLS SHOWING YOU HOW TO USE THE DIFFERENT FLAVORS OF CHECK BOX AND RADIO BUTTON.

See figure 8-4 through 8-6 for some screen shots of really inappropriate uses of check boxes and radio buttons.

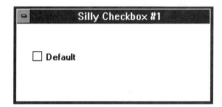

FIGURE 8-4   DON'T DO THIS...

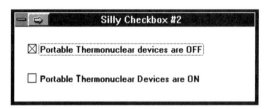

C'mon all you need is a radio button...

FIGURE 8-5   ...OR THIS...

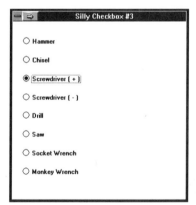

Gosh, wouldn't be simpler to use a listbox?

FIGURE 8-6   ...OR THIS EITHER. REALLY, CAN YOU IMAGINE USING A PRODUCT
THAT HAD ANY OF THESE FLAWS?

Using Radio buttons in your program

Now that we've got a good understanding of how to use (and how not to use) radio buttons in our program, let's build a small application that allows us to see how we manipulate radio buttons. Let's go over each of the listings a little bit, then we'll get into the whys and wherefors of how the thing actually works.

Listings 8-1 through 8-11 contain the source code for a simple application that shows you how to respond to radio buttons in the dialog box.

Listing 8-1, skeleton.cpp is our standard skeleton window application that I've discussed before. Skeleton.cpp (along with several other files) gives us the basic framework for a Windows application that we can get up and running very quickly.

Listing 8-1   Skeleton.cpp

```
//
// SKELETON.CPP
//
//    The skeleton application...
//
//
#include <skeleton.hpp>

//————————
//
// WinMain()
//

    int PASCAL
WinMain ( HINSTANCE    hInstance,
    HINSTANCE        hPrevInstance,
    LPSTR            lpCmdLine,
    int              nCmdShow )
{
    MSG    msg;            // Message holder...

    BOOL   returnCode = TRUE; // Return code...
```

continued

Listing 8-1 *continued*

```
//————————-

hInst = hInstance;    // Save instance handle...

//
// Initialize the application as needed
//

if ( !SkeletonInitApplication ( hInstance,
                    hPrevInstance,
                    &nCmdShow,
                    lpCmdLine ) )
{
    returnCode = FALSE;
    goto Leave;
}

//
// Initialize the class, if necessary...
//

if ( !hPrevInstance )
{
    if ( !SkeletonRegisterClass ( hInstance ) )
    {
        returnCode = FALSE;
        goto Leave;
    }
}

//
// Create the main window...
//

MainhWnd = SkeletonCreateWindow ( hInstance );

if ( !MainhWnd )
{
    returnCode = FALSE;
    goto Leave;
}

//
// Show the window, so that the message loop gets pumped...
```

```
    //

    ShowWindow ( MainhWnd,
               nCmdShow );

    UpdateWindow ( MainhWnd );

    //
    // Now do our message loop
    //

    while ( GetMessage ( &msg,
               0,
               0,
               0 ) )
    {
        TranslateMessage ( &msg );
        DispatchMessage ( &msg );
    }

Leave:

    SkeletonExitApp();     // Cleanup if necessary

    //
    // Give back the proper return code...
    //

    if ( returnCode == TRUE )
    {
        return ( msg.wParam );
    }
    else
    {
        return FALSE;
    }
}

//————————
//
// MainWindowProc()
//
//     Main window callback procedure
//
```

continued

Listing 8-1 *continued*

```
        LONG FAR PASCAL

SkeletonMainWindowProc ( HWND hWnd,
                         UINT  message,
                         UINT  wParam,
                         LONG  lParam )
{
    //————————

    switch ( message )
    {

        case WM_DESTROY:

            PostQuitMessage ( 0 );

            return DefWindowProc ( hWnd,
                                   message,
                                   wParam,
                                   lParam );
            break;

        case WM_COMMAND:
            {
                ModalDialogHandler     modalBox;

                //——————————--

                //
                // Have the modal dialog box
                // handler create the modal
                // dialog box
                //

                modalBox.CreateSelf ( hWnd,
                                      "TestDialog",
                                      FARPROC)SkeletonDlgProc,
                                      hInst );

                return DefWindowProc ( hWnd,
                                       message,
                                       wParam,
                                       lParam );
            }
```

```
        break;


    case WM_CREATE:

        return DefWindowProc ( hWnd,
                               message,
                               wParam,
                               lParam );
        break;

    default:

        return DefWindowProc ( hWnd,
                               message,
                               wParam,
                               lParam );
        break;
    }

    return FALSE;     // Returns FALSE if processed
}
```

Listing 8-2, Skelinit.cpp, contains the routines which let us initialize the skeleton application. Most of this stuff is very straightforward Windows code, and doesn't need to be covered in depth here. The important pieces are the initialization of the four ResBitmap instances, newMoon, quarterMoon, halfMoon, and fullMoon, with their respective bitmaps. These bitmaps are going to be used later in the dialog box in connection with our radio buttons.

Listing 8-2   Skelinit.cpp

```
//
// SKELINIT.CPP
//
//    Initialization routines for the skeleton
// application
//
//
```

continued

Listing 8-2 *continued*

```
#include <skeleton.hpp>


//————————
//
// SkeletonInitApplication()
//
//     Initialize the application.
//

    BOOL
SkeletonInitApplication ( HINSTANCE  hInst,
                    HINSTANCE hPrev,
                    int       *pCmdSHow,
                    LPSTR      lpCmd )
{

    //
    // Load the four moon bitmaps that
    // we'll be displaying in the dialog
    // box.
    //

    newMoon.LoadSelf ( hInst,
                    "NEWMOON" );

    quarterMoon.LoadSelf ( hInst,
                        "QURTMOON" );

    halfMoon.LoadSelf ( hInst,
                    "HALFMOON" );

    fullMoon.LoadSelf ( hInst,
                    "FULLMOON" );

    //
    // Setup the values for the dialog box...
    //

    rbSetting = 0;

    return TRUE;
}
```

```
//—————————-
//
// SkeletonRegisterClass()
//
//    Registers the skeleton class
//

    BOOL
SkeletonRegisterClass ( HINSTANCE    hInstance )
{
    WNDCLASS WndClass;

    //—————————-

    hMBrush = CreateSolidBrush(RGB(192,192,192));

    WndClass.style          = 0;
    WndClass.lpfnWndProc    = SkeletonMainWindowProc;
    WndClass.cbClsExtra     = 0;
    WndClass.cbWndExtra     = 0;
    WndClass.hInstance      = hInstance;
    WndClass.hIcon          = LoadIcon ( hInstance,
                                "SKELETON" );

    WndClass.hCursor        = LoadCursor ( NULL,
                                    IDC_ARROW );
    WndClass.hbrBackground = hMBrush;

    WndClass.lpszMenuName  = "SKELETON";

    WndClass.lpszClassName = "SKELETON";

    return RegisterClass(&WndClass);
}

//—————————-
//
// SkeletonCreateWindow()
//
//    Creates the main skeleton window
//

    HWND
SkeletonCreateWindow ( HINSTANCE    hInstance )
```

continued

Listing 8-2 *continued*

```
{
    HWND    hWnd;

    int     coords[4];

    //————————

    coords [ 0 ] = CW_USEDEFAULT;
    coords [ 1 ] = 0;
    coords [ 2 ] = CW_USEDEFAULT;
    coords [ 3 ] = 0;

    hWnd = CreateWindow (
                "SKELETON",
                "Skeleton Application",
                WS_OVERLAPPED | WS_THICKFRAME | WS_SYSMENU | WS_MINI-
MIZEBOX | WS_MAXIMIZEBOX,
            coords [ 0 ],
            coords [ 1 ],
            coords [ 2 ],
            coords [ 3 ],
            0,               // Parent handle
            0,               // Child id
            hInstance,       // Instance handle
            (LPSTR)NULL );   // No additional info
    return hWnd;
}

//————————-
//
// SkeletonExitApp()
//
//   Does any final cleanup...
//

    void
SkeletonExitApp( void )
{
    //————————-

    if ( hMBrush )
    {
        DeleteObject ( hMBrush );
```

```
        hMBrush = 0;
    }
}
```

Listing 8-3, Skeldlg.cpp is the dialog box handling procedure for our radio button dialog box. This dialog contains four radio buttons, and a static frame that we're going to draw an image into. The code in this listing handles what happens during dialog initialization, as well as what happens when one of the radio buttons has been pressed. It also handles the drawing of the bitmap when a radio button has changed.

Listing 8-3   Skeldlg.cpp

```
//
// Skeldlg.cpp
//
//    Skeleton dialog procedure code
//

#include <skeleton.hpp>

//——————————————
//
// SkeletonDlgProc()
//
//    Dialog box procedure for the cursor control panel
//
//

    BOOL FAR PASCAL
SkeletonDlgProc ( HWND hDlg,
                  UINT message,
                  UINT wParam,
                  LONG lParam )
{

    WORD    screenWidth;
    WORD    screenHeight;

    int     i;
```

continued

Listing 8-3 *continued*

```
RECT    rectal;

//————————

switch ( message )
{
    case WM_INITDIALOG:

        CheckDlgButton ( hDlg,
                         ID_NewMoon,
                         TRUE );

        ChangeMoonButton ( hDlg,
                           ID_NewMoon );

        //
        // This code here allows us to center
        // the dialog in the middle of the
        // screen, regardless of resolution
        //

        screenWidth = GetSystemMetrics ( SM_CXSCREEN );

        screenHeight = GetSystemMetrics ( SM_CYSCREEN );

        GetWindowRect ( hDlg,&rectal );

        screenWidth -= ( rectal.right - rectal.left );

        screenHeight -= ( rectal.bottom - rectal.top );

        screenWidth /= 2;

        screenHeight /= 2;

        MoveWindow ( hDlg,
                     screenWidth,
                     screenHeight,
                     rectal.right - rectal.left,
                     rectal.bottom - rectal.top,
                     TRUE );

        //
        // All done with moving the screen,
```

```
    // now let's setup our buttons
    //

    return TRUE;   // TRUE means Windows will continue processing

    break;

case WM_PAINT:

    PaintMoonImage ( hDlg );

    return FALSE;      // Keep processing

    break;

case WM_COMMAND:

    switch ( LOWORD ( wParam ) )
    {

        case ID_NewMoon:
        case ID_QuarterMoon:
        case ID_HalfMoon:
        case ID_FullMoon:

            ChangeMoonButton ( hDlg,
                        LOWORD ( wParam ) );
            break;

        case IDOK: // All done, cleanup and go home...

            //
            // Ok, all done, punt...
            //

            EndDialog ( hDlg,
                        IDOK );
            break;

        case IDCANCEL:

            EndDialog ( hDlg,
                        IDCANCEL );
            break;
```

continued

Listing 8-3 *continued*

```
            default:
                return FALSE;      // Didn't process message
        }

        break;

    default:

        return FALSE; // Didn't process message...
        break;
    }

    return TRUE;
}

//——————-
//
// ChangeMoonButton()
//
//   Handles what happens when
//   the user changes the moon
//   radio button state
//

    void WINAPI
ChangeMoonButton ( HWND       hDlg,
                   WPARAM  buttonID )
{
    ResBitmap *    bmpToShow = NULL;

    HWND           moonBoxWnd = GetDlgItem ( hDlg, ID_MoonBox );
    CenteredWindow    moonBox ( moonBoxWnd );

    ClientDC       myDC ( moonBoxWnd );

    int            xOff;
    int            yOff;

    //———-

    //
    // Because our radio buttons are
    // auto radio buttons, we don't
    // have to actually check or
```

```
// uncheck the buttons here.
// But we do need to change the bitmap
// that we're displaying.
//

switch ( buttonID )
{
    case ID_NewMoon:

        bmpToShow = &newMoon;
        break;

    case ID_QuarterMoon:

        bmpToShow = &quarterMoon;
        break;

    case ID_HalfMoon:

        bmpToShow = &halfMoon;
        break;

    case ID_FullMoon:

        bmpToShow = &fullMoon;
        break;

    default:
        break;      // This should never execute
}

//
// Now display the bitmap if it's
// not NULL...
//

if ( bmpToShow != NULL )
{
    xOff = 32; // Size of moon bitmap
    yOff = 32; // Size of moon bitmap

    moonBox.FindCenteredRect ( xOff,
                               yOff );

    bmpToShow->DisplaySelf ( myDC.GetHandle(),
```

continued

Listing 8-3 *continued*

```
                                    xOff,
                                    yOff );
    }
}

//————————————-
//
// PaintMoonImage()
//
//    Paints the proper moon image
// on the screen
//

    void WINAPI
PaintMoonImage ( HWND hDlg )
{
    int     check1;
    int     check2;
    int     check3;
    int     check4;

    //—————————-

    //
    // Get the status of each of
    // our three buttons
    //

    check1 = SendDlgItemMessage ( hDlg,
                                  ID_NewMoon,
                                  BM_GETCHECK,
                                  0,
                                  0 );

    check2 = SendDlgItemMessage ( hDlg,
                                  ID_QuarterMoon,
                                  BM_GETCHECK,
                                  0,
                                  0 );

    check3 = SendDlgItemMessage ( hDlg,
                                  ID_HalfMoon,
                                  BM_GETCHECK,
                                  0,
```

```
                                      0 );

    check3 = SendDlgItemMessage ( hDlg,
                                  ID_FullMoon,
                                  BM_GETCHECK,
                                  0,
                                  0 );

    if ( check1 )
    {
        ChangeMoonButton ( hDlg,
                           ID_NewMoon );
    }
    else if ( check2 )
    {
        ChangeMoonButton ( hDlg,
                           ID_QuarterMoon );
    }
    else if ( check3 )
    {
        ChangeMoonButton ( hDlg,
                           ID_HalfMoon );
    }
    else if ( check4 )
    {
        ChangeMoonButton ( hDlg,
                           ID_FullMoon );
    }
}
```

Listing 8-4, Skelvars.cpp, is my standard file for holding all global variables in an application. The three variables that I always use—hMBrush, MainhWnd, and hInst are here, along with any application specific variables. In this case, I've got four instances of a ResBitmap object, which I use for the four phases of the moon that I display in the dialog box.

Listing 8-4   Skelvars.cpp

```
//
// SKELVARS.CPP
//
// Global variables for the skeleton application
```

continued

Listing 8-4 *continued*

```
//
//

#define __SKELETON_GLOBAL_VARS

#include <skeleton.hpp>

//——————————————--
//
// All the following are standard global
// variables used by the skeleton application
//

HBRUSH      hMBrush;   // Brush for window background

HWND        MainhWnd;  // Main window handle

HINSTANCE   hInst;     // Instance handle that we need


//——————————--
//
// Add custom variables here
//

WORD        rbSetting;      // What state is the radio button in?

ResBitmap   newMoon;
ResBitmap   quarterMoon;
ResBitmap   halfMoon;
ResBitmap   fullMoon;
```

Listing 8-5, Skeleton.hpp, is my single point of inclusion for all source (.cpp) files that I have in a project. I talk about why I do this in a fair amount of detail in my book, *Visual C++: A Developer's Guide* (M+T Books, 1994), but the bottom line is this: Having a single point of inclusion for all my source files eliminates several classes of very ugly and difficult to track down bugs.

Listing 8-5   Skeleton.hpp

```
//
// SKELETON.HPP
//
//    Mondo include file for
// the skeleton app.
//
//   __EVERYTHING__ gets included here, ONCE.
//
// That's it.
//

#ifndef __SKELETON_HPP

#define __SKELETON_HPP

//————————————-

#include <WINDOWS.H>

#include <gocl.hpp>        // GOCL definitions

#include <skelextn.hpp>    // Externs for the global variables

#include <skelprot.hpp>    // Prototypes for all functions in skeleton

#include <skelincs.hpp>


//————————————-


#endif // __SKELETON_HPP
```

Listing 8-6, Skeldfns.hpp contains all of the important #defines that I use in this program. All of the dialog control ID's are defined here, so that we can refer to them in both the source (.cpp) files, as well as in the resource (.rc) files. Having one file that gets referred to in both places ensures that I'll always be using the same numbers for the same control.

Listing 8-6 Skeldfns.hpp

```
//
// SKELDFNS.HPP
//
//   Defines used by the skeleton application
//

#ifndef __SKELDFNS_HPP

#define __SKELDFNS_HPP

//————————-

#define CB_ONE      0x01
#define    CB_TWO    0x02

//———

#define    SKELETON_BASE_ID   4000

#define ID_HalfMoon          SKELETON_BASE_ID + 1
#define ID_FullMoon          SKELETON_BASE_ID + 2
#define ID_NewMoon           SKELETON_BASE_ID + 3
#define ID_MoonBox           SKELETON_BASE_ID + 4
#define ID_QuarterMoon       SKELETON_BASE_ID + 5

#define    DIALOG_1   1


//———

#define    ID_SkeletonExit   SKELETON_BASE_ID + 0


//————————-

#endif // __SKELDFNS_HPP
```

Listing 8-7, Skelextn.hpp contains all the externalized references to all variables that are in the program. It provides a "one-stop shopping" method of referring to global variables, again ensuring that everybody's talking about the same thing (you wouldn't believe the number of bugs that can be attributed to the fact that one module thinks it's talking to a WORD, and another one thinks it's talking to a DWORD, or some similar variation. Having this file (along with skelvars.cpp, prevents that.)

Listing 8-7   Skelextn.hpp

```
//
// SKELEXTN.HPP
//
//     External define file for the skeleton app
//
//

#ifndef __SKELETON_GLOBAL_VARS

#define __SKELETON_GLOBAL_VARS

//————————————


extern  HBRUSH      hMBrush;    // Brush for window background

extern  HWND        MainhWnd;   // Main window handle

extern  HINSTANCE   hInst;      // Instance handle that we need


//————————————--


extern  WORD        rbSetting;  // What state is the radio button in?

extern  ResBitmap   newMoon;
extern  ResBitmap   quarterMoon;
extern  ResBitmap   halfMoon;
extern  ResBitmap   fullMoon;

//————————————

#endif // __SKELETON_GLOBAL_VARS
```

Listing 8-8, skelincs.hpp, is a method of packaging the define file skeldfns.hpp in such a fashion that both our source files (which include skeleton.hpp, and so get this file) as well as our resource files (which include this file directly) can include the same sets of definitions for resources.

Listing 8-8 Skelincs.hpp

```
//
// SKELINCS.HPP
//
//   Skeleton includes.
//
//   Packaged this way so that both the
// .cpp files and the .rc files can
// use them.
//

#ifndef __SKELINCS_HPP

#define __SKELINCS_HPP

//——————————

#include <WINDOWS.H>

#include <skeldfns.hpp>      // Resource and other ID defines

//——————————

#endif // __SKELINCS_HPP
```

Listing 8-9, Skelprot.hpp, defines all the functions that are in our program, and plops them into one file, so that (theoretically) any function can be referred to anywhere, in any source module. Having this file ensures that you don't have to worry about being able to call across modules—has the function you need to access been exported to this particular source file? By making sure that every file gets this include file, every file can access every function. Slower? A little, but that's what precompiled headers are for.

Listing 8-9   Skelprot.hpp

```
//
// SKELPROT.HPP
//
//     Prototype file
//

#ifndef __SKELETON_PROTOTYPES_HPP

#define __SKELETON_PROTOTYPES_HPP

//——————————-

//——————--
//
// Extern C wrappers
//

#ifdef __cplusplus

extern "C" {

#endif

//————————-

    int PASCAL
WinMain ( HINSTANCE   hInstance,
    HINSTANCEhPrevInstance,
    LPSTR    lpCmdLine,
    int      nCmdShow );

    LONG FAR PASCAL
SkeletonMainWindowProc ( HWND hWnd,
        UINT   message,
        UINT   wParam,
        LONG   lParam );
    BOOL
SkeletonInitApplication ( HINSTANCE  hInst,
        HINSTANCEhPrev,
        int      *pCmdSHow,
        LPSTR    lpCmd );
    BOOL
SkeletonRegisterClass ( HINSTANCE   hInstance );
```

continued

Listing 8-9 *continued*

```
    HWND
SkeletonCreateWindow ( HINSTANCE      hInstance );

    void
SkeletonExitApp( void );

    BOOL FAR PASCAL
SkeletonDlgProc ( HWNDhDlg,
                UINT message,
                UINT wParam,
                LONG lParam );

    void WINAPI
ChangeMoonButton ( HWND       hDlg,
                WPARAM   buttonID );

    void WINAPI
PaintMoonImage ( HWND hDlg );

//————————————————-

//————————-
//
// Extern C wrappers
//

#ifdef __cplusplus

};

#endif


//————————————-

#endif // __SKELETON_PROTOTYPES__HPP
```

Listing 8-10, skeleton.rc, is our resource file for the application. In this case, there's only a handful of stuff in this file—the definitions for the four bitmaps that we'll be using, along with a very simple menu which allows us to call up the dialog box. The definition of the dialog box itself is in the next listing, skeleton.dlg.

Listing 8-10   Skeleton.rc

```
//
// Skeleton.rc
//

#include <skelincs.hpp>

#include <cppres.rc>

#include <skeleton.dlg>

//—————————-
//
// Bitmaps, icons, cursors
//

SKELETON    ICON       SKELETON.ICO

FULLMOON    BITMAP     fullmoon.bmp
HALFMOON    BITMAP     halfmoon.bmp
NEWMOON     BITMAP     newmoon.bmp
QURTMOON    BITMAP     qurtmoon.bmp

//—————————-
//
// Menus
//

SKELETON MENU
{
 POPUP "Skeleton"
 {
  MENUITEM "Dialog Box", ID_SkeletonExit
 }

}
```

Listing 8-11, Skeleton.dlg, is the source for our dialog box in this sample app. Notice that we've got four radio buttons defined, as well as an OK and a Cancel button. Another important item is the frame that we've got defined. We're going to be using the frame as a place to draw a bitmap into (more on how that works in a minute).

Listing 8-11   Skeleton.dlg

```
//
// Skeleton.dlg
//
//   File which holds the
// dialog definition for
// our standard dialog box.
//

TestDialog DIALOG 34, 34, 199, 124
STYLE DS_MODALFRAME | WS_POPUP | WS_VISIBLE | WS_CAPTION | WS_SYSMENU
CAPTION "Radio Button Dialog"
FONT 8, "MS Sans Serif"
{
 DEFPUSHBUTTON "OK", IDOK, 50, 98, 50, 14
 PUSHBUTTON "Cancel", IDCANCEL, 110, 98, 50, 14
 CONTROL "Quarter Moon", ID_QuarterMoon, "BUTTON", BS_AUTORADIOBUTTON,
19, 35, 83, 12
 CONTROL "Half Moon", ID_HalfMoon, "BUTTON", BS_AUTORADIOBUTTON, 19, 49,
80, 12
 CONTROL "Full Moon", ID_FullMoon, "BUTTON", BS_AUTORADIOBUTTON, 19, 63,
84, 12
 CONTROL "", -1, "static", SS_BLACKFRAME | WS_GROUP, 11, 12, 110, 72
 CONTROL "New Moon", ID_NewMoon, "BUTTON", BS_AUTORADIOBUTTON, 19, 21,
62, 12
 CONTROL "", ID_MoonBox, "static", SS_BLACKFRAME, 150, 52, 31, 31
}
```

SHOOTING THE MOON: OUR APPLICATION IN ACTION

If you take a look at figure 8-7, you'll see a screen shot of our dialog box in action—as you can see, there are four radio buttons, corresponding to four phases of the moon (please, no irate letters from astronomers chastising me for having gotten it wrong—I know there are more than four phases to the moon, and I know that these aren't what they're really called. They're called waxing and waning, or spit and polish, or some such thing).

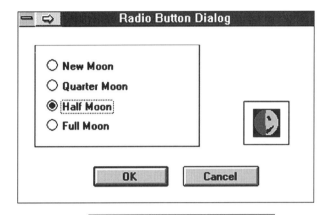

FIGURE 8-7 THE MOON APPLICATION IN ACTION.

In any case, if you run the application you'll immediately see an important point about it—as soon as you click on a radio button for a particular phase of the moon, the bitmap in the frame changes to that lunar phase. This is an important point that I wanted to demonstrate, because it shows that you can respond to changes to a radio button *within* the dialog itself, not just when you exit. Last chapter I showed you how you could tell what the state of a radio button was when you exited a dialog box—but there are some circumstances where you want to know that a radio button has changed immediately. This example shows you how to do that.

Really, it's quite simple. All that's required of you is to be able to respond to the WM_COMMAND message. Of course, we're already doing that, in order to be able to respond to the OK and Cancel buttons. However, the following little piece of magic also lets us respond to the radio buttons:

```
case WM_COMMAND:

    switch ( LOWORD ( wParam ) )
    {
```

```
        case ID_NewMoon:
        case ID_QuarterMoon:
        case ID_HalfMoon:
        case ID_FullMoon:

        ChangeMoonButton ( hDlg,
                      LOWORD ( wParam ) );
            break;

        case IDOK: // All done, cleanup and go
```

As you can see, whenever a radio button is pressed, our little switch statement will detect that fact, and make a call to the function **ChangeMoonButton().** This routine is the one that's responsible for actually changing the graphic that appears in the frame. Just remember, though, that the important piece of responding to a change in the radio button state *in* the dialog box is WM_COMMAND—you just have to check for the radio button ID's in this piece of code, and perform whatever it is that needs doing.

In our case, we want to change the graphic of the moon that appears in the frame rectangle in our dialog box. How do we accomplish this? Here's the routine that does it.

```
//———————--
//
// ChangeMoonButton()
//
//   Handles what happens when
//   the user changes the moon
//   radio button state
//

    void WINAPI
ChangeMoonButton ( HWND        hDlg,
            WPARAM   buttonID )
{
    ResBitmap *    bmpToShow = NULL;

    HWND           moonBoxWnd = GetDlgItem ( hDlg,  ID_MoonBox );
    CenteredWindow     moonBox ( moonBoxWnd );
```

```
ClientDC      myDC ( moonBoxWnd );

int           xOff;
int           yOff;

//————-
```

The first part of this function involves setting up our variables that we're going to be using, mostly the ones that we'll be drawing with. The variable moonBoxWnd is simply the window handle of the frame rect control in our dialog. This window handle is the one we'll be drawing into, using a **ClientDC** object, and a CenteredWindow object.

The **ClientDC** object is one of my GOCL object classes (which you can find on the disk that comes with this book); this one provides us with a ready-made device context into which we can draw. It's called a **ClientDC** because that's the kind of DC that it gives you—the client area of the specified window handle. Of course, 98% of the time that's what you want to be drawing into.

The **CenteredWindow** object (also a GOCL class) performs a nice little bit of trickery—given a window handle, and an x and y size of a bitmap, this class will return the x and y coordinates that the bitmap must be drawn at in order for the bitmap to be centered in the window.

Ok, once more in English—given a bitmap that you want to appear centered in a larger, framing window, the *CenteredWindow* class will hand you back the coordinates at which the bitmap must be drawn in order to appear centered. Of course, one thing you'll notice right away is that my bitmap object classes all have an optional x and y coordinate to begin displaying themselves at. I can use that to good effect here.

```
//
// Because our radio buttons are
// auto radio buttons, we don't
// have to actually check or
// uncheck the buttons here.
// But we do need to change the bitmap
// that we're displaying.
//
```

```
switch ( buttonID )
{
    case ID_NewMoon:

        bmpToShow = &newMoon;
        break;

    case ID_QuarterMoon:

        bmpToShow = &quarterMoon;
        break;

    case ID_HalfMoon:

        bmpToShow = &halfMoon;
        break;

    case ID_FullMoon:

        bmpToShow = &fullMoon;
        break;

    default:
        break;      // This should never execute
}
```

The previous bit of code is the one that's responsible for figuring out which of the four bitmaps should be displayed—I simply fill in the pointer to the appropriate bitmap, and then in the next bit of code, I ask the bitmap to display itself.

```
//
// Now display the bitmap if it's
// not NULL...
//

if ( bmpToShow != NULL )
{
    xOff = 32; // Size of moon bitmap
    yOff = 32; // Size of moon bitmap

    moonBox.FindCenteredRect ( xOff,
                               yOff );

    bmpToShow->DisplaySelf ( myDC.GetHandle(),
```

```
                              xOff,
                              yOff );
     }
}
```

As you can see in the code above, I'm asking the **CenteredWindow** object to give me back the coordinates at which I need to place the bitmap in order for it to be centered in the window. I then have whichever bitmap I've been given a pointer to display itself at that position.

This is all well and good, and as soon as you run the program and start twiddling the radio buttons, you'll become convinced that this little technique works like a charm.

There's a little gotcha, however. The first time I built this program, the bitmap did not appear when the dialog box fired up—it was only after a button was pressed that the bitmap appeared. So I went back, and added this code to the WM_INITDIALOG message:

```
     CheckDlgButton ( hDlg,
                      ID_NewMoon,
                      TRUE );

     ChangeMoonButton ( hDlg,
                        ID_NewMoon );
```

figuring that everything would now work. However, it didn't. You've probably already figured out why, but it took me a bit of head scratching to come up with the answer.

I finally figure out that the code above was kosher as written—and in fact, it was doing exactly the right thing—the first radio button was being checked (i.e., turned on), and then the bitmap was being displayed. But I'd forgotten *when* the WM_INITDIALOG message occurs— *before* the dialog is displayed. Oh, I was drawing the bitmap, all right— but the dialog itself wasn't yet visible! Of course, this meant that the bitmap wasn't visible either.

After smacking my forehead a couple of times, I set out to right the situation. All I needed to do was respond to the WM_PAINT message, and the problem was solved. My code to handle the WM_PAINT message looks like this:

```
case WM_PAINT:

        PaintMoonImage ( hDlg );

        return FALSE;      // Keep processing
```

First, I painted the proper image in the frame rect (more on that in a minute), and then I returned a FALSE, to let Windows know to keep processing the paint message (doing this meant that all my other controls would continue to paint properly).

The guts of **PaintMoonImage()** correspond to the inverse case of WM_COMMAND handler for the radio buttons—in this case, we know that we have to paint something, but not what. In the case of the WM_COMMAND message, we know that the radio button has just changed, which means that we also know what has to be painted.

Since the **PaintMoonImage()** routine has to determine which image to paint, the obvious question is how do we do that? Since the image that needs to be displayed is dependent upon which radio button is currently pressed, it's easy for us to see that the answer is to query the radio buttons, and draw the image based on that. Here's the relevant code:

```
check1 = SendDlgItemMessage ( hDlg,
                              ID_NewMoon,
                              BM_GETCHECK,
                              0,
                              0 );

check2 = SendDlgItemMessage ( hDlg,
                              ID_QuarterMoon,
                              BM_GETCHECK,
                              0,
                              0 );

check3 = SendDlgItemMessage ( hDlg,
                              ID_HalfMoon,
```

```
                                    BM_GETCHECK,
                                    0,
                                    0 );

check3 = SendDlgItemMessage ( hDlg,
                              ID_FullMoon,
                              BM_GETCHECK,
                              0,
                              0 );

if ( check1 )
{
    ChangeMoonButton ( hDlg,
                       ID_NewMoon );
}
else if ( check2 )
{
    ChangeMoonButton ( hDlg,
                       ID_QuarterMoon );
}
else if ( check3 )
{
    ChangeMoonButton ( hDlg,
                       ID_HalfMoon );
}
else if ( check4 )
{
    ChangeMoonButton ( hDlg,
                       ID_FullMoon );
}
```

As you can see, we're querying each of the four radio buttons, and then simply checking each one of the return values in our 'if' statement. We already have the drawing code in place. So, rather than repeat it, I simply call the drawing routine **ChangeMoonButton()** with the id of the proper button. **ChangeMoonButton(),** you'll remember, uses the id of the button to determine which of the four bitmaps to draw with.

If this seems a somewhat roundabout way of drawing the image in response to a paint message, I have to agree. However, I'd much rather call a routine that already does what I want (in this case, drawing the object) than write some new code that duplicates the functionality of what I want to achieve.

CHECKING OUT THE MOON: OUR APPLICATION WITH CHECK BOXES

Having demonstrated how we can respond to radio buttons interactively in a dialog, it's now time to do the same thing for check boxes. Our dialog is going to look very similar—instead of four radio buttons, however, we'll be using four check boxes. The difference here is that each check box is going to turn on or off a phase of the moon display, and we can have up to four of them visible at one time. Let's take a look at how this is going to work. (Note: For brevity's sake I'm only going to give you the listings that have changed. You'll find the complete source and project files for both these applications on your disk.).

Listing 8-12, Skeldlg.cpp contains the new version of the dialog box handler. By far the bulk of the changes have occurred in this one file. There are a number of small changes throughout the other files, but I'm going to basically ignore them. Skeldlg.cpp is where the real action is happening.

Listing 8-12 Skeldlg.cpp

```
//
// Skeldlg.cpp
//
//    Skeleton dialog procedure code
//

#include <skeleton.hpp>

//————————————
//
// SkeletonDlgProc()
//
//    Dialog box procedure for the cursor control panel
//
//

    BOOL FAR PASCAL
SkeletonDlgProc ( HWND hDlg,
                  UINT message,
                  UINT wParam,
```

```
                LONG  lParam )
{

    WORD    screenWidth;
    WORD    screenHeight;

    int     i;

    RECT    rectal;

    //————————————

    switch ( message )
    {
        case WM_INITDIALOG:

            //
            // This code here allows us to center
            // the dialog in the middle of the
            // screen, regardless of resolution
            //

            screenWidth = GetSystemMetrics ( SM_CXSCREEN );

            screenHeight = GetSystemMetrics ( SM_CYSCREEN );

            GetWindowRect ( hDlg,
                            &rectal );

            screenWidth -= ( rectal.right - rectal.left );

            screenHeight -= ( rectal.bottom - rectal.top );

            screenWidth /= 2;

            screenHeight /= 2;

            MoveWindow ( hDlg,
                         screenWidth,
                         screenHeight,
                         rectal.right - rectal.left,
                         rectal.bottom - rectal.top,
                         TRUE );

            //
```

continued

Listing 8-12 *continued*

```
            // All done with moving the screen,
            // now let's setup our buttons
            //

            return TRUE;   // TRUE means Windows will continue processing

            break;

    case WM_PAINT:

            PaintMoonImage ( hDlg );

            return FALSE;      // Keep processing

            break;

    case WM_COMMAND:

            switch ( LOWORD ( wParam ) )
            {

                case ID_NewMoonButton:

                    DrawMoonOrNot ( hDlg,
                                    ID_NewMoonButton,
                                    ID_NewMoonBox,
                                    newMoon );
                    break;

                case ID_QuarterMoonButton:

                    DrawMoonOrNot ( hDlg,
                                    ID_QuarterMoonButton,
                                    ID_QuarterMoonBox,
                                    quarterMoon );
                    break;

                case ID_HalfMoonButton:

                    DrawMoonOrNot ( hDlg,
                                    ID_HalfMoonButton,
                                    ID_HalfMoonBox,
                                    halfMoon );
                    break;
```

```
            case ID_FullMoonButton:

                DrawMoonOrNot ( hDlg,
                                ID_FullMoonButton,
                                ID_FullMoonBox,
                                fullMoon );
                break;

            case IDOK: // All done, cleanup and go home...

                //
                // Ok, all done, punt...
                //

                EndDialog ( hDlg,
                            IDOK );
                break;

            case IDCANCEL:

                EndDialog ( hDlg,
                            IDCANCEL );
                break;

            default:
                return FALSE;        // Didn't process message
        }

        break;

    default:

        return FALSE; // Didn't process message...
        break;
    }

    return TRUE;
}

//————————————-
//
// PaintMoonImage()
//
//   Paints the proper moon image
// on the screen
```

continued

Listing 8-12 *continued*

```
//

    void WINAPI
PaintMoonImage ( HWND hDlg )
{
    //————————

    DrawMoonOrNot ( hDlg,
                    ID_NewMoonButton,
                    ID_NewMoonBox,
                    newMoon );

    DrawMoonOrNot ( hDlg,
                    ID_QuarterMoonButton,
                    ID_QuarterMoonBox,
                    quarterMoon );

    DrawMoonOrNot ( hDlg,
                    ID_HalfMoonButton,
                    ID_HalfMoonBox,
                    halfMoon );

    DrawMoonOrNot ( hDlg,
                    ID_FullMoonButton,
                    ID_FullMoonBox,
                    fullMoon );
}

//————————
//
// DrawMoonOrNot()
//
//    Given the id of a button,
//    this routine will determine
//    if that button is checked.
//    If it is, this routine will use
//    he passed-in bitmap to draw
//    the moon. Otherwise, it will
//    use the global variable 'blank'
//    to draw a blank space in the
//    display.
//
//    It uses the variable windowID to
//    determine which window to draw into.
```

```
//

    void WINAPI
DrawMoonOrNot ( HWND           hDlg,
                WPARAM         buttonID,
                WPARAM         windowID,
                ResBitmap &    myBmp )
{
    int    check1;

    //——————————

    //
    // Find out if this button is checked
    // or not.
    //

    check1 = SendDlgItemMessage ( hDlg,
                                  buttonID,
                                  BM_GETCHECK,
                                  0,
                                  0 );
    //
    // If the button is checked, use
    // the moon bitmap...
    //

    if ( check1 )
    {
        DrawMoon ( hDlg,
                   windowID,
                   myBmp );
    }

    //
    // Ok, button is not checked, so
    // draw a blank.
    //

    else
    {
        DrawMoon ( hDlg,
                   windowID,
                   blank );
    }
```

continued

Listing 8-12 *continued*

```
}

//————
//
// DrawMoon()
//
//    Given a window to draw
//    into, and a resource bitmap
//    to draw, this routine will
//    do just that.
//

    void WINAPI
DrawMoon ( HWND            hDlg,
          WPARAM      windowID,
          ResBitmap & myBmp )
{
    HWND            moonBoxWnd = GetDlgItem ( hDlg,
                                                windowID );
    CenteredWindow    moonBox ( moonBoxWnd );

    ClientDC        myDC ( moonBoxWnd );

    int            xOff;
    int            yOff;

    //————

    xOff = 32; // Size of moon bitmap
    yOff = 32; // Size of moon bitmap

    moonBox.FindCenteredRect ( xOff,
                               yOff );

    myBmp.DisplaySelf ( myDC.GetHandle(),
                        xOff,
                        yOff );
}
```

As you can see from the screen shot of our check box version in action (see figure 8-8), there are now four check boxes, along with four frame windows. Each frame window corresponds to one check box—if the box is checked, then that moon image will appear. If the box is unchecked, then a black square appears.

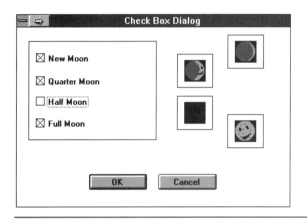

FIGURE 8-8   THE CHECK BOX VERSION OF THE MOON APPLICATION IN ACTION.

Conceptually, here's how our application has changed: In the radio button version of the application, we could check for a WM_COMMAND message to any of our radio buttons, and then simply draw the one bitmap that was called for. The reason we could do this was because of an implicit assumption about the way radio buttons work—when one is checked, all the others are unchecked. Thus, when we get a WM_COMMAND message for one of the radio buttons, it means that only the one that sent the message is checked, and all the others are unchecked.

However, for this version of the application, each of the four check boxes is independent of the other three—we can have none, some or all of the check boxes checked at any given time. This means that we have to be able to independently determine the state of any of the check boxes and act accordingly.

Having said this, however, it also behooves us to look at what it is we need to do for a check box—this turns out to be the same, regardless of which check box we're dealing with. What we need to do is this:

1. Determine if the check box is checked or unchecked.

2. If the box is checked, draw the moon bitmap in the appropriate frame

3. If the box is unchecked, draw the black square in the appropriate frame.

This is what the functions **DrawMoonOrNot()** and **DrawMoon()** are responsible for. **DrawMoonOrNot(),** shown below, sends a message to the ID of the checkbox that has been passed in. If the return value is non-zero (meaning the box is checked), then the routine **DrawMoon()** is called, and is passed the handle of the **ResBitmap** containing the proper moon image (note how I'm using **ResBitmap** &, which allows me to directly access the member function of the **ResBitmap** in question, without knowing in advance which one it is.)

```
        void WINAPI
DrawMoonOrNot ( HWND          hDlg,
                WPARAM        buttonID,
                WPARAM        windowID,
                ResBitmap &   myBmp )
{
    int     check1;

    //———————

    //
    // Find out if this button is checked
    // or not.
    //

    check1 = SendDlgItemMessage ( hDlg,
                                  buttonID,
                                  BM_GETCHECK,
                                  0,
                                  0 );
    //
    // If the button is checked, use
    // the moon bitmap...
    //
```

```
    if ( check1 )
    {
        DrawMoon ( hDlg,
                   windowID,
                   myBmp );
    }

    //
    // Ok, button is not checked, so
    // draw a blank.
    //

    else
    {
        DrawMoon ( hDlg,
                   windowID,
                   blank );
    }
}
```

If the return value of the **SendMessage()** call is zero, then the box is not currently checked, and I call **DrawMoon()** with the handle of the blank bitmap.

By packaging the functionality this way, I've given myself an easy way to handle each button—each button simply has a call of the following form:

```
case WM_COMMAND:

    switch ( LOWORD ( wParam ) )
    {

        case ID_NewMoonButton:

            DrawMoonOrNot ( hDlg,
                    ID_NewMoonButton,
                    ID_NewMoonBox,
                    newMoon );
                    break;
```

As you can see, my **WM_COMMAND** handler simply breaks out each button, and calls **DrawMoonOrNot()** with slightly different parameters.

From there, the routines work identically, regardless of which button I'm actually dealing with.

Packaging my calls this way has the additional benefit of allowing me to repaint all of my check boxes and their frames at any time, simply by calling each one in sequence. This is what the routine **PaintMoonImage()** does. It simply makes four calls to **DrawMoonOrNot(),** each time using a different check box ID, frame ID and ResBitmap handle.

SUMMARY

As we've seen in this chapter, check boxes and radio buttons provide a nice way of handling state information—that is, information which can have several different states, such as on/off, 1/2/3, etc.

It's easy to manipulate radio buttons and check boxes in dialogs—indeed, with the advent of the AUTORADIOBUTTON and AUTOCHECKBOX styles, you don't even have to manipulate the controls directly if you don't want to—Windows will handle the checking and unchecking for you. All you'll need to do is set up the initial state, and check it when you're done.

Of course, you can also interactively determine the state of a radio button or check box at any time, by using the **SendMessage()** call along with the BM_GETCHECK message. Interactively determining this can be useful when you need to know what state a button is in during the execution of your dialog—for example, if you have changing information which needs to be dynamically displayed in response to a button being on or off.

Radio buttons and check boxes provide a good way of presenting small amounts of information. Sometimes, however, you'll need to present larger amounts of information (such as lists of things) to your users. In that case, you'll need to use the controls that are the topic of the next chapter—list boxes and combo boxes.

CHAPTER 9

LIST BOXES AND
COMBO BOXES

In Chapter 8, we talked about radio buttons and check boxes, controls that you use in your dialog to convey state information (i.e., on or off, one of a set of conditions, etc.). In this chapter, we're going to look at list boxes and combo boxes, which are controls which allow you to give the user a method of selecting a broader range of information. This means that instead of a half-dozen choices (which is really about the limit for a set of radio buttons), you can allow the user to select from several dozen (or more) possibilities. You can also allow them to select more than one item from a list box (something not possible with radio buttons).

Figure 9-1 shows a dialog box with two list boxes and two combo boxes. The list boxes show a list of the files in the current directory, and a tree path of the current directory. You can select a file from the left hand listbox, or change what directory you're looking in by manipulating the entries in the right hand listbox.

The combo boxes allow you to choose which kind of files to look at (the combo box on the left) and which drive to look on (the combo box on the right).

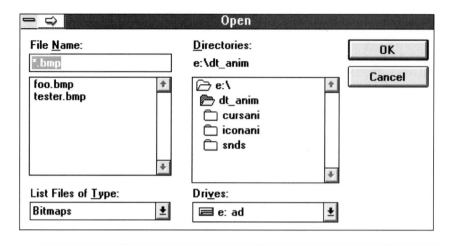

FIGURE 9-1 THE FILE OPEN DIALOG BOX FROM THE MICROSOFT COMMON DIALOGS. IN THE DIALOG THERE ARE TWO LIST BOXES (THE FILE LIST AND THE DIRECTORY LIST) AND TWO COMBO BOXES (THE FILE TYPE SELECTOR, AND THE DRIVE SELECTOR).

LISTBOX AND COMBOBOX DO'S AND DON'TS

As usual, before we go diving into code examples and implementation details, let's take a look at the broader picture, namely, under what conditions should we use a list box or combo box?

Because list boxes and combo boxes are good at holding lots of information, they often get used for displaying things that would be impractical to display in other fashions (such as radio buttons). However, there are still a few caveats to keep in mind.

✦ Don't put too many items into a list box. What's "too many?" In real terms, too many is probably anything over 100-200 entries. Realistically, it begins to become extremely impractical to scroll through that many entries, looking for the one you want. In addition, since list boxes are built-in controls, they have a built-in limit to the amount of text that they can hold.

✦ Make sure that all entries in a listbox can be viewed horizontally. If you don't know in advance how big your entries are going to be, make sure that you enable horizontal scrolling so that the user can see all the entries. One of my absolute favorite "love-to-hate" programs has a vertical list box with a list of files in it—but you can't scroll the listbox horizontally, and the files all have path-names on the front of them. This means that for any file that has a path of more than 2 or 3 letters, part of the file name itself is not visible (it's off to the right of the listbox), and for any file that has a *real* pathname (like D:\myproj\src) the entire filename is not visible. This means that for all intents and purposes you have *no idea* what the files in the listbox really are. This is a fundamental flaw, since this is critical information for this program. You know it's there—you just can't see it, and there's no way to get to it.) Make sure your combo boxes are big enough, too.

✦ If you create a multiple-select listbox for your program, make it support discontiguous selections (LBS_MULTISEL), not just contiguous selections (LBS_EXTENDEDSEL). It's not much more work (in truth, it isn't *any* more work) to do so, and your users will be much happier. Why? Simple—many people want to be able to pick out this item, that item, and the other item, without picking out all the items in between. Forcing them to either select everything or select one thing at a time will make them extremely unhappy.

✦ If you create a combo box with a drop down list box attached, please make sure that the size of the drop down list isn't too small or too big. Too many combo boxes that I've seen have drop down list boxes that are only big enough to hold two or three items, when in fact, the combo box is giving you twenty items to choose from. If you know that you're going to have twenty items, why not size the list box accordingly (make it able to dis-play, say, 8 items at a time)? This way, your users won't be pag-ing through the list forever, trying to find the item that they want. There's another reason for this, too. Since the listbox portion of the combo box is so darned easy to put away, making the listbox portion bigger will reduce the number of times the user has to hit the up or down arrow, and hence reduce the number of times that they accidentally shut down the list box when they were simply trying to scroll through it.

✦ Make your combo boxes and list boxes have the LBS_INTE-GRALHEIGHT style. This ensures that they look good on the screen—nothing's uglier than a listbox with only half an entry showing.

Now that I've given you my philosophy of list and combo boxes, let's take a closer look at list boxes, and how they are used, followed by a closer look at combo boxes, and how *they* are used.

FLAVORS OF LIST BOXES AND COMBO BOXES

There are several flavors of both list box and combo box. These flavors give the boxes rather different behaviors, and can allow you to achieve disparate ends. Let's get a better understanding of each type of box, and what they might be used for. Table 9-1 shows the various parameters that a listbox can be created with. Each style sets certain properties of the listbox, and defines it's behavior.

Table 9-1 List box styles

STYLE	DESCRIPTION
LBS_DISABLENOSCROLL	Normally, a list box that does not have enough entries in it to justify a vertical scroll bar will hide the scroll bar (make it disappear). By using this style flag (or the appropriate dialog editor equivalent), you can make the scroll bar visible

	(but disabled) when there are not enough entries in the list box.
LBS_EXTENDEDSEL	This flag allows the user to 'Shift-click' on an entry, and select several items in the listbox at once. This is not the same as the LBS_MULTIPLESEL flag (below); this flag means that when the user 'Shift-clicks' on an entry, all items between the currently selected one and this one will be selected. (For example, if item 2 is selected, and the user 'Shift-clicks' on item 6, items 2, 3, 4, 5 and 6 will become elected.) For discontiguous selections, use the LBS_MULTIPLESEL flag.
LBS_HASSTRINGS	Specifies that the list box contains items which are strings. Using this flag means that the listbox will handle all the memory and pointer manipulation of the strings (and will clean it all up). You can retrieve the text of a string by using the LB_GETTEXT message. Be default, all list boxes (except owner-draw listboxes) are created with this style.
LBS_MULTICOLUMN	Specifies a listbox that has more than one vertical column of entries. The LB_SETCOLUMN-WIDTH message allows you to set the width of the columns, specified in pixels.

LBS_MULTIPLESEL	Allows the user to select multiple discontiguous (not next to each other) entries in the listbox. Each entry in the listbox acts as a toggle. For contiguous selection of items, use the LBS_EXTENDEDSEL flag.
LBS_NOINTEGRALHEIGHT	Prevents Windows from resizing the listbox when it displays the dialog. Normally, Windows will grow or shrink a listbox slightly, so that the listbox will only display complete items.
LBS_NOREDRAW	Specifies that a list box's appearance is not updated when changes are made. You can change this value at any time via the WM_SETREDRAW message.
LBS_NOTIFY	Notifies the parent window with an input message whenever the user single clicks or double clicks in the listbox.
LBS_OWNERDRAWFIXED	Specifies that the owner of the listbox (i.e., your program) is responsible for drawing the elements in the listbox, and that the items are all the same height. The parent window receives a WM_MEASUREITEM message when the list box is created, and a WM_DRAWITEM message when elements in the box need to be redrawn.
LBS_OWNERDRAWVARIABLE	Same as LBS_OWNERDRAWFIXED, except that the items in the listbox are assumed to be variable

	in height. The parent window receives a WM_MEASUREITEM for each item in the listbox, and a WM_DRAWITEM message when elements in the box need to be redrawn.
LBS_SORT	Sorts the strings in the listbox alphabetically.
LBS_STANDARD	Combination of the LBS_SORT and LBS_NOTIFY flags, and also specifies that the listbox will have a border drawn around it.
LBS_USETABSTOPS	Allows a list box to recognize and expand tab characters when drawing strings. Default tab stops are 32 dialog box units. (This can be converted to pixels using the GetDialogBaseUnits() function).
LBS_WANTKEYBOARDINPUT	Specifies that the owner of the list box receives WM_VKEYTOITEM or WM_CHARTOITEM messages whenever the user presses a key and the list box has the input focus. This allows the application to perform special processing on the keyboard input.

As you can see from the listbox styles, there are basically two varieties of listboxes: those that can have only a single element selected at a time, and those that can have multiple elements selected at a time.

By default, a listbox can only have one entry selected at a time. This is useful for when you're using the listbox as a way of selecting "one of many." For example, Figure 9-2 shows a screen shot of a product I wrote that allows users to apply an animation and a sound to a desktop icon.

There are two listboxes in the dialog—one for animations, and one for sounds. Each listbox can only have one item selected at a time., because the user can apply only one animation and one sound to a particular icon.

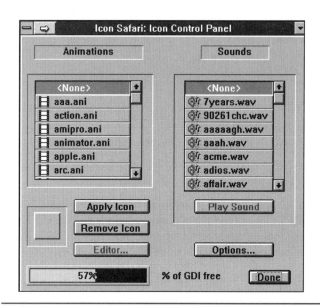

FIGURE 9-2 A SCREEN SHOT OF THE ICON PANEL. BOTH THE ANIMATIONS LISTBOX AND THE SOUNDS LISTBOX AND SINGLE-SELECT, BECAUSE A USER CAN ONLY APPLY ONE ANIMATION AND ONE SOUND TO A GIVEN ICON.

However, you may want the user to be able to select more than one item from the listbox at a time. An example of this is in File Manager, which allows you to select multiple files from the listbox display (the File Manager window is also a multicolumn list box).

In this case, you'll want to use the LBS_EXTENDEDSEL style, which allows the user to select more than one item in the listbox, using the combination of the keyboard <Shift> key and the left mouse button. One thing that you may notice about this style, however, is that it does not allow *discontiguous* selections; that is, selections which are separated by non-selected items. Only selections where you are selecting a range of items are allowed with this style.

If you want to be able to pick and choose among items in the listbox, you'll need to use the LBS_MULTIPLESEL style, which allows you to single click on individual items, and turn them on or off. The type of multiple selection that you're going to want is going to depend upon what you want your users to be able to do—assuming, of course, that you even want them to be able to select multiple items at all.

USING A LISTBOX

The easiest way to learn about listboxes is by giving you some examples. Herewith, then, are a series of code fragments that show you how to handle listboxes, along with a sample program that lets you manipulate them. (Table 9-2 is a list of all the messages that listboxes respond to, along with a quick reference of the wParam and lParam of each message, what the message does, and what it returns.)

To set a text entry in a listbox:

```
SendDlgItemMessage (  hDlg,
                ID_ListBox,
                LB_ADDSTRING,     // Adds it to
                         // the listbox
                0,         // Not used
                (LPARAM)lpString );
```

The message LB_ADDSTRING causes the string to be added to the listbox. If the listbox has the style LBS_SORT, then the listbox is sorted. This has the effect of adding the string in alphabetical order. If the listbox does not have the LBS_SORT style, then the string is added at the end.

Another message that allows you to add strings to a listbox is LB_INSERTSTRING; here's an example of how you use that:

```
SendDlgItemMessage (  hDlg,
                ID_ListBox,
                LB_INSERTSTRING,  // Adds it to
                         // the listbox
                position,              // point to
```

```
                                        // insert at.
                    (LPARAM)lpString );
```

The difference between this call and the previous one is that LB_ADDSTRING puts the string in the listbox, and then re-orders it (meaning you don't know where the string is going to end up), while LB_INSERTSTRING puts it at a specified point.

Suppose we want to get the text of the currently selected item. Here's a piece of code that will do that:

```
char        item [ 128 ];



SendDlgItemMessage ( hDlg,
                    ID_ListBox,
                    LB_GETTEXT,
                    position,
                    (LPARAM)item );
```

This retrieves the text string at position **position**, and puts it into the buffer item. (Actually, this doesn't retrieve the currently selected item automatically—it simply retrieves the text of an arbitrary entry. If you want the current selection, you'd have to first send the LB_GETCURSEL message, and use the return value from that as your position.) If you want to ensure that your buffer is going to be big enough to hold the string, you can send the LB_GETTEXTLEN message, like so:

```
int     tLen;

tLen = SendDlgItemMessage ( hDlg,
                    ID_ListBox,
                    LB_GETTEXTLEN,
                    position,
                    0L );
```

Table 9-2   Listbox messages

Listbox message	wParam	lParam	Returns:	Comments
LB_ADDSTRING				
Adds a string to the listbox	0	lpString	Zero based index of the string in the list box.	Adds a string to the listbox. If listbox is not sorted, the string is added at the end.
LB_DELETESTRING				
Deletes a string from the listbox	index	0L	Count of remaining strings.	Deletes the string specified by the value of index.
LB_DIR				
Fills the listbox with a directory listing of files specified by the lpFileSpec pointer.	attrib-Flags	lpFile-Spec	Zero based index of last file added	If you're adding a file list, you should use LB_RESETCON-TENT to clear out the list box first.
LB_FINDSTRING				
Matches the passed in-string as a prefix to the strings in the listbox. Works even if listbox strings are longer than the passed-in string	start-Index	lpFind-String	Index of the matching item, LB_ERR if there was no match.	If startIndex is -1, the entire list box is searched. lpFindString must be NULL terminated. Not case-sensitive.
LB_FINDSTRINGEXACT				
Matches the passed-in string to the strings in the listbox.	start-Index	lpFind-String	Index of the matching	If the startIndex is -1, the entire list box is

Must be an exact match. (Strings must be same length).			item, LB_ERR if there was no match.	searched. lpFindString must be NULL terminated. Not case sensitive

LB_GETCARETINDEX

Get the item that has the focus rectangle in a multipleselection list box.	0	0L	Zero based index of item that has the focus.	For multiple selection list-boxes,returns the with the focus; item for single selection list boxes, item isthe one currently any. selected, if

LB_GETCOUNT

Returns a count of the number of items in the listbox	0	0L	Number of items in the listbox.	Return count is 1 bigger than the index of the last element.

LB_GETCURSEL

Returns the index of the currently selected item in the listbox. Used for single-selection listboxes only.	0	0L	Zero based index of the current selection.	LB_ERR if there is none. This message cannot be sent to a multiple selection listbox.

LB_GETHORIZONTALEXTENT

Returns the width (in pixels) of the scrollable width of the listbox.	0	0L	Scrollable width of listbox, in pixels.	The listbox must have been defined with the WS_HSCROLL style.

LB_GETITEMDATA

Returns the LONG value that was associated with the item entry.	item-Index	0L	The double-word value associated with the entry.	Use the LB_SETITEM-DATAmessage to set the long word valueof an item.

LB_GETITEMHEIGHT

Returns the height, in pixels, of items in the listbox.	item-Index	0L	Height, in pixels, of item(s) in the listbox.	The wParam value should only be used if the style DRAW-LBS_OWNER VARIABLE is used; otherwise it should be 0.

LB_GETITEMRECT

Fills in the RECT pointed to by lpFarRect with the display bounding box of the item determined by itemIndex.	item-Index	lpFar-Rect	Not meaning-ful if call was OK.	A RECT is: top; left; bottom; right;

LB_GETSEL

Returns the selection state of the item specified by itemIndex.	item-Index	0L	The selection state of the item.	If the item is selected, the return value is positive, other-wise it's zero.

LB_GETSELCOUNT

Returns a count of the number of items selected in a multiple selection listbox.	0	0L	Count of selected items in the listbox.	The return value is LB_ERR if the listbox is a single-selection listbox.

LB_GETSELITEMS

Fill the buffer pointed to by lpItemBuff with a list of integers specifying the selected items.	max-Items	lpItem-Buff	Actual number of items placed in the buffer.	maxItems specifies the maximum num -ber of elements that can be put in lpItemBuff. Return value is LB_ERR if the listbox is a single -selection listbox.

LB_GETTEXT

Retrieves the text string specified by itemIndex, and puts it into the buffer specified by lpStringBuff.	item-Index	lpString-Buff	Length of string (in bytes), not including NULL termina-tion.	If the listbox is ownerdraw, but doesn't have the LBS_HAS-STRINGS style, the buffer recieves the longword associ-ated with the entry.

LB_GETTEXTLEN

Returns the length of the string of the item specified by itemIndex.	item-Index	0L	Length of string (in bytes), not includ-ing NULL

			terminat-ion.	
LB_GETTOPINDEX				
Returns the zero based index of the first visible item in the listbox.	0	0L	Zero-based index of first visible item in the listbox.	
LB_INSERTSTRING				
Inserts the string pointed to by lpString into the listbox at the position indicated by itemIndex. If itemIndex is -1, string is inserted at the end of the listbox	item-Index	lpString	Index of the position at which the string was inserted.	This message doesnot cause a listboxwith the LBS_SORT style to be sortd. Will return LBS_ERRSPACE if there isn't enoughspace for the string.
LB_RESETCONTENT				
Removes all items from a listbox.	0	0L	Nothing	If ownerdraw, but not LBS_-HASSTRINGS, a WM_DELETE-ITEM is sent for each item.
LB_SELECTSTRING				
Search the listbox at the position indicated by indexStart for the string lpFindString, and if found, select that item. The string	index-Start	lpFind-String	Index of selected item	If the string was not found, the current selection is unchanged. The listbox is scrolled, if necessary, to

in the listbox may be longer than the string pointed to by lpFindString.				bring the selected item in view.

LB_SELITEMRANGE

Selects one or more consecutive items in a multiple selection list box. If selectStyle is 0, item(s) are deselected; if selectStyle is non-0, item(s) are selected and highlighted.	select-Style	start/-endSel	Not meaning-ful unless LB_ERR.	The lParam specifies the starting and ending positions ofthe selection; loword is starting position, hiword is ending position; both positions are zero based.

LB_SETCARETINDEX

Set the focus rectangle to the item specified by itemIndex. Use for multiple selection listboxes only.	item-Index	scroll-Flag	Not meaning-ful unless LB_ERR	scrollFlag should be set like this: MAKELPARAM-(flag,0). If scroll-Flag is 0, the tem is scrolled into full view, if non-zero, then theitem is scrolled until at least partially in view.

LB_SETCOLUMNWIDTH

Sets the width, in pixels, of all the columns in a multi-column list box.	clWidth	0L	Nothing	clWidth specifies the width in pixels.

LB_SETCURSEL

Sets the selection in a list box to be the item specified by itemIndex. If itemIndex is -1, the selection is removed.	item-Index	0L	Not meaning-ful unless LB_ERR	This should only be used with singleselection list boxes. The return will be LB_ERR if itemIndex is -1. This is ok, and does not indicate an error.

LB_SETHORIZONTALEXTENT

Sets the width, in pixels, by which a listbox may be scrolled horizon-tally.	cwPixels	0L	Nothing	By default, the horizontal extent of a listbox is set to zero.

LB_SETITEMDATA

Sets the double word value of the item specified by itemIndex	item-Index	dwData	Not meaning-ful unless LB_ERR	The value set here can be retrieved later by using LB_GET-ITEMDATA.

LB_SETITEMHEIGHT

Sets the height, in pixels, of item(s) in the listbox. If listbox is OWNERDRAW-VARIABLE, this only sets the height of this item, otherwise all item's height is set.	item-Index	item-Height	Not meaning-ful unless LB_ERR	The height is specified by the loword of lParam. Use MAKELPARAM (height, 0)

LB_SETSEL

Selects a string in a multiple selection list box. If itemIndex (loword of lParam) is -1, selection is added or removed from all strings, depending upon selFlags.	selFlag	item-Index	Not meaning-ful unless LB_ERR.	If selFlags is TRUE, item is selected and highlighted, if FALSE, deselected and dehighlighted. item-Index should beplaced in the low word of lParam.

LB_SETTABSTOPS

Set the tab stop positions of a list box.The tab stop spacing is specified in dialog units.	numTabs	lpTabs	Nonzero if all tabs were set; 0 otherwise.	The list box must have been created with the LBS_USETAB-STOPS style. lpTabs points to an array of integers specifying tab stops. Array must be in increasing order.

LB_SETTOPINDEX

Ensures that a particular item, specified by itemIndex, is visible in the listbox.	item-Index	0L	Not meaning-ful unless LB_ERR.	Listbox is scrolled so that item is at the top, or the bottom of the listbox is reached.

Notes:

◆ All listbox messages return LB_ERR if there is an error, unless otherwise noted.

◆ Any parameter that is marked as 0 must be set to zero. These parameters are generally unused, but should be set to 0 for future compatability.

Now that we've had a few code fragments, it's time for a full example. As usual, I'll be using my Skeleton application to build a quick framework with which to support our investigations. This version of the Skeleton application is going to allow us to bring up a dialog box that has two list boxes in it. The list box on the left is going to contain all the files in the directory where the program was launched from. We're going to be able to add and delete these files from the listbox on the right. Listings 9-1 through 9-11 give the source code for this version of the skeleton application.

Listing 9-1, Skeleton.cpp is our usual startup and main window handling code. The only really different thing here is my use of my **ModalDialogHandler()** class to create and fire up an instance of the dialog "TestDialog." My **ModalDialogHandler()** class (it's part of the GOCL library) is nice, because it allows me to get rid of all those little function calls that do nothing except start up a particular dialog. Here, all that code is encapsulated in an object (where it should be).

Listing 9-1: Skeleton.cpp

```
//
// SKELETON.CPP
//
//     The skeleton application...
//
//
#include <skeleton.hpp>
//————————
//
```

continued

Listing 9-1: *continued*

```
// WinMain()
//
    int PASCAL
WinMain ( HINSTANCE    hInstance,
          HINSTANCEhPrevInstance,
          LPSTR      lpCmdLine,
          int        nCmdShow )
{
    MSG    msg;              // Message holder...
    BOOL   returnCode = TRUE; // Return code...
    //——————————-
    hInst = hInstance;     // Save instance handle...
    //
    // Initialize the application as needed
    //
    if ( !SkeletonInitApplication ( hInstance,
                                    hPrevInstance,
                                    &nCmdShow,
                                    lpCmdLine ) )
    {
        returnCode = FALSE;
        goto Leave;
    }
    //
    // Initialize the class, if necessary...
    //
    if ( !hPrevInstance )
    {
        if ( !SkeletonRegisterClass ( hInstance ) )
        {
            returnCode = FALSE;
            goto Leave;
        }
    }
    //
    // Create the main window...
    //
    MainhWnd = SkeletonCreateWindow ( hInstance );
    if ( !MainhWnd )
    {
        returnCode = FALSE;
        goto Leave;
    }
    //
```

```
    // Show the window, so that the message loop gets pumped...
    //
    ShowWindow ( MainhWnd,
                 nCmdShow );
    UpdateWindow ( MainhWnd );
    //
    // Now do our message loop
    //
    while ( GetMessage ( &msg,
                 0,
                 0,
                 0 ) )
    {
        TranslateMessage ( &msg );
        DispatchMessage ( &msg );
    }
Leave:
    SkeletonExitApp();     // Cleanup if necessary
    //
    // Give back the proper return code...
    //
    if ( returnCode == TRUE )
    {
        return ( msg.wParam );
    }
    else
    {
        return FALSE;
    }
}
//————
//
// MainWindowProc()
//
//      Main window callback procedure
//
    LONG FAR PASCAL
SkeletonMainWindowProc ( HWND hWnd,
                         UINT  message,
                         UINT  wParam,
                         LONG  lParam )
{
    //————
    switch ( message )
    {
```

continued

Listing 9-1: *continued*

```
        case WM_DESTROY:
            PostQuitMessage ( 0 );
            return DefWindowProc ( hWnd,
                                    message,
                                    wParam,
                                    lParam );
            break;
        case WM_COMMAND:
            {
                ModalDialogHandler    modalBox;
                //————————-
                //
                // Have the modal dialog box
                // handler create the modal
                // dialog box
                //
                modalBox.CreateSelf ( hWnd,
                                    "TestDialog",
                                    (FARPROC)SkeletonDlgProc,
                                    hInst );

                return DefWindowProc ( hWnd,
                                    message,
                                    wParam,
                                    lParam );
            }
            break;

        case WM_CREATE:
            return DefWindowProc ( hWnd,
                                    message,
                                    wParam,
                                    lParam );
            break;
        default:
            return DefWindowProc ( hWnd,
                                    message,
                                    wParam,
                                    lParam );
            break;
    }
    return FALSE;      // Returns FALSE if processed
}
```

Listing 9-2, Skelinit.cpp, is the initialization and cleanup code for the skeleton application. This code handles special stuff that we need on a per-application basis. However, in this case there isn't anything that I need to handle, so the code is unchanged from my standard do-nothing skeleton app.

Listing 9-2: Skelinit.cpp

```
//
// SKELINIT.CPP
//
//     Initialization routines for the skeleton
// application
//
//
#include <skeleton.hpp>


//————————————
//
// SkeletonInitApplication()
//
//     Initialize the application.
//
     BOOL
SkeletonInitApplication ( HINSTANCE  hInst,
             HINSTANCEhPrev,
             int       *pCmdSHow,
             LPSTR     lpCmd )
{
    //
    // Setup the values for the dialog box...
    //
    rbSetting = 0;
    cbSetting = 0;
    return TRUE;
}


//————————-
//
// SkeletonRegisterClass()
//
//     Registers the skeleton class
//
     BOOL
```

continued

Listing 9-2 *continued*

```
SkeletonRegisterClass ( HINSTANCE    hInstance )
{
    WNDCLASS WndClass;
    //————————-
    hMBrush = CreateSolidBrush(RGB(192,192,192));
    WndClass.style        = 0;
    WndClass.lpfnWndProc    = SkeletonMainWindowProc;
    WndClass.cbClsExtra    = 0;
    WndClass.cbWndExtra    = 0;
    WndClass.hInstance     = hInstance;
    WndClass.hIcon         = LoadIcon ( hInstance,
                        "SKELETON" );
    WndClass.hCursor       = LoadCursor ( NULL,
                    IDC_ARROW );
    WndClass.hbrBackground = hMBrush;
    WndClass.lpszMenuName  = "SKELETON";
    WndClass.lpszClassName = "SKELETON";

    return RegisterClass(&WndClass);
}
//————————-
//
// SkeletonCreateWindow()
//
//    Creates the main skeleton window
//
    HWND
SkeletonCreateWindow ( HINSTANCE    hInstance )
{
    HWND   hWnd;
    int    coords[4];
    //————————
    coords [ 0 ] = CW_USEDEFAULT;
    coords [ 1 ] = 0;
    coords [ 2 ] = CW_USEDEFAULT;
    coords [ 3 ] = 0;
    hWnd = CreateWindow (
                "SKELETON",
                "Skeleton Application",
                WS_OVERLAPPED | WS_THICKFRAME | WS_SYSMENU | WS_MINI-
MIZEBOX | WS_MAXIMIZEBOX,
            coords [ 0 ],
            coords [ 1 ],
            coords [ 2 ],
```

```
            coords [ 3 ],
            0,            // Parent handle
            0,            // Child id
            hInstance,    // Instance handle
            (LPSTR)NULL ); // No additional info
    return hWnd;
}
//————————--
//
// SkeletonExitApp()
//
//   Does any final cleanup...
//
    void
SkeletonExitApp( void )
{
    //————————--
    if ( hMBrush )
    {
        DeleteObject ( hMBrush );
        hMBrush = 0;
    }
}
```

Listing 9-3, Skeldlg.cpp, is where all the good stuff is. This is the dialog handler, and associated routines, which deal with the display and selection of items in the list box, and how those items are displayed and moved.

SkeletonDlgProc() itself is the routine which handles all the messages for the dialog box. The address of this procedure is what we pass in to the instance of the **ModalDialogHandler()** class when we create it. **SkeletonDlgProc()** is the one responsible for figuring out if we single-or-double clicked inside a list box, and what to do when that happens. **MoveEntry()**, the other big routine in this file, is responsible for actually removing a text entry from one list box, and putting it in the other list box.

Listing 9-3   Skeldlg.cpp

```
//
// Skeldlg.cpp
```

Listing 9-3 *continued*

```
//
//    Skeleton dialog procedure code
//
#include <skeleton.hpp>
//—————————
//
// SkeletonDlgProc()
//
//    Dialog box procedure for the cursor control panel
//
//
    BOOL FAR PASCAL
SkeletonDlgProc ( HWND hDlg,
                  UINT message,
                  UINT wParam,
                  LONG lParam )
{
    WORD    screenWidth;
    WORD    screenHeight;
    int     i;
    RECT    rectal;
    //—————————
    switch ( message )
    {
       case WM_INITDIALOG:
           //
           // This code here allows us to center
           // the dialog in the middle of the
           // screen, regardless of resolution
           //
           screenWidth = GetSystemMetrics ( SM_CXSCREEN );
           screenHeight = GetSystemMetrics ( SM_CYSCREEN );
           GetWindowRect ( hDlg,
                           &rectal );
           screenWidth -= ( rectal.right - rectal.left );
           screenHeight -= ( rectal.bottom - rectal.top );
           screenWidth /= 2;
           screenHeight /= 2;
           MoveWindow ( hDlg,
                        screenWidth,
                        screenHeight,
                        rectal.right - rectal.left,
                        rectal.bottom - rectal.top,
                        TRUE );
```

```
    //
    //
    // All done with moving the screen,
    // now let's fill the list box on the
    // left.
    //
    AddListBoxElements ( hDlg );
    return TRUE;   // TRUE means Windows will continue processing
    break;
case WM_COMMAND:
    switch ( LOWORD ( wParam ) )
    {
        case IDC_LISTBOX1:
            //
            // HIWORD ( lParam ) gives us
            // the notification code for
            // the listbox...
            //
            switch ( HIWORD ( lParam ) )
            {
                case LBN_SELCHANGE:         // Single click
                    break;
                case LBN_DBLCLK:            // Move entry over
                                            // to other listbox

                    MoveEntry ( hDlg,

                                IDC_LISTBOX1,
                                IDC_LISTBOX2 );

                    break;
                default:
                    return FALSE;           // Not handled
            }
            break;
        case IDC_LISTBOX2:
            //
            // HIWORD ( lParam ) gives us
            // the notification code for
            // the listbox...
            //
            switch ( HIWORD ( lParam ) )
            {
                case LBN_SELCHANGE:         // Single click
                    break;
                case LBN_DBLCLK:            // Move entry over
                                            // to other listbox

                    MoveEntry ( hDlg,
```

continued

Listing 9-3   *continued*

```
                                        IDC_LISTBOX2,
                                        IDC_LISTBOX1 );
                    break;
                default:
                    return FALSE;                // Not handled
            }
            break;

        case ID_AddButton:
            MoveEntry ( hDlg,
                        IDC_LISTBOX1,
                        IDC_LISTBOX2 );
            break;
        case ID_RemoveButton:
            MoveEntry ( hDlg,
                        IDC_LISTBOX2,
                        IDC_LISTBOX1 );
            break;
        case IDOK: // All done, cleanup and go home...
            //
            // Ok, all done, punt...
            //
            EndDialog ( hDlg,
                        IDOK );
            break;
        case IDCANCEL:
            EndDialog ( hDlg,
                        IDCANCEL );
            break;
        default:
            return FALSE;      // Didn't process message
        }
        break;
    default:
        return FALSE; // Didn't process message...
        break;
    }
    return TRUE;
}
//——————————-
//
// AddListBoxElements()
//
```

```
    void WINAPI
AddListBoxElements ( HWND hDlg )
{
    //───────────
    DlgDirList ( hDlg,
                 "*.*",
                 IDC_LISTBOX1,
                 NULL,
                 DDL_READWRITE );
}
//─────────────-
//
// MoveEntry()
//
//    Moves the current selection
// from the source box to the
// destination box.
//
    void WINAPI
MoveEntry ( HWND   hDlg,
            WORD   srcBox,
            WORD   destBox )
{
    int    lResult;
    char   fooBuff [ 128 ];
    //──────────-
    //
    // First, get the current selection
    // in the source list box
    //
    lResult = LOWORD ( SendDlgItemMessage ( hDlg,
                                            srcBox,
                                            LB_GETCURSEL,
                                            0,
                                            0L ) );
    //
    // If the result is LB_ERR, then there
    // is no selection, so don't do anything.
    //
    if ( lResult != LB_ERR )
    {
        //
        // Ok, there is a current selection.
        // Please remove it from the source
        // box, and put it in the destination
```

continued

Listing 9-3   *continued*

```
// box.
//
//
// Make sure the text string isn't too
// long for our buffer.  (This isn't going
// to happen in our example program, but
// it could happen in real life.  Here's
// how to check for it...)
//

if ( LOWORD ( SendDlgItemMessage ( hDlg,
                                   srcBox,

                                   LB_GETTEXTLEN,
                                   lResult,
                                   0 ) ) < 128 )
    {
    //
    // Get the text from the selected
    // item here...
    //
    SendDlgItemMessage ( hDlg,
                         srcBox,
                         LB_GETTEXT,
                         lResult,
                         (LPARAM) fooBuff );
    //
    // Ok, delete the item from
    // the source list box
    //
    SendDlgItemMessage ( hDlg,
                         srcBox,
                         LB_DELETESTRING,
                         lResult,
                         0L );
    //
    // ...and add it to the
    // destination list box
    //
    SendDlgItemMessage ( hDlg,
                         destBox,
                         LB_ADDSTRING,
                         0,
                         (LPARAM) fooBuff );
```

```
        }
    }
}
```

Listing 9-4, Skelvars.cpp, contains all the global variables used by the skeleton application. In this case, since we don't have any custom variables, these are just the three standard variables—hMBrush, a grey brush for drawing the background; MainhWnd, the main window handle; and hInst, the instance of this application.

Listing 9-4: Skelvars.cpp

```
//
// SKELVARS.CPP
//
//  Global variables for the skeleton application
//
//
#define __SKELETON_GLOBAL_VARS
#include <skeleton.hpp>
//——————————————————————--
//
// All the following are standard global
// variables used by the skeleton application
//
HBRUSH      hMBrush;   // Brush for window background
HWND        MainhWnd;  // Main window handle
HINSTANCE   hInst;     // Instance handle that we need

//————————————————--
//
// Add custom variables here
//
```

Listing 9-5, Skeleton.hpp, is my single point of inclusion include file. As I've mentioned elsewhere (and in detail in my book *Visual C++: A Developer's Guide*), I like having a single include file that all source files will include, because it eliminates many kinds of problems that occur when different files have different views of what the rest of the world looks like. Having a single include file ensures that all the source files are speaking the same language.

Listing 9-5   Skeleton.hpp

```
//
// SKELETON.HPP
//
//     Mondo include file for
// the skeleton app.
//
//   __EVERYTHING__ gets included here, ONCE.
//
// That's it.
//
#ifndef __SKELETON_HPP
#define __SKELETON_HPP
//————————————-
#include <WINDOWS.H>
#include <gocl.hpp>              // GOCL definitions
#include <skelextn.hpp>          // Externs for the global variables
#include <skelprot.hpp>          // Prototypes for all functions in skele-
ton
#include <skelincs.hpp>


//————————————-

#endif // __SKELETON_HPP
```

Listing 9-6, Skeldfns.hpp, defines all the numerical identifiers that are used in the dialog box that we are working with. They are packaged in this fashion so that both the resource compiler and the C++ compiler can access them.

Listing 9-6   Skeldfns.hpp

```
//
// SKELDFNS.HPP
//
//     Defines used by the skeleton application
//
#ifndef __SKELDFNS_HPP
#define __SKELDFNS_HPP
//————————————-
#define CB_ONE      0x01
#define CB_TWO      0x02
```

```
//————
#define    SKELETON_BASE_ID   4000
#define IDC_LISTBOX1       SKELETON_BASE_ID + 1
#define ID_AddButton       SKELETON_BASE_ID + 2
#define ID_RemoveButton        SKELETON_BASE_ID + 3
#define IDC_LISTBOX2       SKELETON_BASE_ID + 4
//————
#define    ID_SkeletonExit            SKELETON_BASE_ID + 0

//———————————-
#endif // __SKELDFNS_HPP
```

Listing 9-7, Skelextn.hpp, is the file containing all of our externalized global variables. This allows all source files equal access to the variables, and also ensures that all files think they are the same *kind* of variable.

Listing 9-7   Skelextn.hpp

```
//
// SKELEXTN.HPP
//
//     External define file for the skeleton app
//
//
#ifndef __SKELETON_GLOBAL_VARS
#define __SKELETON_GLOBAL_VARS
//———————————

extern HBRUSH     hMBrush;    // Brush for window background
extern HWND       MainhWnd;   // Main window handle
extern HINSTANCE  hInst;      // Instance handle that we need

//———————————-
//
// Add custom variables here
//
//———————————


#endif // __SKELETON_GLOBAL_VARS
```

Listing 9-8, Skelincs.hpp, is simply a wrapper file that we include in skeleton.hpp. This file, in turn, includes several other files; we've packaged it this way because it allows us to easily have both the resource compiler and the C++ compiler access the same numerical defines without certain other problems. The resource compiler, in particular, cannot handle certain kinds of statements that are legal in C++; if we simply tried to include the same files for the resource compiler as we do the C++ compiler, the resource compiler would choke. So we do it this way:

Listing 9-8   Skelincs.hpp

```
//
// SKELINCS.HPP
//
//    Skeleton includes.
//
//    Packaged this way so that both the
// .cpp files and the .rc files can
// use them.
//
#ifndef __SKELINCS_HPP
#define __SKELINCS_HPP
//———————————
#include <WINDOWS.H>
#include <skeldfns.hpp>        // Resource and other ID defines

//———————————
#endif // __SKELINCS_HPP
```

Listing 9-9, Skelprot.hpp are the prototypes for all the functions that we use in our program.

Listing 9-9   Skelprot.hpp

```
//
// SKELPROT.HPP
//
//    Prototype file
//
#ifndef __SKELETON_PROTOTYPES_HPP
#define __SKELETON_PROTOTYPES_HPP
//———————————--
//———————————--
//
```

```
// Extern C wrappers
//
#ifdef __cplusplus
extern "C" {
#endif
//─────────────────────-
    int PASCAL
WinMain ( HINSTANCE   hInstance,
      HINSTANCEhPrevInstance,
      LPSTR    lpCmdLine,
      int      nCmdShow );
    LONG FAR PASCAL
SkeletonMainWindowProc ( HWND hWnd,
          UINT   message,
          UINT   wParam,
          LONG   lParam );
    BOOL
SkeletonInitApplication ( HINSTANCE   hInst,
          HINSTANCEhPrev,
          int      *pCmdSHow,
          LPSTR    lpCmd );
    BOOL
SkeletonRegisterClass ( HINSTANCE     hInstance );
    HWND
SkeletonCreateWindow ( HINSTANCE      hInstance );
    void
SkeletonExitApp( void );
    BOOL FAR PASCAL
SkeletonDlgProc ( HWNDhDlg,
            UINT message,
            UINT wParam,
            LONG lParam );
    void WINAPI
AddListBoxElements ( HWND hDlg );
    void WINAPI
MoveEntry ( HWND   hDlg,
        WORD   srcBox,
        WORD   destBox );


//───────────────────-
//──────────────────--
//
// Extern C wrappers
//
#ifdef __cplusplus
```

continued

Listing 9-9 *continued*

```
};
#endif

//————————————-

#endif // __SKELETON_PROTOTYPES__HPP
```

Listing 9-10, Skeleton.rc, is the main resource file for our project. Of course, in this project we don't have much in the way of resources (the only really important resource we have is the dialog box, and it's contained in a separate file), so this file is quite small. Still, we have to make sure that we have our menu entry, so that we can fire up our dialog box on request.

Listing 9-10: Skeleton.rc

```
//
// Skeleton.rc
//
#include <skelincs.hpp>
#include <cppres.rc>
#include <skeleton.dlg>
//——————————-
//
// Bitmaps, icons, cursors
//
SKELETON    ICON        SKELETON.ICO

//——————————-
//
// Menus
//
SKELETON MENU
{
 POPUP "Skeleton"
 {
  MENUITEM "Dialog Box", ID_SkeletonExit
 }

}
```

Listing 9-11, Skeleton.dlg, is the file which contains the source code for our dialog box. As you can see, we've got the listbox controls defined with numerically equated ID's—IDC_LISTBOX1 and IDC_LISTBOX2. This allows us to refer to these controls in our source code as well, without having to worry about what the numerical value of the id is. It also allows us to change the id's of the controls (either in a resource editor, or by hand) without having to go into our source code and make changes there.

Listing 9-11: Skeleton.dlg

```
//
// Skeleton.dlg
//
//   File which holds the
// dialog definition for
// our standard dialog box.
//


TestDialog DIALOG 34, 34, 199, 179
STYLE DS_MODALFRAME | WS_POPUP | WS_VISIBLE | WS_CAPTION | WS_SYSMENU
CAPTION "Listbox dialog"
FONT 8, "MS Sans Serif"
{
 DEFPUSHBUTTON "OK", IDOK, 44, 153, 50, 14
 PUSHBUTTON "Cancel", IDCANCEL, 111, 153, 50, 14
 LISTBOX IDC_LISTBOX1, 7, 22, 64, 99, LBS_STANDARD
 PUSHBUTTON ">>>", ID_AddButton, 81, 30, 38, 19
 PUSHBUTTON "<<<", ID_RemoveButton, 82, 59, 38, 22
 LISTBOX IDC_LISTBOX2, 129, 22, 64, 99, LBS_STANDARD
}
```

THE LISTBOX APPLICATION IN ACTION

Now that you've seen the source code for the listbox application (and no doubt tried it out from the disk), it's time to take a look at the really exciting parts internally.

Of course, since this is a modified version of the skeleton application, I'm going to skip over the standard bits about window class initiation, and so on, and jump right into the good stuff—the dialog box handler, and how it works.

There are really two pieces to the dialog box handler that are of interest to us—how the list box gets filled, and how we deal with adding and deleting items from the listboxes. We'll take a look at the second problem first.

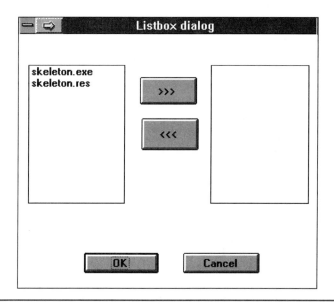

FIGURE 9-3 THE LISTBOX APPLICATION IN ACTION. NOTICE THAT THE LEFT LIST BOX HAS A LISTING OF ALL THE FILES IN THE STARTUP DIRECTORY, AND THE RIGHT LISTBOX DOESN'T HAVE (AS YET) ANY FILES.

Here's the code for the routine **MoveEntry()**. We'll break it down a line at a time.

```
//——————————-
//
// MoveEntry()
//
//   Moves the current selection
```

```
// from the source box to the
// destination box.
//
```

The first thing to notice here is that we are passing three parameters into the function—the dialog window handle, and the ID's of the source and destination list boxes. We're going to be using the source and destination listbox ID's to pass messages to the two boxes. The tricky thing about this is the fact that it doesn't matter which list box is our source and which is our destination; the procedure that we use to remove a string from one list box and put it in the other listbox is exactly the same, whether we're moving a string from the left listbox to the right, or vice versa. We can take advantage of this fact to write a single routine which will move a string from one listbox to the other, and then call the routine with different parameters to move the string either left or right.

```
    void WINAPI
MoveEntry ( HWND    hDlg,
            WORD    srcBox,
            WORD    destBox )
{
    int     lResult;
    char    fooBuff [ 128 ];
    //————————-
    //
    // First, get the current selection
    // in the source list box
    //
```

We need to make sure that there is, in fact, a selection in the source list box. A listbox doesn't always have a selected item in it, and this code tests for that.

```
    lResult = LOWORD ( SendDlgItemMessage ( hDlg,
                                srcBox,
                                LB_GETCURSEL,
                                0,
                                0L ) );
    //
    // If the result is LB_ERR, then there
    // is no selection, so don't do anything.
    //
```

Only if the result of the LB_GETCURSEL message is not LB_ERR will we execute the code in this if statement. This is our test to ensure that the source list box has a selection in it.

```
if ( lResult != LB_ERR )
{
    //
    // Ok, there is a current selection.
    // Please remove it from the source
    // box, and put it in the destination
    // box.
    //
    //
    // Make sure the text string isn't too
    // long for our buffer.  (This isn't going
    // to happen in our example program, but
    // it could happen in real life.  Here's
    // how to check for it...)
    //
```

Since we know that the source listbox has a selection in it, we might be tempted to simply send a LB_GETTEXT message to the listbox to retrieve the text. In this case, that would be fine, since we know that the longest string in the listbox is going to be an 8.3 filename (12 characters at the most), which will easily fit inside our string buffer of 128 bytes. However, for the general purpose case where we don't know how long a string is, it's best to first check how *big* a string is before trying to retrieve it. Failing to do this might result in attempting to retrieve a string that's bigger than our buffer; and since the LB_GETTEXT message doesn't do any bounds-checking, we could blow up if this happened.

```
if ( LOWORD ( SendDlgItemMessage (   hDlg,
                                     srcBox,
                                     LB_GETTEXTLEN,
                                     lResult,
                                     0 ) ) < 128 )
{
    //
    // Get the text from the selected
    // item here...
    //
```

If this statement passes as true, the text string that we want to retrieve is smaller than the size of the buffer that we want to put it in. Go ahead and retrieve the text string here.

```
SendDlgItemMessage ( hDlg,
                srcBox,
                LB_GETTEXT,
                lResult,
                (LPARAM) fooBuff );
//
// Ok, delete the item from
// the source list box
//
```

Now that we've gotten the text string out of the source listbox, we need to delete it from the source listbox. Send the LB_DELETESTRING to the source listbox to cause the string to be deleted.

```
SendDlgItemMessage ( hDlg,
                srcBox,
                LB_DELETESTRING,
                lResult,
                0L );
//
// ...and add it to the
// destination list box
//
```

We've deleted the text string from the source list box, and now we want to add it to the destination listbox. Send the LB_ADDSTRING message to the destination list box to do this. The LB_ADDSTRING message will cause the listbox to be sorted as well, since we created both our listboxes with the LBS_HASSTRINGS style flag.

```
SendDlgItemMessage ( hDlg,
                destBox,
                LB_ADDSTRING,
                0,
                (LPARAM) fooBuff );
        }
    }
}
```

And that's it!

To recap, the process of moving a string from one list box to another is as follows:

1. Get the current selection in the source list box (ensuring that there is, in fact, a selection at all). Message: LB_GETCURSEL

2. Make sure that the currently selected string will fit in our string buffer (alternatively, you could use this size to dynamically allocate some memory for the string. Just be sure to allocate at least 1 more byte than the returned size, since the returned size does *not* include the NULL character at the end of the string.) Message: LB_GETTEXTLEN.

3. If the string will fit in the buffer, retrieve the string. Message: LB_GETTEXT.

4. Delete the string from the source listbox. Message: LB_DELETESTRING.

5. Add the string to the destination listbox. Message: LB_ADDSTRING.

Okay, so that's how our function works, but how do we access it? In other words, under what circumstances should we call this routine? Here's the code from the dialog procedure that's responsible for that:

```
switch ( LOWORD ( wParam ) )
{
    case IDC_LISTBOX1:
        //
        // HIWORD ( lParam ) gives us
        // the notification code for
        // the listbox...
        //
        switch ( HIWORD ( lParam ) )
        {
            case LBN_SELCHANGE:                 // Single click
                break;
            case LBN_DBLCLK:            // Move entry over
                            // to other listbox
```

```
                    MoveEntry ( hDlg,
                            IDC_LISTBOX1,
                            IDC_LISTBOX2 );
                    break;
                default:
                    return FALSE;         // Not handled
            }
            break;
        case IDC_LISTBOX2:
            //
            // HIWORD ( lParam ) gives us
            // the notification code for
            // the listbox...
            //
            switch ( HIWORD ( lParam ) )
            {
                case LBN_SELCHANGE:                // Single click
                    break;
                case LBN_DBLCLK:          // Move entry over
                                    // to other listbox
                    MoveEntry ( hDlg,
                            IDC_LISTBOX2,
                            IDC_LISTBOX1 );
                    break;
                default:
                    return FALSE;         // Not handled
            }
            break;
        case ID_AddButton:
            MoveEntry ( hDlg,
                    IDC_LISTBOX1,
                    IDC_LISTBOX2 );
            break;
        case ID_RemoveButton:
            MoveEntry ( hDlg,
                    IDC_LISTBOX2,
                    IDC_LISTBOX1 );
            break;
}
```

As you can see, we call the **MoveEntry()** function under one of the following four conditions:

◆ Double click in the left listbox

✦ Double click in the right listbox

✦ Single click on the >>> (Add) button

✦ Single click on the <<< (Remove) button

The only difference in how we call **MoveEntry()** is in which listbox is acting as the source, and which is acting as the destination. However, what we want to have happen (deleting the text string from one list box, and putting it into the other listbox) is always the same. Therefore, we can use the same series of messages, and just direct them to the appropriate list box.

USING LISTBOX ITEM DATA ELEMENTS

If you've looked over Table 9-2, or browsed through volume 3 of the Windows SDK, you might be intrigued by the messages LB_SETITEM-DATA and LB_GETITEMDATA. These two messages allow you to set and retrieve a double word value (essentially a long pointer, although you can use it for whatever you want) for each element in the list box.

This can be extremely handy, because it gives you a way of associating data directly with each entry in the listbox. Suppose, for example, each entry had a corresponding data structure associated with it. Rather than building some sort of mapping function between entries and data structures, you could simply put the pointer for the data structure of a particular entry right along with that entry. Then, whenever you wanted the data structure for a particular entry, you could simply retrieve the pointer and use it to access the data structure.

What makes the item data element so powerful is that the listbox handles most of the management of it. If an element in the listbox gets sorted, then the item data of that element goes right along with it.

Of course, you don't have to use the item data DWORD as a pointer. It might simply be a unique token that you've got associated with that entry, acting like a key value. Instead of having to compare strings to find out what entry was selected, you could check the token value.

A couple of points are worth noting—if you are moving an entry from one listbox to another, (as in our example program), you must also *explicitly* move the item data. That is, if you use the steps outlined above to move a string, you must also do this:

◆ Before deleting the string from the source listbox, you must send a LB_GETITEMDATA message to retrieve the value of the DWORD associated with the entry.

◆ After adding the string to the destination listbox, you must use the return value of LB_ADDSTRING (which gives the position of the string in the destination listbox) as the index for the message LB_SETITEMDATA, which you will send to the destination listbox, along with the value of the DWORD data.

In other words, you must not only copy the string itself across, but you must also copy across the item data. Here's an updated version of **MoveEntry()** that copies not only the string element, but the item data element as well.

```
    void WINAPI
MoveEntry ( HWND   hDlg,
            WORD   srcBox,
            WORD   destBox )
{
    int     lResult;
    char    fooBuff [ 128 ];
    LRESULT itemData;
    //———————--
    //
    // First, get the current selection
    // in the source list box
    //
    lResult = LOWORD ( SendDlgItemMessage ( hDlg,
                                    srcBox,
                                    LB_GETCURSEL,
                                    0,
                                    OL ) );
    //
    // If the result is LB_ERR, then there
    // is no selection, so don't do anything.
```

```
//
if ( lResult != LB_ERR )
{
    //
    // Ok, there is a current selection.
    // Please remove it from the source
    // box, and put it in the destination
    // box.
    //
    //
    // Make sure the text string isn't too
    // long for our buffer.  (This isn't going
    // to happen in our example program, but
    // it could happen in real life.  Here's
    // how to check for it...)
    //

    if ( LOWORD ( SendDlgItemMessage (   hDlg,
                                      srcBox,
                                      LB_GETTEXTLEN,
                                      lResult,
                                      0 ) ) < 128 )
    {
        //
        // Get the text from the selected
        // item here...
        //
        SendDlgItemMessage ( hDlg,
                    srcBox,
                    LB_GETTEXT,
                    lResult,
                    (LPARAM) fooBuff );
```

Here, we're going to get the itemData item associated with the currently selected entry.

```
        // New code
        itemData = SendDlgItemMessage ( hDlg,
                                srcBox,
                                LB_GETITEMDATA,
                                lResult,
                                0L );
        //
        // Ok, delete the item from
        // the source list box
```

```
            //
            SendDlgItemMessage ( hDlg,
                         srcBox,
                         LB_DELETESTRING,
                         lResult,
                         0L );
            //
            // ...and add it to the
            // destination list box
            //
            lResult = LOWORD ( SendDlgItemMessage ( hDlg,
                                         destBox,
                                 LB_ADDSTRING,
                                 0,
                         (LPARAM) fooBuff );
```

Now that we've the string to the new listbox, we now have the position that the string occupies in the list box (this is the value returned from the LB_ADDSTRING message); we use this to insert the item data at the right point, using the LB_SETITEMDATA message.

```
            // New code
            SendDlgItemMessage ( hDlg,
                         destBox,
                         LB_SETITEMDATA,
                         lResult,
                         itemData );
        }
    }
}
```

Now that we've examined how to manipulate the strings inside a list-box, let's take a look at how we got the strings in there in the first place. The following function **AddListBoxElements()** does this

```
    void WINAPI
AddListBoxElements ( HWND hDlg )
{
    //─────────
    DlgDirList ( hDlg,
             "*.*",
             IDC_LISTBOX1,
```

```
            NULL,
            DDL_READWRITE );
}
```

As you can see, there's really very little here—just a call to **DlgDirList()**, which fills the listbox with a directory listing.

DLGDIRLIST: A WARNING

The Windows call **DlgDirList()** is used to fill a listbox with a file or directory listing. In essence, it provides a simple way for you to fill a listbox with a set of filenames. I've used this function to provide a list of filenames for users to select (I used **DlgDirList()** in my IconPanel program to allow users to select animation files and sound files). Of course, we also just used it in our sample program. Here's the format of the call:

```
DlgDirList (   hDlg,       // Dialog window handle
          lpFilePath,// Pointer to string with
                     // file path info in it
          ID_ListBox,// ID of listbox to be
                     // used
          ID_Static, // ID of static control
                     // to receive current
                     // drive
                     // and directory
          fileAttribs ); // List of file
                     // attributes.
```

Everything about this looks pretty straightforward. You provide the parent window handle (the dialog box containing the list box control), the string which specifies the file and/or path (i.e., "e:\\sounds*.wav" or "*.*"), the ID of the list box, the ID of the static control which will get the current drive and path, and the attributes of the files that you want displayed (such as hidden, read-only, etc.).

If you read the Windows documentation, you'll find that the **DlgDirList()** function sends the messages LB_RESETCONTENT and

LB_DIR messages to the list box. If you're not using the static control to display the file path, you might be tempted to substitute the following lines of code:

```
SendDlgItemMessage (  hDlg,
                      ID_ListBox,
                      LB_RESETCONTENT,
                      0,
                      0L );
SendDlgItemMessage (  hDlg,
                      ID_ListBox,
                      LB_DIR,
                      0,
                      (LPARAM)lpFilePath );
```

and expect to get pretty much the same results. In fact, you do—the list-box will be filled with the same files, and everything will look just fine. However, all is not well.

In particular, the current working directory of your program is *not* the same. If you use the **DlgDirList()** example, above, and then perform a file open, the working directory will be e:\sounds. If you use the two messages below, and perform a file open, the working directory will be simply e:, or wherever your program originally executed from. In other words, **DlgDirList()** not only fills your listbox with the files you want, but it *also* sets your current working directory to be the directory you specified in the lpFilePath parameter.

In contrast, simply sending the two messages shown above will *not* set your current working directory to the path specified by lpFilePath. If you simply use the two messages, nothing at all is done to your current working directory.

I once changed over from the **DlgDirList()** method to the two message method, and discovered that I could no long open the files that I was seeing in the listbox. This is because my working directory was no longer being set to the place I thought it was. I spent a good deal of time scratching my head, and debugging my code, trying to figure out what was going wrong. All the code was working fine—it just could no longer open the file that I'd just obtained from the listbox. It finally dawned on me that maybe **DlgDirList()** was doing something *other* than simply sending those two messages.

Not having the working directory set may or may not be good for you—there can be times when not having the current working directory set can be an advantage-—but it certainly isn't documented anywhere that I've ever seen, and it sure caused me some headaches until I figured out what was going on.

The solution I used was to use both the two messages *and* **DlgDirList()**; the two messages caused the listbox to be filled, and the new version of **DlgDirList()** set the current working directory to the proper place. It turns out that you can not specify either the listbox or the static control to **DlgDirList**; when you do that, it doesn't fill in any controls, but simply sets the current working directory to the specified path. Here's how that call looks now:

```
DlgDirList (   hDlg,
        lpFilePath,
        NULL,
        NULL,
        DDL_READWRITE );
```

This has the effect of setting the current working directory to be whatever the path is specified by lpFilePath; however, nothing visible happens, since we've specified neither a listbox or a static control.

You may be wondering *why* I'm doing this—after all, doesn't **DlgDirList()** work just fine? Yes, it does, provided that you're using a standard listbox control. However, I was using a third-party listbox control—one that looked and behaved exactly like a list box, but which had additional capabilities. The problem with using **DlgDirList()** under those circumstances is that under the debugging kernel of Windows (or under a debugger such as BoundsChecker for Windows), using **DlgDirList()** on a control which is not a standard

Windows list box causes a fatal error to occur (you know, the "Fatal Error, Abort, Break or Ignore?" message). Mind you, there's nothing actually wrong—the third party listbox *works* just like a listbox control—it's just that it will generate this message.

People running the retail version of Windows will never know, or care, of course; however, it's good practice to make sure that you program doesn't crash or croak when put under the debugging kernel, or a really serious debugger.

LISTBOXES AND THIRD PARTY CONTROLS

Incidentally, the reason I was using the third party control was that it provided great owner draw listbox capabilities. Take a look at figure 9-4, and you'll see what I mean. On the right is a standard listbox, and on the left is the third-party listbox.

The third party controls that I use are the Blaise custom controls, from Innovative Data Concepts (122 North York Road, Suite 5, Hatboro, PA 19040, (215) 443-9705). Their listbox provides an easy method for doing owner-draw listboxes without much of the sweat involved in calculating font sizes and attributes. You simply respond to a series of messages that ask you to provide a bitmap for the current item, and the listbox control takes care of the rest. (In fact, you'll find my **ListboxBitmap()** class in the GOCL library. This class makes it even simpler to use the Blaise listbox, by doing all the work of creating the selected and unselected bitmaps for you.)

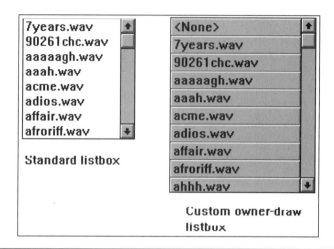

FIGURE 9-4   A STANDARD LISTBOX, AND A THIRD PARTY CUSTOM CONTROL LISTBOX. THE THIRD
PARTY CONTROL PROVIDES SIGNIFICANTLY ENHANCED FUNCTIONALITY WHEN IT
COMES TO DRAWING THE LISTBOX ELEMENTS

I've been using the Blaise controls for over three years, and have found them to be extremely useful and reliable. If you're looking for a good third party custom control library that will give you good looking 3-D controls (there are radio buttons, check boxes, and all the usual Windows controls), then I'd recommend Blaise highly. (I paid my own money for them, too—that's how good I think they are.)

COMBO BOXES

Now that we've explored list boxes in depth, it's time to take a look at combo boxes. Fortunately we've already covered a great deal of the ground with the list boxes.

Why is this? Simple. A combo box is nothing but a combination of a list box and a control—either an edit control or a static text control. Take a look at figure 9-5, which shows the three different kinds of combo boxes.

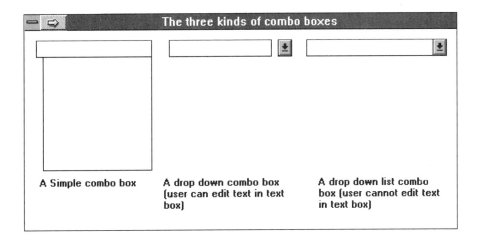

FIGURE 9-5   THE THREE TYPES OF COMBO BOXES—SIMPLE, DROP DOWN, AND DROP DOWN LIST. THE DROP DOWN LIST COMBO BOX HAS A STATIC EDIT CONTROL (MEANING THE USER CANNOT EDIT WHAT'S IN THERE), WHILE THE OTHER TWO HAVE EDIT CONTROLS ALONG WITH THE LIST BOX.

What do you use combo boxes for? Really, there are a couple of answers, depending upon what style of combo box you choose. Working backwards, here's a list of the combo box styles, and some of the things that people have done with them.

> *Drop down list combo box.* Used to select "one of a" kinds of things; that is, one of a set of several possible options. This is a nice way of letting the user select a particular item without having the entire list of selections around all the time. Drop down list combo boxes are also popular in file open dialogs, and other dialogs which require browsing the user's drives.
>
> *Drop down combo box.* Like the drop down list combo box, the drop down combo box is used to select "one of a" kinds of things. Unlike the drop down list, however, this kind of box also lets the user enter their own information into the edit field of the combo box. This is useful where there are several sets of information that can be variable in nature and length. For example, this kind of

combo box is used by the Borland 4.0 C++ IDE to display source and include path information; you can select from a path that you've already typed in, or you can type in a new path.

Simple combo box. This kind of combo box is like a drop down combo box, except that the list box portion of the control is visible all the time. This means that this kind of combo box is good for the same things that the drop down is—selecting single-choice information, where that information is variable in length and can be edited by the user. However, because of the larger screen requirements of this control versus the drop down combo box, I see very few applications that use it.

Now that we've taken a look at the three styles of combo box, let's take a look at the various style flags that combo boxes can be created with. These styles can be set in the **CreateWindow()** call, or using a dialog editor.

Table 9-3 Combo box styles

STYLE	DESCRIPTION
CBS_AUTOHSCROLL	Automatically scrolls the text in the edit control to the right when the user types a character. If this style isn't set, then only text that fits inside the confines of the edit box is allowed.
CBS_DISABLENOSCROLL	Normally, a list box that does not have enough entries in it to justify a vertical scroll bar will hide the scroll bar (make it disappear). By using this style flag (or the appropriate dialog editor equivalent), you can make the scroll bar visible (but disabled) when there are not

	enough entries in the list box portion **of** the combo box.
CBS_DROPDOWN	The list box portion of the combo box is not visible unless the user presses the "down arrow" next to the edit control portion of the combo box.
CBS_DROPDOWNLIST	Same as CBS_DROPDOWN, except that the edit control portion of the combo box is replaced by a static text control that shows the current selection of the list box portion of the combo box.
CBS_HASSTRINGS	Specifies that the list box portion of the combo box contains items which are strings. Using this flag means that the listbox will handle all the memory and pointer manipulation of the strings (and will clean it all up). You can retrieve the text of a string by using the CB_GETLB-TEXT message.
CBS_NOINTEGRALHEIGHT	Prevents Windows from resizing the listbox portion of the combo box when it displays the listbox. Normally, Windows will grow or shrink a listbox slightly, so that the listbox will only display complete items. (Using this flag allows the display of partial items, which I don't recommend.)
CBS_OEMCONVERT	Converts text entered in the combo box edit control from the Windows character set to the OEM character

set, and then back to the Windows set. This ensures proper character conversion when the application calls the AnsiToOem() function to convert a Windows string in the combo box to OEM characters. Applies only to CBS_SIMPLE and CBS_DROPDOWN styles.

CBS_OWNERDRAWFIXED	Specifies that the owner of the combo box (i.e., your program) is responsible for drawing the elements in the edit control and listbox, and that the items are all the same height. The parent window receives a WM_MEASUREITEM message when the list box is created, and a WM_DRAWITEM message when elements in the box need to be redrawn.
CBS_OWNERDRAWVARIABLE	Same as CBS_OWNERDRAW-FIXED, except that the items in the listbox are assumed to be variable in height. The parent window receives a WM_MEASUREITEM for each item in the listbox, and a WM_DRAWITEM message when elements in the box need to be redrawn.
CBS_SIMPLE	The listbox portion of the combo box is displayed at all times. The current list box selection is displayed in the edit control.
CBS_SORT	Sorts the strings in the listbox alphabetically.

As with listboxes, combo boxes are manipulated primarily be sending messages to them. If you look over table 9-4, you'll see that many combo box messages are analogous to list box ones. LB_GETCURSEL and CB_GETCURSEL, for example, both return the current selection in the list box, if there is one. There are slight differences, of course—the list box in a combo box cannot have more than one selection, for example. However, if you know how to manipulate a list box, you're well on the way to manipulating a combo box.

Table 9-4   Combo box messages

Listbox message	wParam	lParam	Returns:	Comments
CB_ADDSTRING				
Adds a string to the listbox portion of the combo box	0	lpString	Zero based index of the string in the list box.	Adds a string to the listbox. If listbox is not sorted, the string is added at the end.
CB_DELETESTRING				
Deletes a string from the listbox portion of a combo box.	index	0L	Count of remaining strings.	Deletes the string specified by the value of index.
CB_DIR				
Fills the listbox portion of the combo box with a directory listing of files specified by the lpFileSpec pointer.	attrib-Flags	lpFile-Spec	Zero based index of last file added	If you're adding a file list, you should use CB_RESET-CONTENT to clear out the list box first.

CB_FINDSTRING

Matches the passed in-string as a prefix to the strings in the listbox. Works even if listbox strings are longer than the passed-in string	start-Index	lpFind-String	Index of the match-ing item, CB_ERR if there was no match.	If startIndex is -1, the entire list box is searched. lpFindString must be NULL terminated. Not case-sensitive.

CB_FINDSTRINGEXACT

Matches the passed-in string to the strings in the listbox. Must be an exact match. (Strings must be same length).	start-Index	lpFind-String	Index of the matching item, CB_ERR if there was no match.	If the startIndex is -1, the entire list box is searched. lpFind-String must be NULL ter-minated. Not casesensitive

CB_GETCOUNT

Returns a count of the number of items in the listbox.	0	0L	Number of items in the listbox.	Return count is 1 bigger than the index of the last element.

CB_GETCURSEL

Returns the index of the currently selected item in the listbox..	0	0L	Zero based index of the current selection. CB_ERR if there is none.	There may not be a currently selected item.

CB_GETDROPPEDCONTROLRECT

Retrieves the screen coordinates of the visible (dropped down) list box of a combo box.	0	lpRect	Always CB_OKAY	Lparam is a pointer to a RECT struct.

CB_GETDROPPEDSTATE

Detemines whether or not the list box portion of a combo box is visible (dropped down).	0	0L	Non zero if listbox is visible, Zero if listbox is not visible.	

CB_GETEXTENDEDUI

Detemines whether the combo box has the default user interface or the extended user interface.	0	0L	Non-zero if extended UI, zero if default UI.	Extended UI changes the behavior of the combo box slightly.

CB_GETITEMDATA

Returns the LONG value that was associated with the item entry.	item-Index	0L	The double-word value associated with the entry	Use the CB_SETITEM-DATA message to set the long word value of an item.

CB_GETITEMHEIGHT

Returns the height, in pixels, of items in the listbox.	item-Index	0L	Height, in pixels, of item(s) in the listbox.	The wParam value should only be used if the style CBS_OWNER-

				DRAWVAR-IABLE is used; otherwise it should be 0.

CB_GETLBTEXT

Retrieves the text string specified by itemIndex, and puts it into the buffer specified by lpStringBuff.	item-Index	lpString-Buff	Length of string (in bytes), not including NULL termination.	If the listbox is ownerdraw, but doesn't have the CBS_HAS-STRINGS style, the buffer recieves the longword associated with the entry.

CB_GETTEXTLEN

Returns the length of the string of the item specified by itemIndex.	item-Index	0L	Length of string (in bytes), not including NULL termination.	

CB_INSERTSTRING

Inserts the string pointed to by lpString into the listbox at the position indicated by itemIndex. If itemIndex is -1, string is inserted at the end of the listbox.	item-Index	lpString	Index of the position at whichthe string was inserted.	This message does not cause a listbox with the CBS_SORT style to be sorted. Will return CBS_ERRSPACE if there isn't enough space for the string.

CB_LIMITTEXT

Limits the length of the text entry that a user may type into the edit control of the combo box	text-Limit	0L	1 if the message was successful	This message only limits what a user may type—it does not limit strings already in the list box.

CB_RESETCONTENT

Removes all items from the listbox and edit control of a combo box.	0	0L	Nothing	If ownerdraw, but not CBS_-HASSTRINGS, a WM_DELETEI-TEM is sent for each item.

CB_SELECTSTRING

Search the listbox at the position indicated by indexStart for the string lpFindString, and if found, select that item and copy it to the edit control. The string in the listbox may be longer than the string pointed to by lpFindString.	index-Start	lpFind-String	Index of selected item	If the string was not found, the current selection is unchanged. If indexStart is -1, the entire listbox is searched.

CB_SETCURSEL

Sets the selection in a list box to be the item specified	item-Index	0L	Not meaning-ful unless	This should only be used with single-selection

			LB_ERR	list boxes. The
by itemIndex. If itemIndex is -1, the selection is removed. If the listbox is visible, it will be scrolled to bring the selection into view.				return will be LB_ERR if itemIndex is -1. This is ok, and does not indicate an error.

CB_SETEDITSEL

Selects characters in the edit control of a combo box. If starting postion is -1, selection is removed. If ending position is -1, all text from starting position to the end is selected	0	start/end	Nonzero if the message was successful.	The application should use the macro MAKELPARAM (start, end) to generate the starting and ending postion value.

CB_SETEXTENDEDUI

Sets or removes the extended ui style for a combo box that has the DROPDOWN or DROPDOWNLIST attributes.	fEx-tended	0L	CB_OKAY if the message was successful.	Sending TRUE will set the extended ui attribute; sending FALSE will set the default attribute.

CB_SETITEMDATA

Sets the double word value of the item specified by itemIndex.	item-Index	dwData	Not meaning-ful unless CB_ERR	The value set here can be retrieved later by using CB_GET-ITEDATA.

CB_SETITEMHEIGHT

Sets the height, in pixels, of item(s) in the listbox. If listbox is OWNERDRAW-VARIABLE, this only sets the height of this item, otherwise all item's height is set.	item-Index	item-Height	Not meaning-ful unless CB_ERR	The height is specified by the loword of lParam. Use MAKELPARAM (height, 0). If itemIndex -1, then this sets the height of the edit control.

CB_SHOWDROPDOWN

Shows or hides the drop down list box of a combo box that has the DROPDOWN or DROPDOWNLIST attribute.	fShow	0L	Always non-zero.	TRUE shows the listbox, FALSE hides it.

Notes:

✦ All listbox messages return CB_ERR if there is an error, unless otherwise noted.

✦ Any parameter that is marked as 0 must be set to zero. These parameters are generally unused, but should be set to 0 for future computability.

✦ Messages that specify the list box are talking about the list box portion of the combo box.

DEALING WITH COMBO BOXES: SOME EXAMPLES

Here are some of the basic types of interactions that you can do with a combo box:

To set a text entry in the listbox portion of the combo box:

```
SendDlgItemMessage (  hDlg,
                ID_ComboBox,
                CB_ADDSTRING,     // Adds it to
                        // the listbox
                0,        // Not used
                (LPARAM)lpString );
```

The message CB_ADDSTRING causes the string to be added to the list-box portion of the combo box. Note that this *doesn't* mean that it's visible—if the listbox is not dropped down, the user won't see the new addition until the next time he or she drops the list box. If the combo box has the style CBS_SORT, then the listbox is sorted. This has the effect of adding the string in alphabetical order. If the combo box does not have the CBS_SORT style, then the string is added at the end.

As you probably remember, we can also add strings to a listbox by using the LB_INSERTSTRING message. Combo boxes have an analogous message, CB_INSERTSTRING. Here's how you use that:

```
SendDlgItemMessage (  hDlg,
                ID_ComboBox,
                CB_INSERTSTRING,  // Adds it to
                        // the listbox
                position,          // point to
                        // insert at.
                (LPARAM)lpString );
```

The difference between the two calls is that CB_ADDSTRING puts the string in the listbox, and then re-orders it (meaning you don't know where the string is going to end up), while CB_INSERTSTRING puts it at the specified point. This is the same as the LB_ADDSTRING and LB_INSERTSTRING messages, too.

Suppose we want to get the text of an item in the combo box. Here's a piece of code that will do that:

```
char        item [ 128 ];


SendDlgItemMessage (   hDlg,
                    ID_ComboBox,
                    CB_GETTEXT,
                    position,
                    (LPARAM)item );
```

This retrieves the text string at position position, and puts it into the buffer item. If you want to ensure that your buffer is going to be big enough to hold the string, you can send the CB_GETTEXTLEN message, like so:

```
int      tLen;


tLen = SendDlgItemMessage (    hDlg,
                    ID_ComboBox,
                    CB_GETTEXTLEN,
                    position,
                    0L );
```

Of course, that's not all you can do with a combo box. Let's take a look at a complete example of a combo box in action. (Since this is another application based on my skeleton framework, I am (for the sake of brevity) going to omit all the source except the dialog code and related pieces. Everything else is the same. You can find the complete source for the project on the accompanying disk.)

Listing 9-12   Skeldlg.cpp

```
//
// Skeldlg.cpp
```

continued

Listing 9-12 *continued*

```
//
//    Skeleton dialog procedure code
//
#include <skeleton.hpp>
//—————
//
// SkeletonDlgProc()
//
//    Dialog box procedure for the cursor control panel
//
//
    BOOL FAR PASCAL
SkeletonDlgProc ( HWND hDlg,
                  UINT message,
                  UINT wParam,
                  LONG lParam )
{
    WORD    screenWidth;
    WORD    screenHeight;
    int     i;
    RECT    rectal;
    //—————
    switch ( message )
    {
        case WM_INITDIALOG:
            //
            // This code here allows us to center
            // the dialog in the middle of the
            // screen, regardless of resolution
            //
            screenWidth = GetSystemMetrics ( SM_CXSCREEN );
            screenHeight = GetSystemMetrics ( SM_CYSCREEN );
            GetWindowRect ( hDlg,
                            &rectal );
            screenWidth -= ( rectal.right - rectal.left );
            screenHeight -= ( rectal.bottom - rectal.top );
            screenWidth /= 2;
            screenHeight /= 2;
            MoveWindow ( hDlg,
                         screenWidth,
                         screenHeight,
                         rectal.right - rectal.left,
                         rectal.bottom - rectal.top,
                         TRUE );
```

```
        //
        //
        // All done with moving the screen,
        // now let's fill the list box on the
        // left.
        //
        AddListBoxElements ( hDlg );
        return TRUE;   // TRUE means Windows will continue processing
        break;
    case WM_COMMAND:
        switch ( LOWORD ( wParam ) )
        {
            case IDC_LISTBOX2:
                //
                // HIWORD ( lParam ) gives us
                // the notification code for
                // the listbox...
                //
                switch ( HIWORD ( lParam ) )
                {
                    case LBN_SELCHANGE:          // Single click
                        break;
                    case LBN_DBLCLK:             // Move entry over
                                                 // to other listbox
                        MoveEntryToComboBox ( hDlg );
                        break;
                    default:
                        return FALSE;            // Not handled
                }
                break;

            case ID_AddButton:
                MoveEntryFromComboBox ( hDlg );
                break;
            case ID_RemoveButton:
                MoveEntryToComboBox ( hDlg );
                break;
            case IDOK: // All done, cleanup and go home...
                //
                // Ok, all done, punt...
                //
                EndDialog ( hDlg,
                            IDOK );
```

continued

Listing 9-12 *continued*

```
                    break;
                case IDCANCEL:
                    EndDialog ( hDlg,
                                IDCANCEL );
                    break;
                default:
                    return FALSE;        // Didn't process message
            }
            break;
        default:
            return FALSE; // Didn't process message...
            break;
    }
    return TRUE;
}

//————————-
//
// AddListBoxElements()
//
    void WINAPI
AddListBoxElements ( HWND hDlg )
{
    //————————
    DlgDirListComboBox ( hDlg,
                         "*.*",
                         IDC_COMBOBOX1,
                         NULL,
                         DDL_READWRITE );
}
//————————-
//
// MoveEntryFromComboBox()
//
//    Moves the current selection
// from the source box to the
// destination box.
//
    void WINAPI
MoveEntryFromComboBox ( HWND  hDlg )
{
    int     lResult;
    char    fooBuff [ 128 ];
    int     srcBox =  IDC_COMBOBOX1;
```

```
int    destBox =   IDC_LISTBOX2;
//——————--
//
// First, get the current selection
// in the source list box
//
lResult = LOWORD ( SendDlgItemMessage ( hDlg,
                                        srcBox,
                                        CB_GETCURSEL,
                                        0,
                                        0L ) );
//
// If the result is LB_ERR, then there
// is no selection, so don't do anything.
//
if ( lResult != CB_ERR )
{
    //
    // Ok, there is a current selection.
    // Please remove it from the source
    // box, and put it in the destination
    // box.
    //
    //
    // Make sure the text string isn't too
    // long for our buffer.  (This isn't going
    // to happen in our example program, but
    // it could happen in real life.  Here's
    // how to check for it...)
    //

    if ( LOWORD ( SendDlgItemMessage ( hDlg,
                                       srcBox,
                                       _GETLBTEXTLEN,
                                       lResult,
                                       0 ) ) < 128 )
    {
        //
        // Get the text from the selected
        // item here...
        //
        SendDlgItemMessage ( hDlg,
                             srcBox,
                             CB_GETLBTEXT,
                             lResult,
                             (LPARAM) fooBuff );
```

continued

353

Listing 9-12   *continued*

```
            //
            // Ok, delete the item from
            // the source list box
            //
            SendDlgItemMessage ( hDlg,
                                 srcBox,
                                 CB_DELETESTRING,
                                 lResult,
                                 0L );
            //
            // ...and add it to the
            // destination list box
            //
            SendDlgItemMessage ( hDlg,
                                 destBox,
                                 LB_ADDSTRING,
                                 0,
                                 (LPARAM) fooBuff );
        }
    }
}

//——————————--
//
// MoveEntryToComboBox()
//
//   Moves the current selection
// from the source box to the
// destination box.
//
    void WINAPI
MoveEntryToComboBox ( HWND    hDlg )
{
    int     lResult;
    char    fooBuff [ 128 ];
    int     srcBox  =   IDC_LISTBOX2;
    int     destBox =   IDC_COMBOBOX1;
    //——————————-
    //
    // First, get the current selection
    // in the source list box
    //
    lResult = LOWORD ( SendDlgItemMessage ( hDlg,
                                            srcBox,
```

```
                                        LB_GETCURSEL,
                                        0,
                                        0L ) );
//
// If the result is LB_ERR, then there
// is no selection, so don't do anything.
//
if ( lResult != LB_ERR )
{
    //
    // Ok, there is a current selection.
    // Please remove it from the source
    // box, and put it in the destination
    // box.
    //
    //
    // Make sure the text string isn't too
    // long for our buffer.  (This isn't going
    // to happen in our example program, but
    // it could happen in real life.  Here's
    // how to check for it...)
    //

    if ( LOWORD ( SendDlgItemMessage ( hDlg,
                                       srcBox,
                                       LB_GETTEXTLEN,
                                       lResult,
                                       0 ) ) < 128 )
    {
        //
        // Get the text from the selected
        // item here...
        //
        SendDlgItemMessage ( hDlg,
                             srcBox,
                             LB_GETTEXT,
                             lResult,
                             (LPARAM) fooBuff );
        //
        // Ok, delete the item from
        // the source list box
        //
        SendDlgItemMessage ( hDlg,
                             srcBox,
                             LB_DELETESTRING,
```

continued

Listing 9-12 *continued*

```
                                lResult,
                                0L );
        //
        // ...and add it to the
        // destination list box
        //
        SendDlgItemMessage ( hDlg,
                             destBox,
                             CB_ADDSTRING,
                             0,
                             (LPARAM) fooBuff );
    }
  }

}
```

The big changes here are the way the controls are handled, and the method of copying items. First off, you'll notice that I've gotten rid of the **MoveEntry()** function, and replaced it with two, **MoveEntry-ToComboBox()** and **MoveEntryFromComboBox()**. I had to eliminate MoveEntry(), because it expected both the source and destination controls to be listboxes. In this case, that's no longer true—one's a listbox, and one's a combo box (albeit containing a list box). If I moved to having *two* combo boxes, I could again have single purpose call to do the trick. After all, it doesn't really matter what kind of control we're using, as long as the same messages work for both. However, I wanted to show the case where you're talking to two different types of controls at the same time.

That said, the two **Move()** functions still look pretty much the same; only the type of message has changed. The underlying algorithm hasn't changed at all:

1. Get the current selection.

2. Make sure that the currently selected string will fit in our string buffer.

3. If the string will fit in the buffer, retrieve the string.

4. Delete the string from the source control.

5. Add the string to the destination control.

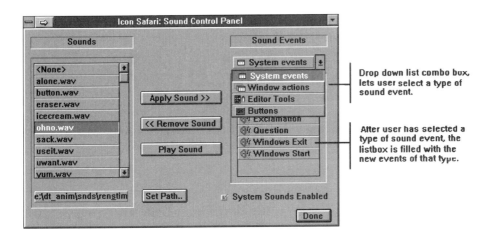

FIGURE 9-6   SCREEN SHOT OF AN APPLICATION THAT'S USING BOTH A DROP DOWN LIST COMBO BOX
AND A LISTBOX AT THE SAME TIME.

(If you look, you'll see that this is the same procedure that we used when we had two listboxes.)

Another thing to notice is that I don't respond to *any* command messages from the combo box. I only check it's state when we want to add or remove an item from it (either the add and remove buttons, or a double click in the listbox). In real life, if the user has selected an entry in the combo box, you probably want to react to it. Here's one way of doing that:

```
case ID_ComboBox:
    switch ( HIWORD ( lParam ) )
    {
        case CBN_CLOSEUP: // List box is closing
                          // back up, so get the
                          // selection
            curSel = SendDlgItemMessage ( hDlg,
                              ID_ComboBox,
                              CB_GETCURSEL,
```

```
                              NULL,
                              NULL );
         if ( curSel != CB_ERR )
         {
             // Do something in response
             // to the selection change
             // here.  curSel contains the
             // index of the new item.
         }
         break;
      default:
         break;
   }
   break;
```

As you can see, the way I respond to the combo box is by checking to see if the list box is closing; if it is, then the user may have made a new selection. By getting the current selection (via the CB_GETCURSEL message), I can then determine what action to take.

COMBO BOXES AND ITEM DATA

Since combo boxes contain a list box, you might expect them to be able to handle an item data entry for each list box entry. You'd be right. Just as the messages LB_GETITEMDATA and LB_SETITEMDATA allow you to get and set a DWORD value for each list box entry, the messages CB_GETITEMDATA and CB_SETITEMDATA allow you to get and set a DWORD for each entry in the list box of the combo box.

Here's how those messages look:

```
itemData = SendDlgItemMessage (      hDlg,
                       ID_ComboBox,
                       CB_GETITEMDATA,
                       itemPosition,
                       0L );
```

gets the item data associated with an entry, and:

```
SendDlgItemMessage (   hDlg,
                    ID_ComboBox,
                    CB_SETITEMDATA,
                    itemPosition,
                    itemData );
```

sets the item data associated with an entry. Just as with listboxes, it's important to remember that if you extract a string from a combo box, it's associated item data has *not* been extracted; you have to do that manually if you want the item data to go with the string.

SUMMARY

In this chapter we've looked at the different ways of using listboxes and combo boxes for presenting information. Listboxes and combo boxes, we've discovered, are very useful tools for presenting the user with broad sets of information, and letting them choose one or more pieces of that information. We've also seen how we can associate data with elements of the listbox, enabling us to have each element "carry along" it's own data structure.

In looking back over this chapter, and back over the whole book, it's important to keep in mind what good user interface design is really all about—making it simple for your users to accomplish their tasks. The best user interface is the one that users don't even notice, one which quietly and competently assists them in getting their work done. User interface design can sometimes be a thankless job, because the best interfaces are the ones that aren't noticed. But if your users say things like "It just works right" and "It's so easy to use," you'll know you've done your job well. Good luck!

INDEX

A

_lstrlen() function, 121

adding

    power to applications, 29-33

    strings to combo box list boxes, 341, 344, 348

    text entries to list boxes, 293-295, 325-326

AddListBoxElements() function, 331-332

AlertBox() function, 198

AnsiToOem() function, 339-340

applications

    closing, 85

    translating to other languages, 194-195

auto radio buttons, 221-222

B

bitmaps

    BmButton class instances, 175

    changing radio button, 266-273

    definitions for radio button, 264-265

Blaise custom controls, 335-336

BmButton class

    creating instances of, 144

    internal operation of, 146-181

BMBUTTON.CPP file, 158-175

BMBUTTON.HPP file, 147-158

BM_GETCHECK message, 233

BM_SETCHECK message, 234

BS_AUTORADIOBUTTON style flag, 223

BS_OWNERDRAW style flag, 176

BS_PUSHBUTTON style flag, 120

bugs

    externalized references to global variables, 260-261

    linear programs and, 42

    multiple include file versions, 91-92

BuildButtonWindow() function, 176

BuildSelf() function, 144

buttons. *See also* Cancel button; graphic buttons; OK button; radio buttons; text buttons

    appearance vs. functionality of graphic, 112-117

    avoiding ambiguity on, 192-193

    message box, 199

    text vs. graphic, 110-112

C

C++ language, advantages of, 67, 96-97

C++ object classes, 66-67

C++ source code access to definitions file, 93-94

C language, C++ advantages over, 67, 96

CALLBACK.CPP, 134-137

Cancel button, 191-192, 192-193

CB_ADDSTRING message, 341, 348

CB_DELETESTRING message, 341

CB_DIR message, 341

CB_ERR message, 347

CB_FINDSTRING message, 342

CB_FINDSTRINGEXACT message, 342

CB_GETCOUNT message, 342

CB_GETCURSEL message, 342, 358

CB_GETDROPPEDCONTROLRECT message, 343

CB_GETDROPPEDSTATE message, 343

CB_GETEXTENDEDUI message, 343

CB_GETITEMDATA message, 343, 358

CB_GETITEMHEIGHT message, 343

CB_GETLBTEXT message, 339, 344

CB_GETTEXTLEN message, 344

CB_INSERTSTRING message, 344, 348

CB_LIMITTEXT message, 345

CB_RESETCONTENT message, 341, 345

CBS_AUTOHSCROLL style flag, 338

CBS_DISABLENOSCROLL style flag, 338-339

CBS_DROPDOWN style flag, 339

CBS_DROPDOWNLIST style flag, 339

CB_SELECTSTRING message, 345

CB_SETEDITSEL message, 346

CB_SETEXTENDEDUI message, 346

CB_SETITEMDATA message, 346, 358

CB_SETITEMHEIGHT message, 347

CBS_HASSTRINGS style flag, 339

CB_SHOWDROPDOWN message, 347

CBS_NOINTEGRALHEIGHT style flag, 339

CBS_OEMCONVERT style flag, 339-340

CBS_OWNERDRAWFIXED style flag, 340

CBS_OWNERDRAWVARIABLE style flag, 340

CBS_SIMPLE style flag, 340

CBS_SORT style flag, 340, 348

CenteredWindow class, 269

ChangeMoonButton() function, 273

changing

    menu entries, 104-105

    message box text strings, 200

    radio button bitmaps, 266-273

character sets, converting, 339-340

check boxes

    responding to, 274-284

    saving state of, 233-234

    vs. radio buttons, 237-242

checked menu entries

    clearing check marks from, 104

    code listing, 104

CheckRadioButtons() function, 233

class definition files, DisplayInfoLine() class, 61-66

class libraries, references to, 90

classes, C++ object, 66-67

CLASSES.HPP file, 90

clearing check marks from menu items, 104

ClientDC object, 269-2671M

clipboard, Windows, 58-59

closing applications, 85

code listings. *See also entries for specific files*

BmButton class, 147-175

BuildButtonWindow() function, 176

changing radio button bitmaps, 268-269

check boxes, 274-280, 282-283

checked menu entries, 104

class library references, 90

combo boxes, 348-358

CreateGraphicButtons() function, 144

determining graphic button ID matches, 179-180

dialog boxes, 203-219

display information line skeleton application, 78-85, 86-88, 90-91

DisplayInfoLine() class C++ source code, 67-77

DisplayInfoLine() class member function definitions, 61-66

displaying radio button bitmaps, 270-273

enabling/disabling OK buttons, 234-235

external definitions of global variables, 93

function prototypes, 94-96

global variable definitions, 89

graphic buttons, 124-143

include file for all source files, 92

list box, 303-321

main window text buttons, 118-119

message box wrapper, 196, 197-198

moving items between list boxes,

322-327

packaging Windows.h and SKELDFNS.HPP files, 94

pairing Undo with Redo menu entries, 104-105

PerformActionIfID() function, 176-177

radio buttons, 223-233, 243-266

responding to dialog box text buttons, 117

columns, multiple list box, 289, 300

combo box item data elements, 246, 343, 358-359

combo boxes

described, 336-338

do's and don'ts, 286-288

overview, 285

responding to selections in, 357-358

source code, 348-358

styles, 288-291

common dialog boxes

implementing design consistency, 12

list and combo boxes in, 286

compiler, resource, 93-94, 318

consistency, design, 11-14

control events, 49

controls. *See also entries for specific controls*

handling dialog box, 221-235

initializing dialog box, 201-202

selecting appropriate dialog box, 191-193

as sources of messages, 49

third party list box, 335-336

coordinates, screen, 269-271

Copy (Edit) menu entry, 58-59

CreateGraphicButtons() function, 144-145

CreateSelf() function, 176

CreateWindow() function

graphic buttons, 176

text buttons, 119-121

creating

DIL skeleton application, 77-97

DILs (display information lines), 61-103

graphic buttons, 123-145

menus, 51-107

skeleton application window, 85

text buttons in dialog boxes, 117-123

cursors, 27-28

Cut (Edit) menu entry, 58

D

data elements

combo box item, 343

list box item, 328-332

defaults, providing sensible, 29-33

defining

classes, 66

dialog box controls, 259-260

global variables, 88-89, 93

hInst variable, 89

hMBrush variable, 89

list box ID numbers, 321

MainhWnd variable, 89

numeric values, skeleton application, 90-91

deleting. *See also* clearing check marks from menu items

    combo box items, 341, 345

    list box items, 295, 299, 325

designing user interfaces

    advantages of event-driven interfaces, 47

    overview, 7-10

    philosophy, 11-33

The Design of Everyday Things, 8

DetermineCheckBoxState() function, 233

DetermineDisplayState() function, 178-179, 180

DetermineRadioButtonState() function, 233

determining. *See also* retrieving

    check box state, 281-283

    combo box list box visibility, 343

    combo box text string position/length, 344, 349

    combo box user interface, 343

    graphic button ID number matches, 179-180

    graphic button state, 178-179, 180

    list box item selection state, 297, 323-324

    list box text string position/length, 294, 298, 324-325

    radio button/check box state, 233

    which radio button bitmap to display, 272-273

dialog boxes. *See also* common dialog boxes; *entries for specific controls*

    complex, 201-202

    designing, 186-193

    as feedback from user actions, 22

    message boxes, 194-201

    overview, 183-186

    responding to radio button changes within, 267

    text buttons in, 110, 117-123

    types of, 193-194

DIL class, 61

DIL.CPP file

    DisplayInfoLine() class member functions, 66

    source code, 67-77

DIL.HPP file, 61-66

dilIDs array, 98, 99

DILs (display information lines)

    creating, 61-103

    greyed menu entries, 106

dilStrings array, 98, 99

directories, displaying

    in combo boxes, 341

    in list boxes, 295, 332-335

disabling. *See also* greying out control labels

    combo box scroll bars, 338-339

    OK buttons, 234-235

display information lines (DILs)

    creating, 61-103

    greyed menu entries, 106

DisplayInfoLine() class

adding functionality to, 102-103

class definition file, 61-66

mapping ID numbers to text strings, 98-101

displaying

directories, 295, 332-335, 341

display information lines (DILs), 61-103

DlgDirList() function, 332-335

double word values

combo box items and, 346

list box items and, 328-329

DoubleClickAction() function, 177

drag-right menus, 59, 100

DRAWITEMSTRUCT pointer, 178, 180

DrawMoon() function, 282, 284

drop down combo boxes, 337-338

drop down list combo boxes, 337

DWORDs

combo box entries, 358-359

list box, 297, 301, 328-329, 331

E

edit boxes, requiring entries in, 234-235

Edit menus, 53, 57-59

EnableMenuItem() function, 106

enabling

keyboard input in list boxes, 291

list box scroll bars, 287, 288-289

menu entries, 106

multiple selections in list boxes, 287, 290, 291-293

OK button, 234-235

toggling prompts off, 54

errors. *See also* LB_ERR message

combo box messages, 347

LB_GETCURSEL message triggering, 296

event handlers, 44-45

Event Manager, Windows, 44

event-driven programming, 41-50

events

defined, 50

types of, in Windows, 48-50

Exit (File) menu entry, 56

external global variable definitions, 93. *See also* SKELEXTN.HPP file

F

feedback

aiding user learning process, 23-24

checked menu entries, 103-104

display information lines, 61-103

greying menu entries, 105-106

indicating results of actions, 24-28

overview, 21

as result of user actions, 22-23

File menus, 52, 53-57

files, users creating new, 54

flags. *See entries for specific style flags;* style flags

focus rectangle, setting list box, 300

fonts, 121

framework applications. *See* skeleton applications

function keys, consistency and, 11-12

function pointers, calling NULL, 177

functions

defining, 262-264

prototypes of skeleton application, 94-96

G

GetDialogBaseUnits() function, 291

GetDilIndex() function, 100

GetMenuMapIndex() function, 100-101

global variables

defining, 88-89

DisplayInfoLine() class instance, 67

external definitions, 93

externalized references to, 260-261

list boxes, 315

radio buttons, 257-258

graphic buttons

BmButton class, 144, 146-181

creating, 123-145

drawing selves, 145-146, 176, 178

visual representations of functionality of, 112-117

vs. check boxes, 240

vs. text buttons, 110-112

graphic user interfaces. *See* GUIs (graphic user interfaces)

greying out control labels. *See also* disabling

Copy (Edit) menu entry, 59

Cut (Edit) menu entry, 58

menu entries, 105-106

Paste (Edit) menu entry, 59

Save (File) menu entry, 55

Undo (Edit) menu entry, 58

grouping interface elements

check boxes, 240

dialog box controls, 187-189

guiding user choices by, 17-19

menu entries, 56

radio buttons, 223

guiding user choices, 15-19, 187-189

GUIs (graphic user interfaces), advantages of event-driven, 47

H

header files, 122

height

combo box item, 340, 343

list box item, 290-291, 297, 301

main window text button, 121

.h files, 122

hInst variable

defining, 89

list boxes, 315

radio buttons, 257-258

hMBrush variable

defining, 89

list boxes, 315

radio buttons, 257-258

I

icons, message box system, 199

ID numbers

defining dialog box control, 259-260

display information line, 77, 91, 98-101

graphic button, 177, 178, 179-180

list box control, 321

main window text buttons, 122

source/destination list boxes, 323

include files for all source files, 91-92, 258, 315

initializing

dialog boxes, 201-202

instance variables, 85

radio buttons, 247-251

InitSelf() function, 98-101

Innovative Data Concepts, 335

inserting. *See* adding; CB_INSERT-STRING message; LB_INSERT-STRING message

instance variables, initializing, 85

itemAction style flag, 180

itemState style flag, 180

L

laying out interface elements

dialog box controls, 187-190

preventing user confusion, 20-21

LB_ADDSTRING message, 293, 294, 295, 325, 331

LB_DELETESTRING message, 295, 325

LB_DIR message, 295, 332-333

LB_ERR message

LB_GETCURSEL message and, 296

list box messages and, 303

LB_FINDSTRING message, 295

LB_FINDSTRINGEXACT message, 295-296

LB_GETCARETINDEX message, 296

LB_GETCOUNT message, 296

LB_GETCURSEL message, 294, 296, 326

LB_GETHORIZONTALEXTENT message, 296

LB_GETITEMDATA message, 297, 328-329

LB_GETITEMHEIGHT message, 297

LB_GETITEMRECT message, 297

LB_GETSEL message, 297

LB_GETSELCOUNT message, 298

LB_GETSELITEMS message, 298

LB_GETTEXT messaage, 298, 324

LB_GETTEXTLEN message, 294, 298, 326

LB_GETTOPINDEX message, 299

LB_INSERTSTRING message, 293-294, 299

LB_RESETCONTENT message, 299, 332-333

LBS_DISABLENOSCROLL style flag, 288

LB_SELECTSTRING message, 299

LB_SELITEMRANGE message, 300

LB_SETCARETINDEX message, 300

LB_SETCOLUMNWIDTH message, 300

LB_SETCURSEL message, 301

LB_SETHORIZONTALEXTENT message, 301

LB_SETITEMDATA message, 301, 328-329, 331

LB_SETITEMHEIGHT message, 301

LB_SETSEL message, 302

LB_SETTABSTOPS message, 302

LB_SETTOPINDEX message, 302

LBS_EXTENDEDSEL style flag, 287, 289, 292. *See also* LBS_MULTIPLE-SEL style flag

LBS_HASSTRINGS style flag, 289, 325

LBS_INTEGRALHEIGHT style flag, 288

LBS_MULTICOLUMN style flag, 289

LBS_MULTIPLESEL style flag, 290, 293. *See also* LBS_EXTENDEDSEL style flag; LBS_MULTISEL style flag

LBS_MULTISEL style flag, 287. *See also* LBS_EXTENDEDSEL style flag; LBS_MULTIPLESEL style flag

LBS_NOINTEGRALHEIGHT style flag, 290

LBS_NOREDRAW style flag, 290

LBS_NOTIFY style flag, 290

LBS_OWNERDRAWFIXED style flag, 290

LBS_OWNERDRAWVARIABLE style flag, 290-291

LBS_SORT style flag, 291, 293

LBS_STANDARD style flag, 291

LBS_USETABSTOPS style flag, 291

LBS_WANTKEYBOARDINPUT style flag, 291

linear (traditional) programming, 42-43

list box item data elements, 301, 328-332

list boxes. *See also* combo boxes
adding text entries to, 293-295
do's and don'ts, 286-288
internal operation of, 321-328
messages, 295-303
moving items between, 322-331
multiple selections in, 287, 290, 291-293
overview, 285
source code, 303-321
style flags, 288-291
third part controls, 335-336

ListboxBitmap() class, 335

LoadResource() function, 196

_lstrlen() function, 121

M

MainhWnd variable
defining, 89
list boxes, 315
radio buttons, 257-258

maintaining programs, 42

MainWindowProc() function, 77

mapping ID numbers to text strings, 98-101

MB_ABORTRETRYIGNORE style flag, 198

MB_APPLMODAL style flag, 198

MB_DEFBUTTON*n* style flags, 198

MB_ICONASTERISK style flag, 199

MB_ICONEXCLAMATION style flag, 199

MB_ICONHAND style flag, 199

MB_ICONINFORMATION style flag, 199

MB_ICONSTOP style flag, 199

MB_OK style flag, 199

MB_OKCANCEL style flag, 199

MB_RETRYCANCEL style flag, 199

MB_SYSTEMMODAL style flag, 199

MB_TASKMODAL style flag, 199

MB_YESNO style flag, 199

MB_YESNOCANCEL style flag, 199

MD_ICONQUESTION style flag, 199

memory, text strings in DGROUP segment, 195

menu entries
  checked, 103-104
  defining values for, 91
  Edit menus, 57-59
  File menus, 53-57
  greying out, 105-106
  grouping by function, 57
  standardizing, 52

menu structures, 60

menus
  (DILs) display information lines, 61-103
  drag-right, 59, 100
  importance of, 51-52
  providing user feedback from, 103-104
  standard entries, 52-59

message boxes, 194-201

messages. *See also entries for specific messages*
  combo box, 341-347
  dialog box, 201-202
  list box, 295-303
  types provided by Windows, 48-50

MF_BYCOMMAND style flag, 104

MF_CHECKED style flag, 104

Microsoft Windows. *See* Windows, Microsoft

ModalDialogHandler()
  dialog boxes, 220
  list boxes, 303

MoDisplayInfoLine() classyMenu() function, 105

mouse events
  event handlers for, 44-47
  graphic buttons, 145

MoveEntry() function, 322-323, 327-328, 329-330

MoveEntryFromComboBox() function, 356

MoveEntrytoComboBox() function, 356

moving
  combo box items, 356
  display information lines, 101-102
  list box items, 322-331

multiple-select list boxes
  selecting strings in, 302
  setting focus rectangle, 300
  supporting discontiguous selections, 287, 290, 291-293

N

New (File) menu entry, 53-54

Norman, Don, 8

O

OEM character sets, 339-340

OK button

    enabling/disabling, 234-235

    improper use of, 192

Open (File) menu entry, 55

options, user

    to cancel operations, 191-192

    to change default settings, 30-32

    dialog boxes permitting choice of, 183

    to disable file operation prompts, 54-56

overwrite file queries, 55-56

P

packaging Windows.h and SKELDFNS.HPP files, 93-94

PaintMoonImage() function, 272-273, 284

parameters, list box message, 303

Paste (Edit) menu entry, 59

PerformActionIfID() function, graphic buttons, 176-177

philosophy, user interface design

  adding power to applications, 29-33

    consistency, 11-14

    guiding user choices, 15-19

preventing confusion, 19-21

  providing feedback, 21

pointers, list box items and, 328-329

pop-up menus, 100

positioning

    display information lines, 101-102

    main window text buttons, 120

preventing

  confusion, 19-21

  Windows from resizing list boxes, 290

productivity, enhancing user, 29-33, 116

programming, event-driven vs. linear, 41-50

programs

  closing, 85

    translating to other languages, 194-195

prompts, 54-56. *See also* message boxes

prototypes, Skeleton application function, 94-96. *See also* SKELPROT.HPP file

protyping applications, 35-40

Q

Quit (File) menu entry, 56

R

radio buttons

    incorporating into programs, 243-266

list and combo boxes vs., 240

responding to mouse clicks on, 266-273

saving state of, 233-234

turning on/off, 221-233

vs. check boxes, 237-242

Redo (Edit) menu entry

described, 58

pairing Undo with, 104-105

RenderSelfIfID() function, graphic buttons, 146, 178-179

ResBitmap object

access member functions, 282-283

loading instances of, 85

radio buttons, 257-258

resource compilers, 93-94, 318

resource files. *See also* SKELETON.RC file

message box text strings in, 194-196

radio buttons, 264-266

retrieving. *See also* determining

combo box data items, 343, 358-359

combo box list box item counts, 342

combo box strings, 339, 349

default desktop font size, 121

graphic button ID numbers, 179

list box data items, 330-331

list box item count, 296

list box text strings, 294

S

Save As... (File) menu entry, 55

Save (File) menu entry, 55

screen coordinates, 269-271

scrolling

combo boxes, 338-339

list box text, 287, 296, 301

selecting

combo box strings, 345

list box item strings, 299-300

multiple list box items, 300, 302

SendMessage() function

check box states, 282

setting radio button state, 234

setting

combo box DWORDs, 358-359

combo box list box selections, 345-346

combo box text entries, 348

directories in list boxes, 333-335

focus rectangle in listboxes, 300

list box column width, 300

list box height, 301

list box scrollable width, 301

list box tab positions, 302

list box text entries, 293

radio button states, 234

simple combo boxes, 338. *See also* combo boxes; drop down combo boxes; drop down list combo boxes

SingleClickAction() function, graphic buttons, 177

sizing

combo box drop down lists, 287-288

main window text buttons, 120-121

SKELDFNS.HPP file

dialog boxes, 271

display information lines, 90-91, 93-94

graphic buttons, 138-139

list boxes, 316-317

radio buttons, 259-260

SKELDLG.CPP file

    check boxes, 274-280

    combo boxes, 349-356

    dialog boxes, 210-213

    list boxes, 309-315

    radio buttons, 251-257

    turning radio buttons on/off, 223-233

skeleton applications

    dialog boxes, 203-219

    display information lines, 77-97

    graphic buttons, 124-129

    list boxes, 303-306

    radio buttons, 243-247

SKELETON.CPP file

    dialog boxes, 203-207

    display information lines, 77-85

    graphic buttons, 124-129

    list boxes, 303-306

    radio buttons, 243-247

SkeletonCreateWindow() routine, described, 85

SKELETON.DLG file

    dialog boxes, 218-219

    dialog boxes with radio buttons, 265-266

    list boxes, 321

SkeletonDlgProc() function, 309

SkeletonExitApp() routine, described, 85

SKELETON.HPP file

    dialog boxes, 213

    display information lines, 91-92, 92

    graphic buttons, 137

    list boxes, 315-316

    radio buttons, 258-259

SkeletonInitApplication() routine, calling, 85

SKELETON.RC file

    dialog boxes, 217-218

    graphic buttons, 142-143

    list boxes, 320

    radio buttons, 264-266

SkeletonRegisterClass() routine, described, 85

SKELEXTN.HPP file

    dialog boxes, 213-214

    display information lines, 93

    graphic buttons, 139-140

    list boxes, 317

    radio buttons, 260-261

SKELINCS.HPP file

    dialog boxes, 216-217

    list boxes, 317-318

SKELINICS.HPP file

    display information lines, 93-94

    graphic buttons, 138

    radio buttons, 261-262

SKELINIT.CPP file

    dialog boxes, 207-209

display information lines, 85, 86-88

graphic buttons, 129-133

list boxes, 307-309

radio buttons, 247-251

SKELPROT.HPP file

   dialog boxes, 214-216

   display information line, 94-96

   graphic buttons, 140-141

   list boxes, 318-320

   radio buttons, 262-264

SKELTON.HPP file, 93

SKELVARS.CPP file

   dialog boxes, 209-210

   display information lines, 88, 89

   graphic buttons, 133-134, 144

   list boxes, 315

   radio buttons, 257-258

sorting list box strings

   CBS_SORT style flag, 340, 348

   LBS_SORT style flag, 291, 293

source files, single include file for all, 91-92, 258, 315

static text strings

   combo box, 339

   disadvantages of, 195-196

status lines. *See* DILs (display information lines)

string tables, advantages of, 195

strings

   alphabetically sorting list box, 291, 293, 340

   combo box, 339, 342, 345

   list box, 289, 293-295, 299

selecting, in multiple-select list boxes, 302

UpdateDisplay function and, 103

style flags

   combo box, 338-340

   graphic button states, 178, 180

   list box selection, 287

   main window text buttons, 120

   menu entries, 104

   message box, 198-199

style sheets, 32

system events, 48-49

T

tab stops, list box, 291, 302

tabbed dialog boxes, grouping information in, 190

tasks, user

   prototyping applications based on, 35-40

   simplicity of frequently performed, 29-33

text buttons

   dialog box, creating, 117-123

   main window, creating, 117-123

   vs. check boxes, 240

   vs. graphic buttons, 110-112

text strings

   combo box, 344

   converting character sets of combo box, 339

   display information line, 77, 98-101

   edit control, 234, 235

explaining graphic buttons, 116

main window text buttons, 120

message box, 194-196, 200-201

toolbar buttons

equivalent menu entries for, 59

graphic vs. text, 110-111

visual feedback from, 22-23

tools

consistency and, 13

feedback from selection of, 24-27

guiding users to use of, 17-19

U

Undo (Edit) menu entry

described, 58

pairing with Redo, 104-105

UpdateDil() function, 102

UpdateDisplay function, 103

user events, 49. *See also* user-defined events

user interface design

advantages of event-driven interfaces in, 47

overview, 7-10

philosophy, 11-33

user-defined events, 50. *See also* user events

V

variables. *See also* global variables

instance variables, 85

OK/Cancel buttons and, 193

Visual C++: A Developer's Guide, 315

W

width

list box scrollable, 296, 301

main window text button, 121

windows

dialog boxes as, 201-202

SkeletonCreateWindow() routine creating, 85

text buttons in main, 118-123

Windows, Microsoft. *See also* clipboard, Windows

advantages of designing applications for, 47

character set conversion, 339-340

common dialog boxes, 12

Event Manager, 44

types of events in, 48-50

Windows.h file, packaging of, 93-94

WinMain() function, 77

WMCHARTOITEM message, 291

WM_COMMAND message

BmButton class receiving, 175

check boxes, 283-284

dialog box text buttons, 117

dialog boxes, 219-220

graphic buttons, 145, 146, 176-177

main window text buttons, 123

responding to radio buttons, 267-268

WM_CREATE message, 102

WM_DRAWITEM message

graphic buttons, 146, 178, 180

list boxes, 290

WM_INITDIALOG message
  centering dialog boxes, 220-221
  enabling/disabling OK buttons, 234-235
  initializing dialog boxes, 201-202
  radio button bitmaps, 271
WM_MEASUREITEM message, 290, 340
WM_MENUSELECT message
  greyed menu entries, 106
  menu entry ID numbers, 98
  UpdateDil() function and, 102
WM_PAINT message, 271-272

WM_SETREDRAW message, 290
WM_SIZE message, 101-102
WM_VKEYTOITEM message, 291
wrappers
  list box, 317-318
  message box, 194-201
WS_CHILD style flag, 120
WS_OWNERDRAW style flag, 145-146, 175
WS_VISIBLE style flag, 120

X

x-y coordinates, 269-271

ABOUT THE DISK

This disk contains the source code for the book Designing GUI Applications in Windows, by Alex Leavens.

What you need:

Hardware: Minimum 386 PC with hard drive, capable of running Windows 3.1

Software: Windows 3.1 with Borland 4.0 C++

All the source code on the disk is contained in subdirectories for each chapter (i.e., \CHAP5 contains the source code for Chapter 5). The directory \GOCL contains the header files, source files, and library for GOCL, my Graphics Objects Class Library. You'll need GOCL for a number of the projects that I've built. You don't need to re-build GOCL, because I've included the library (gocl.lib). However, if you want to use some of the GOCL classes for your own programs, and you don't happen to be using large model, you'll need to re-compile.

To install the source code on your hard drive, do the following:

1. Make a directory on your hard drive, where you want the source code to go. For example, you might want to place the code on your C: drive, in the directory called "BOOK". First, create the directory on your C: drive.

2. Change to that directory.

3. Use the DOS command XCOPY to copy the contents of the entire floppy onto your hard drive. For example, if the floppy were in drive A: and the directory you wanted was listed as above (C:\book), you'd type the following from the C:\book directory:

   XCOPY A:*.* . /S/E/V

   This copies all of the contents of the floppy, including the subdirectories, onto your hard drive

4. Run the batch program called "expand", which will now be in the c:\book directory (or wherever you chose to put the contents of the disk).

5. This batch file will move into each subdirectory, and expand the source files in that directory. Note that the source each directory contains a self-extracting zip file, so that if you need to extract one at a later time, you can do so individually.

That's it!

Using the code

All of the code on this disc was developed under and compiled with Borland C++ 3.x and 4.0. I've include the .ide files for Borland 4.0, since that's the latest version, but there's no problem using Borland 3.x, either (I just didn't include the .prj files). Since the place where my compiler lives (e:\bc4\bin) is almost certainly different than the place where your compiler lives, you'll need to change the place that the project is looking for things (these settings are available in the "Directories" portion of the "Options | Project" menu.